THE TENTH MUSE

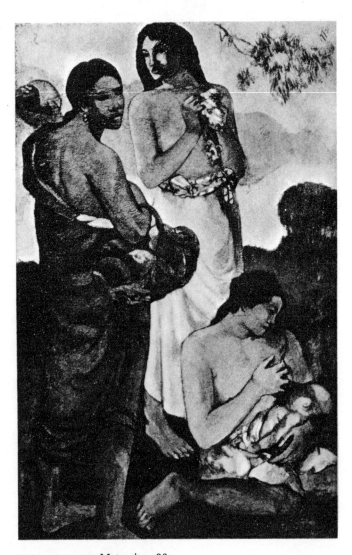

PAUL GAUGUIN: *Maternity* 1889

THE

TENTH MUSE

Essays in Criticism

by

SIR HERBERT EDWARD READ

Essay Index Reprint Series

 BOOKS FOR LIBRARIES PRESS
FREEPORT, NEW YORK

STANDARD BOOK NUMBER:

8369-1427-9

LIBRARY OF CONGRESS CATALOG CARD NUMBER:

73-99646

PRINTED IN THE UNITED STATES OF AMERICA

To
W. G. ARCHER, O.B.E.
who suggested this book

CONTENTS

CONTENTS

ILLUSTRATIONS

"Yes," said Goethe to Eckermann, "I may have missed writing many a good thing, but when I reflect, I am not sorry. I have always regarded all I have done solely as symbolical; and, in fact, it has been tolerably indifferent to me whether I have made pots or dishes."

May 2, 1824

THE

TENTH MUSE

I

On Something in Particular

"AT PRESENT the essay, as a serious, yet personal, intimate, and friendly way of public utterance, is at a low ebb. Those who write 'easy' essays write idly about trifles, often with some elegance, in the tone of polite society; but these things are essentially empty. The tendency is to write articles, not about things in general, about life as it is lived and thought about, or lived and not thought about by the essayist, but about something in particular—literature let us say—from a rather expert or professional point of view."

Thus writes one of the most graceful of living essayists on the modern English essay,[1] and I, as another and less graceful essayist, must confess that the criticism is just. I tend to write "about something in particular", and from a *rather* expert or professional point of view; and generally my essays are called articles, perhaps because they are not personal enough, certainly not intimate enough, to deserve the grander name. An "essay"—that undoubtedly is a form not merely of literature, but of *belles lettres*; an article—that is something paid for at so many guineas a thousand; an article, indeed, of commerce.

[1] Bonamy Dobrée, in *English Essayists*. London, 1946.

I doubt if I could write an *easy* essay, just to express my thoughts about life in general. The only essays in this volume that were not written about something in particular, on a particular occasion and for a particular purpose, were written as pegs to hang my coat on; and even then I was creating my own particular purpose. The rest were written to command—the command of editors and talks producers—as reviews and broadcasts. Each had a particular subject and in each I tried to express a critical opinion. And that is the way of writing forced on one by the circumstances of our time. It may be a bad way of writing, but at least it belongs to the pattern of our way of life.

The circumstances which dictate the form of the modern essay to the writer are economic. The writer cannot dictate to the public: most certainly he cannot dictate to the editors who interpret the demands of the public. Even if the writer is a man of financial independence and ample leisure, and can sit quietly in some country retreat rounding off his five or ten thousand words in the manner of Hazlitt or Macaulay, what is he then to do with the product? No journals like the old *Quarterly* or *Edinburgh* now exist to accommodate such essays; and if some idealist were to cause one to come into existence, such is the pace of modern life that no one would have time to read it. The *Criterion* made an attempt to restore the serious essay, and I took part in that forlorn effort. We failed because we were travelling in a coach-and-four along a first-class motor road, where speed and the number of passengers were the prime essentials. We were often complimented on our elegant turn-out, but there were few who wanted to adopt our pace.

I believe that in the coming years the essay will change even more decisively through the influence of broadcasting. The good talk is a spoken essay, and it usually reads well when printed. That depends, of course, on one's definition of a good talk; personally I am glad to see the last of the mannered talks —the groans and hesitations, the pompous deliberation and fatuous intonations, which passed for a good broadcasting style in the early days. Directness and sincerity have been recognized as the essential qualities of good broadcasting, and these are the essential qualities of good essay writing. But broadcasting imposes standard lengths and usually short lengths, and it imposes a particular subject. The radio does not exist to put across trifles (though it might well be a little less serious): it does not exist to propagate a personal view of life. It encourages intimacy of approach (which is all to the good), and it magnifies and makes intolerable any form of affectation. When one can afford to be serious, or even idle with elegance, as on the Third Programme, then broadcasting is an ideal medium for the essayist.

Must the modern essayist be an expert, as Professor Dobrée suggests? It depends on what is meant by an expert. An expert is usually a man who knows everything about one thing, and nothing much about anything else—he has a fanatical single-track mind: he burrows in a tunnel where no side-passages admit light and air. His counterpart is a man who knows a little about everything and nothing much about anything in particular. I myself am sometimes accused of eclecticism. I do not object to the charge. The essayists I most admire—Bacon, Hazlitt, Bagehot—they too were eclectic. If one has a beam of intelligence, let it play where it lists, so long as it has power and penetration, and a fixed centre.

The intensity and restlessness of modern life forces the essayist to dubious shifts: he is commanded by pressures and exigencies which distort the true picture of his interests. I have been persuaded to write on some subjects beyond my competence, and by chance I have never been asked to write on subjects near my heart. But the longer one lives and the more one writes, the more complete the pattern becomes.

I do not pretend that there is any pattern discernible in the miscellany that follows this opening essay—indeed, if the title had not already been used by Paul Valéry, I might have called it *Variety*. I do not even claim the virtue of consistency, and I am sure a logician could have fine intellectual sport in exposing my contradictions—my paralogisms, as he might call them. I am not in desperate search of what Mr. Crawshay-Williams has called "the comforts of unreason": rather, I am a pluralist, content to let loose a number of truths with no desire to bring them within a house of correction, no itch to reduce them to some "unifying formula". The quotation from C. F. Ramuz's *Journal* which I put in front of a previous collection of this kind, *A Coat of Many Colours*, was meant as a warning, an excuse, a confession of this possible deficiency. That quotation, which I left in French because I found it too difficult to translate into adequate English, is a fairly exact and very compact summary of my general outlook—of an attitude I would never venture to call a philosophy. I might paraphrase it thus: Never yield to habit, especially to habits of thought which polish away the rough edges of truth; remain open, innocent, original. Put away childish things, but retain, all the same, a core of childhood, a slender vein of vital sap which the rings of growth may hide, but must never destroy. Keep a reserve of simplicity, even of primitiveness, so that you do not meet elementary situations with sophistication. Your aim should be, not simply to be, but rather to be ever capable of becoming—not at rest, but moving with the moving world—always in touch with what is changing, changing oneself—open, like the child, to the whole world without, but with an inward reserve which the child does not yet possess, where one gathers a little strength, a certain order.

4

2

The Art of Art Criticism

BY ART CRITICISM in the accepted sense, we mean the current criticism of painting, sculpture, architecture and other visual arts. But what is "criticism"? There is ambiguity in this very word, for it is obvious that the nature of criticism must be determined by the nature of the audience to which it is addressed. A teacher, moving from easel to easel in the life class, will be critical in one manner—pointing to faulty composition in one case, to an insensitive line in another, to inadequacies of all kinds; at the same time praising the successes where they exist, and always urging on his pupils by communicating to them his sympathy and enthusiasm. That I would call *professional* criticism, and with its technicalities and jargon it should be confined to its proper sphere, the studio or the school of art.

There is another kind of criticism which should also be confined to a school. Though it can be applied to contemporary art, it is, properly speaking, *historical* criticism, by which I mean the delineation of movements and groups, the description of styles, the analysis of techniques and materials—in general, the post-mortem attitude to art.

Finally, there is what I would call the *aesthetical* or philosophical criticism of art. In so far as aesthetics is a science, and philosophy a discipline, this also is a form of criticism that calls for a specialized terminology and a concentrated manner of thought. The best art critics have, of course, a philosophical background: their criticism is an *applied* philosophy, but is not in itself a philosophical activity.

What, then, are we left with that might be called simply art criticism? It must be an activity addressed, not to a professional minority of any kind, but to the general body of educated opinion, and it must give its public something it wants—something it is not capable of finding for itself—in one word, enlightenment.

Such a criticism will be either *informative* or *interpretative*. It will not assume that everyone has seen the work of art the critic is talking about; on the contrary, it will try to give everyone a vivid image of the object in question. Having done this, the critic will proceed to interpret the artist's intention, and in the end he may express his own view of the artist's achievement, and this view need not necessarily be favourable. But most critics, I am afraid, never stop to ask what the artist was trying to do; they assume that there is only one way of doing a particular job (painting a landscape, building a cathedral) and they proceed to criticize the artist for not doing the job as *they* would have done it.

But some critics make a practice of imputing to the artist motives which he never had in mind; and they criticize him for not doing what he never intended to do. There can be no true interpretation without complete sympathy and understanding. The lack of sympathy, and therefore of understanding, may be due to the confusing variety of modern styles. Ruskin was faced by an extreme deviation from one style, which we call realism; a modern critic has to cope with a wide variation of execution in at least four distinct styles—realism, super-realism, expressionism and abstract art. He may have sufficient sympathy for realism to make a good critic of realistic painting, but be so completely out of sympathy with abstract art as to be quite incapable of writing anything sensible about it. Few critics would refrain on that account from criticizing abstract art.

I think the modern art critic fails most conspicuously on the descriptive or visualizing side of his activity. Perhaps the verbal description of a painting, a piece of sculpture or a building, is regarded as somewhat old-fashioned. "It seems all right," as Georges Duthuit says, "to speak *because* of a picture, but speaking *of* it must be avoided as much as possible." Photographs and various methods of reproduction have made it easy—in periodicals and in television, but not in broadcasting—to dispense with a lot of verbal description; it is assumed that the reader can grasp from the illustration what the picture or piece of sculpture is about; as well as various details of its composition. Here, maybe, we are near the heart of the present malady, for I believe that the critic ought to be capable of giving an exact verbal description of the object which has caused him aesthetic pleasure or displeasure—only in that way can he be sure that his experience is a complete one, and that the necessary transformation has taken place in his mind which will enable him to criticize the processes of one art (say painting) in the terms of another art (the art of writing).

That, at any rate, was the method of the old art critics—of Hazlitt and Ruskin, of Diderot and Baudelaire. They were all masters of the art of writing, and to them a work of art—a painting or a building—was first and foremost something to be described, something to be *realized in words*, just as a painting in its turn had been something to be realized in paint. One might take, as a perfect example of this type of art criticism, Hazlitt's essay "On a Landscape of Nicolas Poussin"—an essay of some three to four thousand words, first published in *The New Monthly Magazine* for August, 1821. I emphasize that fact to show that it was written as journalism. It deals with Poussin's "Orion", painted in 1658, which Hazlitt had seen in an exhibition at the British Institution. The whole process of

7

criticism is, for Hazlitt, infinitely leisurely. There was no paper shortage in 1821, no restriction of space, and the public had leisured vacancies to fill. So he begins with some account of the legend of "Orion", so that we can appreciate the justness of the painter's selection of a particular incident and scene, and the pertinency with which it has been treated. Then there is a disquisition on the relation of art to nature—to make the point that Poussin's art is "a second nature, not a different one". By this he means that a painter like Poussin—he calls him an "historic" painter, meaning what we should now call a "literary" painter—that such a painter "does not neglect nature, but follows her more closely into her fantastic heights, or hidden recesses. He demonstrates what she would be in conceivable circumstances, and under implied conditions". Hazlitt then interpolates an attack on the lifeless imitators, the dull traducers of nature, and by this time he is half-way through his essay, and must come to his main point, which is: that Poussin was, of all painters, the most poetical. To prove this point will demand a lot of significant detail, not only from the picture under observation, but from Poussin's work in general. Subsidiary points will be made—for example, that Poussin succeeded better in classic than in sacred subjects. A comparison with Rubens is called for, and then we come to a definition which shows the bias of Hazlitt's own mind. "Pictures," he says, "are a set of chosen images, a stream of pleasant thoughts passing through the mind. . . . A life passed among pictures, in the study and the love of art, is a happy noiseless dream: or rather, it is to dream and to be awake at the same time; for it has all 'the sober certainty of waking bliss' with the romantic voluptuousness of a visionary and abstracted being. Pictures are the bright consummate essences of things. . . ." And then Hazlitt checks his eloquence to return to "Orion", and to the gallery in which he had seen the picture,

8

and with a final tribute to the private patrons of art and to the enterprise of those who had organized the exhibition of loans from their collection, he ends his essay.

A leisurely performance, indeed; not apt for the fraction of a newspaper column which is now all that is at the disposal of the modern art critic, nor even for the twenty minutes or so that is put at the disposal of a broadcaster.

The critic in the daily newspaper or the weekly review does not *describe* the works he criticizes, simply because it is not possible to do so in the space at his disposal; so he resorts, either to the supposition that his readers have seen what he is criticizing, or to shorthand symbols which only the initiated understand.

In broadcasting the position should be easier: the time given to an art talk is equivalent to quite a lengthy critical review, but the critic often seems to carry over into the medium of broadcasting the clipped and emaciated language of the Press.

Let me now quote two examples of the kind of criticism that can be read at any time in a weekly periodical. I shall not mention the names of the critics, because they are irrelevant; and I freely admit that I myself might have spoken in a similar vein. The first is from *The Listener* and was not broadcast:

At the Lefèvre Gallery Hans Tisdall has enlarged his scope by a remarkable act of self-abnegation. For him, a full range of colour was always a temptation to turn a picture into a decoration, and, having a daring sense of colour, he succumbed to the temptation. Perhaps, realizing his weakness, he has gone deliberately into a kind of aesthetic retreat, or perhaps he has tired of the seductions of a rainbow palette. Whatever the reason, his recent paintings—still-lifes mainly—are worked out in a monochrome tempered with accents of pale colour. The result is a new range of expressiveness. The familiar rococo pattern is impregnated with space and light and density. The eye no

9

longer slides off into patterned surface but explores the shapes and is drawn in between them.

That is very different from Hazlitt's style of criticism, but it is quite typical of present-day art criticism. I personally do not experience any difficulty in understanding what the critic is saying, for I have studied the private language in which it is written. Not knowing that language, you might protest that if a picture is not a decoration, then what is it; and why shouldn't it be decorative? But I, as one of the initiated, know that a theoretical distinction has been made by modern art critics between painting and decoration, and it is one of the accepted clichés of modern art criticism. We do not stop to discuss the distinction: we assume that the reader is in the secret, and will not stop to question what we mean.

Again, when the critic tells us that "the familiar rococo pattern is impregnated with space and light and density" and that "the eye no longer slides off into patterned surface but explores the shapes and is drawn in between them", I know what these rather mixed metaphors mean. My knowledge of the history of art has given me a general idea of "rococo pattern", but I wonder how many readers know the difference, for example, between a rococo and a baroque pattern?

As for the difficult feat of impregnating such a pattern, not only with space and light, but at the same time with density; and the still more mysterious business of an eye that slides off surfaces, explores shapes and ends by getting drawn in between them—all that will require, on the part of the poor blind reader—I call him blind because he has never seen the painting in question—a prodigious power of visualization.

Now let me take another example—from a broadcast talk which I personally found very illuminating, but which at the time baffled some listeners:

In looking at some of Bacon's paintings we are conscious at first only of the paint, seeing it as some amorphous, ectoplasmic substance floating aimlessly on the canvas. It takes a little time before this stuff that is paint crystallizes into an image. But as soon as it does crystallize, the once vague and shifting shapes become volumes modelled with a wonderful sensitivity and situated with extreme precision in space.

The certainty with which Bacon creates volumes, volumes that are tangible, is largely due to his uncanny sense of the exact degree of tension along each form.

Admittedly there is some jargon here: "volumes" are not "modelled" in any precisely visual sense: they may be suggested by certain pictorial means: and only in some metaphorical sense could such volumes become "tangible". We don't "touch" volumes; we fill them, either really or imaginatively. But apart from such impressions, the language is such as might be used by a lecturer in a physics laboratory. If you protest that art is not physics, I think the critic would be justified in retorting that that is just what it is—the manipulation of physical substances to create the illusion of physical elements like space and colour. And it is perfectly legitimate to use a physical concept like "tension", for it is the physical experience that the painter wants to convey—Francis Bacon, for example, wants to recreate in the spectator the actual feeling of the stretched-out armpits and biceps conveyed in his painting of the Crucifixion. In describing the painter's intention in terminology taken from the science of physics, this particular critic was, I would say, using precise analytical language. It would seem, therefore, that what we really distrust—and by "we" I mean the general public—is the analytical method itself: we remember Wordsworth's phrase, "we murder to dissect", and we would rather be left with a living unity, however baffling it might be. Should not criticism confine itself to giving us the sense of wholeness, the sense of richness, the sense of interest—which was the impression Hazlitt gave us of Poussin's "Orion"?

The critic might reply: "Give me a Poussin, and I will rival Hazlitt: but I can't do a Hazlitt over the amorphous ectoplasm of modern art."

The material the modern art critic has to criticize is not the same—we could hardly describe Francis Bacon's paintings, for example, as "a stream of pleasant thoughts passing through the mind!" And an abstraction by Ben Nicholson does not offer quite the same opportunities for poetic disquisition as "blind Orion hungry for the morn". In deserting Nature, in the sense in which Hazlitt understood that term, the modern artist has left the critic speechless, or at any rate in need of a new language. This, of course, is not true of all types of modern art; the surrealist painters gave their critics plenty of poetic grist; and the more recent return to the old English habit of anecdotage in paint might eventually inspire a corresponding loquacity in criticism—given the space for it. But so far there is no sign of it.

It has been said that there is nothing more boring to listen to than the relation of other people's dreams. The modern anecdotal painting has that dream-like quality, and I can imagine the listener becoming very restive if submitted to a descriptive essay in the manner of Hazlitt on, say, a landscape by Salvador Dali. This is not necessarily an adverse comment on the work of those two painters; it merely implies that different kinds of subject demand different critical approaches. Still, let us face this problem; the problem of critical procedure in relation to works of art which do not lend themselves to direct description.

I believe that a solution of this problem does exist, though it has yet to be proved that people will accept it. It consists in shifting the critical attention from the work of art as object, to the work of art as symbol: from the meaning of the work of art to its motive: in other words, for *description* the critic substitutes *interpretation*. This is not only more difficult than description or analysis: as a method it is woefully subject to error; and by descending so deeply into the psychological realm, the critic may fail in his first duty, which is to keep a sensuous eye on the work of art.

This kind of criticism began, I suppose, with Walter Pater, and his famous prose-poem on the "Mona Lisa", or the equally beautiful description of Botticelli's "Venus", would illustrate what I mean. Pater gives us not only a perfectly conveyed description of the painting, so that we can visualize it although we may never have seen the original or a reproduction, but at the same time an interpretation of its meaning or significance; and all done without any of the machinery of analysis. And it is beautiful to read and to listen to; it is criticism raised in itself to an art, the art of prose, the least appreciated but the most essential of all human arts, for it is the daily bread of communication.

But Pater, you will say, was a genius, and therefore an exception. But I do not think his method of criticism is exceptional, even today. It is merely not fashionable. I might quote a contemporary critic like Adrian Stokes, but that would not be a fair test, for he writes about the same kind of art as Pater—on Giorgione, Desiderio, Piero della Francesca; and with a not incomparable eloquence. I shall take instead a French critic whose name I have already mentioned— Georges Duthuit. His book on *The Fauvist Painters* is a brilliant illustration of what I mean by interpretative criticism: interpretative even when negative. You must not expect a Pateresque passage: it is eighty years since Pater wrote his criticism and since then one of the greatest revolutions in the history of art has taken place. Duthuit's best pages are devoted to the praise of Matisse, but I find it difficult to detach one of these. Here, instead, is a passage in dispraise of Vlaminck, who is compared with Van Gogh:

And now I am afraid, not of being unjust, but of not having insisted enough on the paintings, and there are a certain number of them, in which Vlaminck shows disgust with his usual concoctions, hastily spiced, daubed and peppered, and served up cold; in which, miraculously, he lets his colour carry him along. But what obsesses me is this Van Gogh, to whom his adoptive son, self-adopted, without asking anybody's permission, never ceases to burn incense, with the utmost cordiality, the better to burn incense to himself, immoderately. How can one help being irritated? And as ill-luck would have it, just as I was writing this chapter, I came across some of his feeblest paintings, inexpressibly pretentious and facile. In nothing do they recall, except in such a way as to arouse our indignation, the consternation of the sacrificial victim of the sun of Saint-Rémy, the desperate decisions of the man who preferred not to sign his work, and who, with a shattering humility, compared his most successful paintings to "rough and bungled sketches". Specifically I have in mind two dead fish on a dish-clout, and dead is the word, two varnished corpses. Plush tablecloth of a rather crude dye, laboured with knife and brush, heroically, as though this flaccid material could not be mastered in any other way. With cold-blooded fury Vlaminck has triturated certain passages, in order to ape the passion of Vincent the predestined, who died of his passion, and who with a single lash of the whip could destroy and transfigure the whole of a heterogenous world. Vlaminck, the prudent pugilist, stamps in a pre-arranged space, taking care not to go beyond it, respecting its conventional limits and reinforcing them if need be. He rumples his clout, but his two whitings have been set neatly upon it by an eternal housekeeper, who always manages to slip away before the painter has set up his easel. What, then, is the meaning of these incendiary lights that illumine the eyes, border the gills and fins of these edibles, ready to be rolled in flour? The skin does not even remotely suggest the rainbow. One suspects that the scandal is due only to the smell of fried fish that has invaded the salon; for it is on a fine piece of plush, prize-winner at the Universal Exhibition of 1900, that the chef has set his livid animalcula, beside an overflowing Sunday fruit bowl. A blow from which the glittering drawing-room and the fish will not recover. Soon the painter will give up and bring back his whole bag of tricks to the kitchen gloom. Meanwhile the pair of bi-coloured whitings, horror-stricken, show themselves off on this wisp of silk that makes van Gogh's sunflowers look like old junk.[1]

That, I think, will give the reader a vivid idea of Vlaminck's painting, and, by implication, a better understanding of the essential quality of van Gogh's work. The words convey the very processes of the painter's mind, the physical transmutation of these processes into paint. The metaphors are sometimes far-fetched, but there is no technical jargon—one is made to experience, through another medium, the literary medium, the emotional impact of an object seen by the critic, and if the critic can do that for us, he has served well, not only the reading public, but also, and this is surely important, the artist.

I warned the reader that an interpretative criticism of a modern artist would not be so easy to take in as Hazlitt's descriptive criticism of Poussin. More imaginative effort is required because the mind is being asked to reconstruct, not a familiar myth or a second nature, but a reality. "A new reality"—how easy it is to utter a phrase like that: how difficult it is for the public to know what it means, or if it means arything. We follow Alice into a Wonderland willingly enough, in spite of the Dodo and the Ugly Duchess and the terrors of a contracting and expanding universe; we are glad to meet Renoir and Matisse, but we are less anxious to meet the grimmer creations of Picasso or Francis Bacon.

[1] *The Fauvist Painters* by Georges Duthuit. Translated by Ralph Manheim. New York, 1950.

The task of the modern critic of art is difficult, but that must not be used as an excuse for an obscurity which is a retreat into jargon, nor for a snobbism which is an attempt to reserve certain pleasures for a minority. The "difficulty" of modern art must be accepted by the critic as a challenge—a challenge to his powers of interpretation, a challenge to his capacity for communication. We live in an epoch in which people *must understand*: deep no longer calleth unto deep—symbols must be translated into concepts. That is the critic's job: to take the symbols of the painter or sculptor and translate them, if not into intellectual concepts, then into poetic metaphors. Art criticism can be conducted on the level of explanation; but also on the level of translation. The best art criticism reaches both levels, and to the clarity of a rational discourse, adds the colour of a sensuous style. Inspired by the love of truth, it can rise to the greatest heights of thought and eloquence, and in the hands of a Ruskin or a Pater, proffer tributes to a tenth muse.

II

It is sometimes said that there is no art criticism to compare with the greatest literary or philosophical criticism. That is a prejudice due, I believe, to our academic neglect of art. Our schools and universities recognize literature and literary criticism as worthy subjects of study, but painting, sculpture and architecture are either completely ignored, or treated as elegant optional additions to the normal curriculum. The result is a general depreciation of the literature of art; its very existence, on a scale comparable to the literature of poetry or drama, might be denied. If, however, we look at the general body of criticism, not only in England, but in western and central Europe, we find that a considerable proportion of the best of it has in fact been directed to the visual arts.

I have already suggested that in the hands of a master—and I mentioned the names of Ruskin and Pater—criticism can become in itself another art. In citing these two names I did not mean to imply that the work of art would serve as well as any other subject to inspire good prose, or that a good style would justify any kind of criticism. A good style, I would say, is the product of a well-ordered mind moved by a worthy passion. Ruskin had enthusiasm, passionate enthusiasm, for Turner's paintings, but he also thought clearly about art in general, and was therefore able to relate his immediate experience to basic principles. The experience was deeply sincere, and because Turner was suffering from the misunderstanding that is the usual fate of original artists, Ruskin was moved to a passionate defence of him. But the analysing mind kept pace with the sympathetic heart, and the result was not only great English prose, but also great art criticism.

In this field I would place Ruskin's achievement above all other criticism of whatever kind written in the English language. Where is the work of literary criticism that can compare with *Modern Painters* or *Stones of Venice*—compare in scope and eloquence and in what, in the original sense of the word, one might call righteousness? Coleridge's *Biographia Literaria* is perhaps philosophically more profound, but that philosophy is in part borrowed from Schelling, so Coleridge cannot have all the credit for it. As for the rest of Coleridge's great argument, one might say that it secured for Wordsworth almost exactly the same kind of understanding that Ruskin secured for Turner. These two achievements might be considered as of almost equal value in the history of English culture. But nowhere in *Biographia Literaria*—and I say this in spite of the fact that it is a book to which I am intensely devoted—nowhere will you find those mounting themes of imaginative splendour into which Ruskin's criticism

17

lifts itself, not once, but a hundred times. We may read Ruskin's art criticism as great literature, but if we do not at the same time recognize it as great criticism, it is because of some deep-seated indifference to art. For as criticism it is supreme.

I will quote, as an example of Ruskin's criticism, a passage which he himself looked back upon with satisfaction—his description of the painting he regarded as Turner's greatest— "The Slave Ship":

But, I think, the noblest sea that Turner has ever painted and, if so, the noblest certainly ever painted by man, is that of the "Slave Ship", the chief Academy picture of the Exhibition of 1840. It is a sunset on the Atlantic, after prolonged storm; but the storm is partially lulled, and the torn and streaming rainclouds are moving in scarlet lines to lose themselves in the hollow of the night. The whole surface of sea included in the picture is divided into two ridges of enormous swell, not high, nor local, but a low broad heaving of the whole ocean, like the lifting of its bosom by deep-drawn breath after the torture of the storm. Between these two ridges the fire of the sunset falls along the trough of the sea, dyeing it with an awful but glorious light, the intense and lurid splendour which burns like gold, and bathes like blood. Along this fiery path and valley, the tossing waves by which the swell of the sea is restlessly divided, lift themselves in dark in-definite, fantastic forms, each casting a faint and ghastly shadow behind it along the illumined foam. They do not rise everywhere, but three or four together in wild groups, fitfully and furiously, as the under strength of the swell compels or permits them; leaving between them treacherous spaces of level and whirling water, now lighted with green and lamp-like fire, now flashing back the gold of the declining sun, now fearfully dyed from above, with the un-distinguishable images of the burning clouds, which fall upon them in flakes of crimson and scarlet, and give to the reckless waves the added motion of their own fiery flying. Purple and blue, the lurid shadows of the hollow breakers are cast upon the mist of night which gathers cold and low, advancing like the shadow of death upon the guilty ship as it labours amidst the lightning of the sea, its thin masts written upon the sky in lines of blood, girded with condemnation in that fearful hue which signs the sky with horror, and mixes its flaming flood with the sunlight, and, cast far along the desolate heave of the sepulchral eaves, incarnadines the multitudinous sea.

I believe, if I were reduced to rest Turner's immortality upon any single work, I should choose this. Its daring conception, ideal in the highest sense of the word, is based on the purest truth and wrought out with the concentrated knowledge of a life; its colour is absolutely perfect, not one false or morbid hue in any part or line, and so modulated that every square inch of canvas is a perfect composition; its drawing as accurate as fearless; the ship buoyant, bending, and full of motion; its tones as true as they are wonderful; and the whole picture dedicated to the most sublime of subjects and impressions (completing thus the perfect system of all truth, which we have shown to be formed by Turner's works)—the power, majesty, and deathliness of the open, deep, illimitable sea.

In that last sentence, you may have noticed, there is a parenthesis in which Ruskin claims to have shown that Turner's works form "the perfect system of truth"—an achievement which, in Ruskin's opinion, he shared with only a few choice spirits such as Homer, Shakespeare, Milton and Pope. We cannot stop to examine the validity of this claim: I merely draw attention to it to show that art criticism, no less than literary criticism, can have a philosophical scope.

For another example of art criticism that rises to the heights of literary art I would like to suggest Ruskin's contemporary, Charles Baudelaire. A good deal of the poetry that went into Ruskin's prose Baudelaire reserved for his verse; but his art criticism has the same largeness of view, the same philosophical scope. Baudelaire once said that art criticism ought to be partial, passionate and political—made from an exclusive point of view, but from the point of view that opens up the widest horizons. His own criticism has that enlightening quality; and in his case again there was a particular cause for enthusiasm, a subject for passionate advocacy—the art of Delacroix. Here is a passage from one of his essays on that painter:

In order to complete the analysis, it remains for me to draw attention to a final quality in Delacroix—the most remarkable of all his qualities and the one that makes him the true nineteenth-century painter. It is the strange persistent melancholy which broods over all his work and which is expressed by his choice of subject, by the expression on his people's faces, by gesture and by the way he uses colour. Delacroix is an admirer of Dante and Shakespeare, two other great painters of human suffering. He understands them perfectly and is able to draw on them freely. When we look at a collection of his paintings—"Dante and Virgil", "The Massacre of Scio", "Christ in the Garden of Olives", "St. Sebastian", "Medea", "The Shipwrecked" and "Hamlet", so derided and so little understood—we have the impression that we are attending the celebration of some sad rite. We notice in several of them, as though it were the result of some perpetual chance, one figure which is more stricken, more weighted down by grief than all the rest and which seems to contain in it all the surrounding suffering. We see it in the woman kneeling with her hair hanging down in the foreground of "The Crusaders at Constantinople"; in the mournful wrinkled features of the old woman in "The Massacre of Scio". His melancholy envelops even "The Women of Algiers" the most stylish and decorative of all his pictures. This little poem of an interior, so restful, so bathed in silence, so stuffed with rich furnishings and odds and ends of finery, exudes the strong indefinable odour of an evil place which quickly leads us to unplumbed depths of sadness. In general, he does not paint pretty women, at any rate not pretty by the standards of fashionable society. Nearly all of them are sick and glow with a certain inner beauty. He does not express strength by swelling muscles, but by nervous tension. It is not only suffering that he expresses better than anyone else, but above all—supreme secret of his art—moral suffering! This grave, lofty melancholy shines with a sombre splendour in his very

colouring which like that of all the great colourists is broad, simple
and rich in harmonic masses, but plaintive and deep-toned as a
melody of Weber's.

Each of the old masters had his kingdom and his prerogative which
he was often compelled to share with illustrious rivals. Raphael's was
form; that of Rubens and Veronese, colour; that of Rubens and
Michelangelo, imaginative design. A portion of the empire remained
where Rembrandt alone had made a few incursions—drama, natural
living drama, terrible and sombre drama which was often expressed
by means of colour, but always by means of gesture . . .

This quality, which is essentially modern and new, makes Delacroix the final expression of progress in art. The heir of a great
tradition—the tradition of breadth, nobility and grandeur of composition and the worthy successor of the old masters, he excels them
in his mastery of suffering, passion and gesture. That is the real significance of his greatness. Suppose, for example, the work of one
of the celebrated old masters were to be lost. There would nearly
always be someone like him whose work would explain his and
enable the historian to grasp what had been lost. Take away Delacroix,
and the great chain of history snaps and falls to the ground.

I believe that Ruskin and Baudelaire are the two greatest
art critics of modern times, and they are both distinguished by
the quality of *enthusiasm*. It is a quality from which academic
minds shrink, and it can indeed involve a writer in mistakes
and even in absurdities. These do not matter in the long run.
There are dozens of names in Baudelaire's *Salons*—the notices
of exhibitions which he wrote between 1845 and 1859—
which are now completely forgotten. Most of them he dismissed with a withering phrase; others he praised for qualities
that were merely topical. Ruskin's mistakes were more disastrous, especially in his later days—I need mention only the
name of Whistler. The contemporary scene is always a turmoil, and he who ventures into it, brandishing a sword in the
cause of truth, is sure to hit a few of the wrong people on the

head. But the critic must enter that turmoil—however much one's principles have been formed by the study of the history of art, or by the study of the science of art, those principles do not deserve the name of criticism until they are applied to the living reality of art. Criticism is discrimination, is guidance, and it is useless if it never ventures outside a museum. Every age has its own sense of beauty, and it is the critic's business to isolate and define that particular nuance—if only for the purpose of condemning it.

I cannot think of any great critic—great in the sense I have defined, great as an artist in his own rights—who has not found some good in the art of his own age. It is true that there have been critics who have not found anything particularly interesting to say about the art of their own time, but I do not think one can put them on the same level as Ruskin or Baudelaire. A good example is Eugene Fromentin, himself a disappointed painter, out of sympathy with contemporaries like Delacroix and Courbet, a man without passions, nervous and feminine, as Baudelaire said of him. He had a sensitive talent for description, and wrote a novel of great charm, as well as two or three books of travel. But he also wrote a book on Dutch and Flemish painting from Van Eyck to Rembrandt—*Les Maîtres d'autrefois,* which is undoubtedly one of the masterpieces of art criticism. But it is again a triumph of the art of writing, and if Fromentin is not a critic of the art of his own time, he does manage, by his method of writing, to bring the old masters into the contemporary context. For example, before writing about Rembrandt he describes Amsterdam—not the Amsterdam of Rembrandt's time, but the Amsterdam he himself saw in 1875, and very beautiful and evocative it all is! And he is, as a writer (and even as a painter) a romantic of his time. The best example of his style is his description of Rembrandt's "Night Watch":

There remains an episodic figure which up to the present has baffled all conjectures, because it seems to personify in its traits, its dress, its strange brilliance, and its little bearing on the subject, the magic, the romantic meaning, or, if you like, the counter-sense of the picture. I mean the little person with the look of a witch, childish yet very old, with comet-like head-dress and ornamented tresses, who glides, we scarcely understand why, among the legs of the guards, and who—a thing no less inexplicable—wears suspended from her waist a white cock, which we might take at first for a purse.

Whatever reason it may have had for mixing with this assembly, this small figure seems to have nothing human about it at all. It is colourless, almost shapeless. Its age is doubtful because its traits are indefinable. Its appearance is that of a doll and its behaviour automatic. It has the ways of a beggar, and something like diamonds all over the body—the air of a little queen, with garments like rags. One might say that she came from the Jewish quarter, from the old clothes shop, from the theatre or some Bohemian place, and that, awakening from a dream, she dressed herself in the most singular fashion. She has the glimmerings, the uncertainty and the flickerings of pale fire. The more one examines the less can one seize the subtle lineaments which serve as a covering for her incorporeal existence! We come to see in her nothing but a sort of extraordinarily strange phosphorescence which is not the natural light of things, nor yet the ordinary brilliancy of a well-regulated palette, and which adds a witchery the more to the strangeness of the physiognomy. Note that in the place she occupies in one of the dark corners of the canvas, rather low, in the middle distance, between a man in dark red and the captain dressed in black, this eccentric light has the more activity, that the contrast with the surroundings is more sudden, and that, without extreme precautions, this explosion of accidental light would have been enough to disorganize the whole picture.

What is the meaning of the little being, imaginary or real, which, though but a supernumerary, seems to have taken possession of the principal role? I cannot undertake to tell you. Men more skilful than myself have not failed to ask themselves what this might be, what it is doing there, and have not been able to discover a satisfactory solution.

One thing astonishes me, and that is that people argue with Rembrandt as if he himself were a reasoner. They are enraptured with the novelty, the originality, the absence of all rule, the free flight of an entirely individual imagination, which make up, as has been well said, the great attraction of this venturesome work; and it is precisely the fine flower of his somewhat disordered imagination, which people subject to an examination by logic and pure reason. But if, to all these rather vain questions about the why and wherefore of so many things which probably have none at all, Rembrandt were to reply thus: "This child is a caprice, no less odd than, and for that matter quite as plausible as, many others in my engraved and painted work. I have set it there, as a narrow light between great masses of shade, because its slightness gave it more vibration, and it suited me to enliven one of the dark corners of my picture with a streak of light. Its get-up is, moreover, the ordinary dress of my figures of women, great or small, young or old, and you will find in it the type which, more or less like, is continually found in my works. I like whatever shines brightly, and that is why I have dressed it in brilliant apparel. As to the phosphorescent glimmer which seems to cause you so much astonishment here, while in other places it passes unnoticed, it is in its colourless sparkle, and in its supernatural quality, the light that I usually give my personages when I want them to shine rather vividly." Don't you think that such an answer would have in it sufficient to satisfy the most exacting, and that finally, the rights of the producer being reserved, he would have nothing to answer to us for save on one point; the manner in which he has treated the picture?

The point I want to make about this extract is that the sensibility which Fromentin brings to the appreciation of Rembrandt was the romantic sensibility of 1875, and not some passionless and disinterested analysis of the academic kind. How easy it would have been, before 1875, to have ignored the very existence of that mysterious little witch in Rembrandt's otherwise very solemn picture—or if not easy to have ignored her presence, to have missed her significance! In his way, therefore, Fromentin is as contemporary as Baudelaire or Ruskin. What is odd is that the eye that could appreciate Rembrandt's little witch could not appreciate Manet's *Bon Bock*.

I would say that a blindness to contemporary modes of expression, in any of the arts, is generally due to some psychological inhibition in the spectator, but that is a generalization that would have to be supported by more evidence than I can command at present. The whole problem of inhibition in relation to both the creation and appreciation of art is one which calls for scientific research. I think one might as well face the fact that no amount of interpretative criticism is going to make certain types of people like certain types of modern art. The momentum of the realistic tradition is too great for them—they are not prepared, either by education or environment, for an art that rejects realism. Now the kind of art criticism written by Ruskin, Pater and Baudelaire was always concerned with what might be broadly called pictorial motives. (Every picture tells a story, and criticism has often been the retelling in the critic's words of the theme of the painting.) There is no story in an abstract painting by Ben Nicholson, and the story in many other types of modern art is not of the kind that lends itself to *expatiation*. A still-life by Braque, an odalisque by Matisse, one of Henry Moore's reclining figures—the modern critic cannot approach them as the critics of former days approached Rembrandt, Turner or Delacroix. Even Fromentin when he came to deal with Rembrandt's colour, felt that he had to "leave the easy paths, enter the thicket, and 'talk shop'". But "shop" in 1875 was a fairly simple language of tones and tints, of high-lights and chiaroscuro. A succession of critics—Burckhardt, Wölfflin, Berenson, Roger Fry—enormously extended this scientific terminology, made it into a very exact instrument of formal analysis. Certain of the earlier phases of modern art—the paintings of Cézanne, those of the Cubists—lent themselves all too easily to the formalistic method. But this method becomes meaningless when applied to a picture like Picasso's "Guernica"; to a painting by Klee or Max Ernst, to Kokoschka's "Windbraut" or Chagall's "Russian Village"; or generally to the art of the last thirty years. Such artists are using other means, other conventions, to secure the desired effect, and a new type of art must call into existence a new type of art criticism.

We have, in fact, returned to a phase of art—the Byzantine period is an example in the past—in which the work of art is essentially a symbol and no longer a sign: that is to say, it attempts to express a meaning that cannot be expressed by realistic images. Once realism is abandoned most of the technical jargon of the old art criticism is beside the point, and a new critical vocabulary has to be invented. We live in a transitional period in which such a new language of criticism is gradually being evolved, and some of the difficulty of contemporary art criticism is due to that fact—there is no adequate terminology that is universally accepted. I can perhaps illustrate this difficulty by quoting a typical example of the formalistic criticism which has prevailed for the past half-century and then asking you to admit how impossible it would be to apply the same kind of criticism to a Byzantine mosaic or a painting by Picasso—I will take a short passage from Wölfflin's *Classic Art*, a book which along with the same author's *Principles of Art History* did so much to establish the terminology of modern art criticism:

The head emerges from the darkness of the background, not sharply relieved against a black foil as is sometimes the case with Perugino, but, as it were, encompassed in the greenish half-light and

the highest light does not fall on the face but on a scrap of shirt acci-
dentally displayed at the neck. The hood and collar are dull grey and
brown in colour. The large eyes look calmly out of their orbits. With
all its vibrantly painterly handling the effect of the whole is stabilized
by the vertical position of the head, the simple, full-face view and
the gentle fall of light which brings out exactly half the head and
illumines exactly the necessary points. The head seems to turn with
a quick movement and to be holding, just for a moment, the pose
which gives absolutely pure vertical and horizontal axis, the vertical
being continued right up to the peak of the cap. The simplicity of line
and reposeful masses of light and shadow unite with the clear definition of form of Andrea's developed style, with the bony structure
clearly understood. The way in which the angle at the junction
of nose and eye is brought out, the modelling of the chin, the indica-
tion of the cheek-bone are all strongly reminiscent of the style
of the "Disputa", which was clearly painted at about the same
time.

Wölfflin is describing, and criticizing, a typical Renaissance
portrait. His main concern is with the way the artist has
illuminated his subject, with the clear definition of natural
form, and with a certain ideal of humanism which is represented by these means. A Byzantine artist would not be pre-
occupied with a merely human ideal, but with a divine one;
and to represent such an ideal he would create a symbol, rigid
and hieratic, dominating the spectator by its suggestion of
supernatural power and mystery. Subtleties of modelling and
of light and shade would be irrelevant; the whole vocabulary
perfected by the critics of Renaissance art is irrelevant. Here,
however, is a passage from a contemporary art critic, and one
whose eloquence is not incomparable to Baudelaire's or
Ruskin's, which in the process of describing the essential
qualities of Byzantine art, renounces all jargon and returns
once more to poetry—it comes from the second volume of
André Malraux's *Psychology of Art*:

In the process of becoming Byzantinized, art sets out to destroy the independence of the depicted figure. The Roman painters had made it stand out against a neutral background like that of the classical stage-play. The semblance of a wall, a patch of landscape, sometimes even (as in the Timomachus copies) a hint of perspective, form set scenes in front of which the figures show up like statues in public squares. Christian art makes this background even more abstract; but sometimes makes it *solid,* and joins it up with the figures, which seem to sink back into it like foundering ships. It rediscovers darkness; the desert stars reappear in the night sky above "The Flight into Egypt" The dark, leaden blues of the backgrounds of frescoes and mosaics tend not only to suggest the tragic aspect of the universe, but also to immure the figures within a closed world, to wrest them from their independence, in much the same way as Christianity wrests man's life both from its individuality and from the empire, so as to link it up with the Christian destiny, with the serpent and with Golgotha. For Christianity claims to be the Truth; not Reality. To Christian eyes the life the Romans saw as real was no *true* life. Thus if the true life is to be portrayed, it must break free from the real. The task of the Christian artist is to depict, not this world, but the world to come, and a scene is only worthy of portrayal in so far as it partakes in that other world. Hence the golden backgrounds which create neither real surface nor real distance, but another universe; hence that style, incomprehensible so long as we insist on reading into it a quest of any sort of realism; for always it is an effort towards transfiguration. This does not apply solely to the figures; Byzantium aims at expressing the world viewed as a mystery. Its palace, politics, diplomacy reverted (as did its religion) to that time-old craving for secrecy (and subterfuge) so characteristic of the East. Superficial indeed would be an art portraying emperors and queens, were it confined to the mere display of pomp; but this was only, so to speak, the small change of the art of the great mystery, the secular extension of an art which did not hesitate to annex the profane to the sacred, as is evident when we compare the bust of a Roman empress with Theodora's portrait of the Sainte-Pudentienne "Virgin" with the

"Saint Agnes" in Rome, and with the Torcello "Virgin". The whole significance of Byzantine art is incarnate in this last-named figure, standing aloof in the recess of the dark cupola so that none may intrude on its colloquy with fate. Under the Virgin are aligned the saints and prophets; still lower, we see the crowd of mundane worshippers in prayer. On high, looms the immemorial Eastern night, which turns the firmament into a phantasmagoria of wandering stars, and the earth into as vain a sight as the shadow of armies battling with the void; unless this passing show be mirrored on the meditative visage of a god.

Once again a different kind of art has evoked a different method of appreciation. Modern art—the art of artists like Picasso, Braque, Klee, Henry Moore—is far more akin to Byzantine art than to the art of any intervening period. It is true, of course, that it in no way shares the religious basis of Byzantine art; but its philosophical basis—and for a modern man his philosophy is often his religion—is equally a denial of the validity of the real, and art is consequently an attempt to express a mystery, which we have not confidence enough to call the Truth. One of the most significant modern movements in art adopted the name Surrealism, but all that is essentially modern in contemporary art is in some sense super-realistic. I am not now concerned with the reasons why it is super-realistic—there is surely cause enough in the conditions of modern life to instil in man a longing for the serenity of the absolute—that is to say, of the abstract, the ideal; and if modern man, in his isolation and scepticism, cannot share an ideal or accept a tradition, then that visionary life will rise unaided from the depths of his unconscious, the original source of all myth and symbol.

The modern critic can never for a moment ignore the purely plastic values by means of which aesthetic pleasure is communicated; but these plastic values are now used once more in the service of what might be called metaphysical values, and the critic's function is again to render in adequate words the significance of the symbols created by the artist.

The first qualification for the criticism of modern art is perhaps a realization of the tragic situation of modern man. From that basis the critic can proceed to speak with authority, with feeling, and with simplicity.

3

Gauguin : The Return to Symbolism

IN ANY exhibition of nineteenth-century painting the work of Gauguin seems to emerge with a distinction for which we vainly seek the appropriate word. "Monumentality" is one label conveniently waiting to be applied, but in a sequence that stretches from David to Toulouse-Lautrec there are several artists whose work it would fit—to seek no farther there are the neighbouring canvases of Cézanne and Van Gogh. If we stand back, and as far as possible take in the whole range of the gallery, the Gauguins are immediately noticeable by the weight and brilliance of their colours, and by a significance that is easy to read at a distance. In this sense they have the characteristics of a good poster—of one of Toulouse-Lautrec's posters, to be precise. This at once suggests a depreciation, but in the same moment the glowing colours have reminded us of another kind of poster, the medieval stained-glass window, and our respect is restored.

Of all the influences that went to the shaping of Gauguin's style, it is certain that the medieval one was the strongest. He had no yearning for the Christian sentiment of the Middle Ages—he was a pagan, and his specifically religious subjects, like the "Yellow Christ" or "Jacob wrestling with the Angel", are parodies rather than re-interpretations. A Tahitian myth would serve his purpose just as well—indeed, rather better, for there was no traditional composition to travesty. Deeply as he believed in the creation or representation of symbolism, he had no coherent system of transcendental values to embrace them. The coherence belonged to the paintings—was aesthetic and not religious: a *formal* coherence. At the same time, his art is humanistic; the inherent values are those of vitality and beauty, and these are human values.

A painting he called "Maternity" (*Frontispiece*) may be taken as typical of his greatest achievement. What I have already called "monumentality" is always a question of composition —in this case the interweaving, by gesture and attitude, of three human figures into a rhythmical unity, a plastic volume that rises gigantically against the summary background. Not that the background plays an insignificant part in the composition—its wavy rhythms echo horizontally the vertical structure of the human group, and the yellow, pink and greens contrast harmoniously with the dominant notes of blue, red and brown. But ingenious and plangent as it all is, as a composition in colour, the attention is held, and Gauguin meant it to be held, by the symbolic significance of the group.

Maternity could not be more directly, more naïvely, indicated than by the seated woman giving her breast to the child: it is the archetypal symbol of the subject, and one can only emphasize the perfect simplicity and tenderness with which Gauguin has rendered it. The standing figures, the woman with the basket of fruit, the man with the spray of flowers, reinforce the general significance of the painting with their subsidiary symbolism. The tropical setting, the semi-naked bodies, the rich saturation of the colours—every element contributes to the essential idea of fertility and fruitfulness.

Such is the painting that is offered to the world in an epoch of naturalism, realism and expressionism—in an epoch, that is to say, that was in one way or another devoted to a factual analysis of feeling and observation, that had renounced symbolic artifice and that insisted on the values, whatever they may be, that emerge from the immediate consciousness of life as such. We can, of course, find symbolism of a far more blatant kind in the academic painting of the period, and Puvis de Chavannes is an artist who on this level of symbolism may be fairly compared with Gauguin. We are almost driven to the conclusion that Gauguin, far from being a modernist of his time, was a traditionalist and even an archaicist. He did not object, as did the Impressionists, to the *aims* of the academic painter, but only to the means. Symbolism had been corrupted by realism, illusionism, vulgarity of vision: it was necessary to restore to it its primitive force, to make the embodied idea as clear and as moving as it had been in medieval painting. The corruption of the image had begun in Renaissance times, with irrelevant notions of perspective, of social realism, of ecclesiastical pomp. Mannerism and academicism had destroyed the virtue of the symbol by making it too complex, too consciously artificial, too worldly. Romanticism had not really improved matters: Ingres and Delacroix had merely substituted their own kind of artifice, an illusion of historic realism. Courbet had rejected symbolism, and Manet and Degas had sacrificed everything for the triviality of the immediate vision, the direct sensation, "fiddling with details". Gauguin had learned much from the Impressionists, from Degas and particularly from Pissarro, but already by 1886 he had shown his independence, to become what Pissarro called "an austere sectarian".

Gauguin was not right in his diagnosis, and had no desire to be fair. He did not realize that an object held in pure consciousness, if it be only an apple, may be more symbolic of reality than an idea, however clearly "realized" that idea may be (that is to say, however completely and convincingly represented in visual images). A part of reality—a segment, a fragment—stands for the whole, but only on condition that it is present to consciousness as a thing-in-itself, desentimentalized, dehumanized. That was to be Cézanne's discovery. When Gauguin paints a still-life it is merely decorative: this aspect of his art belongs to the iconography of *l'art nouveau*.

We must recognize Gauguin's limitations, therefore, and then return to an emphasis on his great strength, which lies in his symbolism. But then we must ask whether these isolated icons, of maternity or of fate, add up to any significant vision of life. We misrepresent the nature of symbolism, as Gauguin conceived it, if we think of it exclusively in terms of general concepts like maternity or fate. The great composition at Boston (*D'où venons-nous? Que sommes-nous? Où allons-nous?*) might be taken as an allegory of life, and as in some sense representative of a philosophy of life; but the greater part of Gauguin's paintings do not translate so easily into conceptual notions. Some of them represent symbolic scenes to which Gauguin himself no doubt attached a particular significance ("L'Apparition" of 1902, for example); others are illustrations of Tahitian myths or legends; but for the most part Gauguin is content to ask a silent question, to pose an enigma. It is a questioning face that looks out of such canvases as "Never More" (1897), "The Idol" (1897), "Et l'or de leur corps" (1901) and "Contes Barbares" (1902). By reading Gauguin's own books and letters, we can sometimes discover the symbolic meaning of such paintings, but we are none the wiser, because the legends are too remote from our modes of thought or feeling. This group of paintings attracts us by its overtones of mystery and magic. But far more characteristic of Gauguin's work as a whole are the early "Nude" (1880) at Copenhagen, the Breton and Martinique landscapes, and paintings such as "Conversation à Tahiti" (1897) and "Les seins aux fleurs rouges" (1899), in which the symbolism is simply sensuous or vital. Such paintings are not really distinct from a painting like "Maternity" or "Et l'or de leur corps", but instead of a symbol of easily recognized significance, we have the representation and affirmation of a life of sensation.

It might be asked in what way does such an affirmation differ from that of Renoir's? Only, I think, in a quality of generalization. The gold is certainly present in the flesh of Renoir's nudes, but it is a particular woman that is characterized, not a general quality. The sensuousness in Gauguin's painting is a derivative of the symbolic statement: the breasts are fruitlike and are associated with fruits. The sensuousness in Renoir's painting is a luminous and carnal warmth in the paint itself; we do not "associate", even unconsciously, the body with any symbolic objects: it is immediately present as a particular being, human and vital.

All symbolism is at a remove from the immediate present —that is its function: to enable us to discourse without the associations and distractions of sensation. This does not mean that a symbolic painter is trying to evade "life" or "reality". He is like a mathematician or a logician who can deal more effectively with life or reality by means of signs. But the visual signs of painting and sculpture are more like the characters of a fable. The story of the Good Samaritan, or of the man who went forth to sow seed—such fables are strictly comparable to Gauguin's pictures, and when we read them we do not think of real men with distinctive features, but of typical men with conventional features. To load it with detail would detract from the universality of the fable. In the same way, Gauguin does not need to create an illusion of particular presence, or even of a particular time and place: his discourse is universal and must be expressed in symbolic signs, which are never aspects of reality.

It is for this reason that Gauguin, for all his exoticism, is a popular artist—an artist easily accessible to the man in the street. There have been other exotic artists in our time, most of them influenced in some degree by Gauguin—Emil Nolde, Paula Modersohn, Max Pechstein—but though there are good and even great artists among them, they have not the same appeal as Gauguin because they lacked the same bold grasp of universal themes.

Nevertheless, Gauguin too has his limitations. We have only to compare him with a universal artist like Rembrandt to see how limited was the range of his intelligence. Gauguin was capable of creating universal symbols, but selectively, discreetly. Rembrandt was himself a universal spirit, and this spirit informs everything that he painted, so that a biblical legend, a carcass of an ox, a naked woman, his own self-portrait—all stand as symbols of an all-embracing sympathy. Perhaps only Shakespeare, in another art, has that kind of universal intelligence. But Gauguin, on his more limited frontage, reaches the same heights; as does his friend Van Gogh.

But these comparisons reveal another distinction. A self-portrait by Van Gogh, like a self-portrait by Rembrandt, is a self-analysis, a revelation of the innermost self. A self-portrait by Gauguin is a persona, a mask—that is to say, again a symbol. The symbol may represent what is universal in the man —of evil and of good; but it does not reveal the particularities that are neither good nor evil, that are uncharacterized, but that nevertheless are a segment of the living reality.

In the end symbolism and realism are incompatible. The symbol is an intuitive grasp of realities that remain beyond the range of analytical intelligence. One cannot say that a symbolic art is therefore greater or more intensive than an art that reveals a particular segment of the visible world. These are merely alternative ways of presenting reality, like myth and history. The myth is not historical: it is the archetypal form into which historical events are moulded, for convenience of popular understanding, for ease of memory, for endurance in tradition. History has no archetypal form in this sense: it is diffuse and incoherent, and the historian is an impressionist. But an artist can present a segment of the panorama, and it will be like a "still" snatched from the restless reel. These stills can be arranged like a book of illustrations, and we call the result history. But history is not reality, nor is myth: as efforts of human comprehension they are complementary.

Gauguin's work is symbolic, and he himself is a myth. He rejected the values of bourgeois society and of a machine civilization. His gesture had its sordid side, but retrospectively it seems to have been appropriate, coming at a time when the world was preparing for annihilating wars. It was not a useful example: we cannot all go and live on South Sea islands, and, as I have said before in this connection, modern man carries his civilization like a pack on his back, and cannot cast it off. But he can protest against the burden, and state the real values of life. That is what Gauguin did, in paintings that are symbols of eternal truths, images of great beauty and serenity. He is not a painter's painter, and his influence is not to be found in schools and academies, but in hearts weary of the burden of modernity and enticed for a moment of contemplation into an Earthly Paradise. A cowardly escape? The realist and the politician might think so, but Gauguin's paintings already have the authority of monuments that will outlast our time and its mournful anxieties.

4

The Inspired Tinker

ALEXANDER CALDER was born in Philadelphia more than fifty years ago, and his parents, who were artists, misread his childish proclivities and tried to make an engineer of him. But left to himself Sandy—as he is always called by his friends —began to draw, and when he was free to follow his own bent, he joined an art school. By 1924 he was supporting himself by free-lance work—work which included the regular provision for the *National Police Gazette* of what journalists called a half-page spread. In the course of his job he was asked to cover the circus, and this proved to be the decisive event in his career. He couldn't keep away from the circus, and from drawing the animal and clowns he turned to modelling them in wire and any available bits and pieces. The first time I met Sandy—it was about twenty years ago— he asked those present to sit round him in a circle on the studio floor. He then unrolled and spread in front of him a piece of green baize. Out of a bag he brought the segments of a ring, two or three feet in diameter, which he joined together on the baize, and then he treated us to all the ritual and riotous fun of a circus. The performers—clowns, acrobats, horses, elephants—were all made of wire, and they all

37

went through their turns with a degree of realism that would have to be seen to be fully appreciated. I can't remember all the turns, but his friend James Johnson Sweeney, who has written a book about him and has often seen the performance, tells us that "there were acrobats; tumblers; trained dogs; slack-wire acts *à la japonaise*; a lion-tamer; a sword-swallower; Rigoulot, the strong-man; the Sultan of Senegambia who hurled knives and axes; Don Rodriguez Kolynos who risked a death-defying slide down a tight wire; 'living statues'; a trapeze act; a chariot race; every classic feature of the tan-bark programme".

And Sweeney adds this perceptive comment: "These toys . . . were not mechanical. They had a living quality in their uncertainty. The dog might not succeed in jumping through the paper hoop. The bareback rider might not recover her balance. The aerialists might land in the net beneath, or might succeed in catching the swinging bars with their toes. The number of failures was uncertain; but an eventual success brought relief and restored equilibrium."

This circus was only a rather elaborate toy, but I see in it the beginning of the later "mobiles", those wavering structures of wire and metal that have delighted us at the Lefévre Gallery in 1951. In introducing these mobiles in the catalogue of the exhibition, this same quotable James Johnson Sweeney surprised me with a reference to the machine age. "Calder," he said, "has accepted as the material of his art some of the most crude and obvious features of our mechanical heritage and forged them into a graceful, individualized sculptural expression. . . . He has taken the principle of the unwieldy machine and employed it as the basis of his delicate 'toys'; he has taken the toy and built it on the scale of the machine."

Perhaps before I explain why I disagree at this point with

my friend Sweeney, with whom I usually find myself in an embarrassing fulness of agreement, I ought to assume that some of my readers have never seen a Calder mobile, and therefore attempt a verbal description of this new type of art. It may hang from the ceiling or project from a wall, but generally speaking a mobile stands on three legs—an irregular tripod rising to a sharp point on which balances and rotates an assemblage of wires and pieces of sheet-metal. These pieces may be discs or crescents or rhomboidal shapes, and one rather heavy piece of metal at the end of a short wire will often be balanced against a widespread constellation of small discs, the constellation itself being made up of a series of balances and counter-balances. The tripod is generally, but not necessarily, black; the discs and other counterweights may be white or yellow or red or blue, and the wires are also painted. One has only to tap a disc or a crescent to set the whole system in a swaying, swinging motion, which may last for a considerable time. In suitable weather the soft breezes that come in at the window keep the mobile in continuous movement, and occasionally there will be a tinkle as two discs touch each other or come into contact with a neighbouring object. This gives a lively quality to mobiles such as no other works of art possess: they seem to have a life of their own, and are no trouble at all—they do not need watering, as plants do; they do not even need oiling! If you keep one on your writing-table, as I do, it is always amusing to see what the mobile has been up to since you last looked at it. You can even use it as a kind of divining-rod, to point in the direction in which you should seek inspiration. Finally, it is a fascinating object for a kitten to play with; and even my sophisticated cat will sometimes sit on the table and give it a playful push.

But must we take such art seriously? you might ask.

Modern art, you have been told, is anything but a joke—it is a reflection of the tragic age we live in, something that can only be explained by an existentialist philosophy and a psychology of the unconscious. Of course, there are critics of modern art who say that the whole movement is a gigantic hoax, and that clever fellow Picasso, for example, is simply pulling our insensitive legs. Calder, by making no pretence to profundity, seems, to such people, to be giving the game away. He is one of the playboys of the western world, and if we had not been assured of his direct Scottish descent, we might suspect him of being another Irishman—another Christy Mahon.

But Sandy Calder is a simple man—rather like the Big Bear in the story of the Three Bears, but kindlier to little girls. He lives near Roxbury, Connecticut, in an old farmhouse, and by the side of the farmhouse is a building that was once a barn, but the clapboards have been replaced by glass and the place is in fact a studio, but a studio with a forge at one end and an indescribable clutter of tools and sheets of tin, coils of wire and cans of paint. Suspended from the beams hang scores of tinkling mobiles—the whole room is full of a pretty music as they gently sway in the draughts. I didn't think of the machine age when I visited Calder some years ago: I thought rather of the village blacksmith and the spreading chestnut-tree; of fairy grottoes and crystal chandeliers; of weathercocks and windmills; and of the *Three Bears*. But I also recognized in what I saw the work of one of the most original artists of our time, and I want to try and explain why I think such a playboy can be so important.

There is in modern art an element of *protest*. It is perhaps its most characteristic element. As we are so often told, we live in an age of transition: some of us would say that transition is an optimistic word, for it implies that we are going

ALEXANDER CALDER with *Myxomatose* 1953–4

to get somewhere—not that we are merely going from bad to worse. In a stable civilization we always find an intimate and sympathetic link between art and society—art embodies the ideals of that civilization, gives confident expression to its aims. But for many years now artists have felt no sympathy for the society into which they have been born, and they have tended to use their art either to criticize and mock that society, or to protest against the fate that has condemned them to such a malign destiny. The extreme form of this protest-art was the Dada movement of 1914, which was a declaration of spiritual bankruptcy—a bankruptcy whose receivers were the corrupt and cynical powers that just at that time were letting loose the First World War. After that war the genuine artists of the period continued to protest, though in less obvious terms. What is the art of Picasso, from 1914 to the present day, but an immense and deeply moving protest against the indignity of modern life, and against the falsity of those who attempt to give it a façade of academic respectability?

Calder is also an artist of protest. Verbally he is not very articulate, but I can imagine him saying to Picasso: "Don't get so hot under the collar. *They* will only laugh at you. Take it easy. You might as well have some fun, and let the politicians and philosophers get on with the job of putting the world to rights."

Does this mean that Calder is an escapist? At this point I must venture a statement which may sound rather mystical. It is impossible for any genuine work of art to be escapist. There is in art a principle of obliqueness, indirection, distance —call it what you will—but a law which says that art is most effective when least purposive. Keats expressed this truth when he said that "we hate poetry that has a palpable design on us, and if we do not agree, seems to put its hand in its breeches pocket". Calder's design is not palpable. It is like Mozart's music, or Cervantes' story-telling. In its subtle way such art mocks the false complacency of the official and academic world just as effectively as Goya's art or Picasso's; but by keeping cool and detached it enters the public consciousness by open doors: it amuses before it amazes. The catharsis comes as a secondary and completely unconscious effect.

It is characteristic of all such art that it does not strike an attitude. Picasso strikes an attitude in such a painting as "Guernica"—a direct indictment of tyranny and inhumanity. I am not criticizing Picasso for giving expression to his righteous emotions in this direct way: it is a question of temperament rather than a question of art, and one artist may have a temperament that finds expression in satire while another may have a temperament that finds expression in humour; one may be conscious of his environment, another completely oblivious of it. "I never wrote one single Line of Poetry with the least Shadow of public thought," said Keats. Calder would say the same of his sculpture. "When I am writing for myself for the mere sake of the Moment's enjoyment," continues Keats, "perhaps nature has its course in me." That is the whole point. A moment ago I imagined someone asking me if we should take such art as Calder's seriously. If "seriously" means "solemnly" the answer is No! But after all there may be something to be said for the English habit of taking our pleasures seriously, because it is then, and perhaps only then (I mean when we are enjoying ourselves) that nature takes its course in us.

Such, at any rate, is my justification for taking the art of Alexander Calder seriously. I do not believe that it has anything to do with the machine age, or any mechanism invented later than the Bronze Age. I do not suggest that these playful mobiles are even a reaction to the American "way of life", or to an existentialist *Angst*. Archimedes might have made them: they may have been inspired by the fluttering leaves of the spreading chestnut-tree. And when I think of Sandy Calder, it is not of a modern sculptor exhibiting his novelties in the refined atmosphere of Bond Street or the rue de la Boëtie. Rather I think of him as an inspired tinker whose caravan has come to rest in Roxbury, Connecticut, but whose gaiety has penetrated to the ends of the earth and shattered for a blissful moment the gloom of our scientific civilization.

5

Goethe and Art

MY TITLE IS NOT *Goethe's Philosophy of Art* nor *Goethe's Theory of Art*, for the most significant thing about Goethe is his integrity—the fact that we cannot detach any part of his thought and consider it in isolation. Art and Morality, Science and Philosophy, Religion and Politics—all are knit into one consistent fabric. The part is only fully significant in relation to the whole; there are no boundaries or fences. If we want to know what Goethe thought about a subject like art, we must look with equal expectation on every page he ever wrote— not only in his diaries and letters, his books of travel or of maxims, but also in his novels, his books about the morphology of plants and animals, in his *Theory of Colour* and, of course, in his poems. When we have done that—and it would be almost a life's work to do it competently—then I think we

43

should be in possession of a complete understanding of the nature and significance of art. It may be that with such an understanding we could then formulate a science of art, a theory of aesthetics. But that is not what Goethe did—on the contrary, that is just what he deliberately refrained from doing. For he realized—and these are his own words—"that our understanding of a work of art, as of a work of nature, always remains incommensurable. We contemplate it; we feel it; it is effective; but it eludes exact cognition, and its essence, its quality, cannot be expressed in words".

And yet nothing intrigued Goethe so much as the problem of art. He spent a considerable part of his life in the study of a subject for which he invented a new name—morphology. A science, you will say. Indeed, it has become a science in the limited, specialized sense we give to science nowadays, but to Goethe it meant the study of *form* (which is what the word means) and Goethe realized that form in his sense was present, not only in the crystal and the bone, in the leaf and the cloud, but also in the painting and the poem. Further, and this is the most important point of all, he realized that there is no essential difference between any of these manifestations of form—that the form discoverable in nature is the same as the form revealed by art. There is one creative process—formation and transformation, and at no point can we detect a caesura, a break. Nature and art are linked in one continuous chain of being, and morality, freedom, God—all values are inherent in that reality.

In considering specific works of art, Goethe would always go to the Ancient Greeks for his touchstone, but never in a spirit of imitation. "We always advocate the study of the ancients," he said to Eckermann, "but what does this mean other than: Concentrate upon the real world and seek to express it? For that is what the ancients did in their day." Art

is never born of art. "Art is constitutive—the artist deter-
mines beauty. He does not take it over." So reads one of
Goethe's notes, and in another he points out that *style,* the
characteristic quality of a work of art, "rests on the deepest
foundations of cognition, *on the inner essence of things,* in so far
as this is given us to comprehend in visible and tangible
forms". Nowhere in Goethe do we find any justification for
the conception of art as the slavish imitation of the external
appearances of nature. Art is an intuitive act, a leap beyond the
phenomenal world, into "the realm of what lies beyond words
to utter". But this realm, the realm of what we would
nowadays call archetypal forms, is still a part of the natural
world. But it needs a special faculty—or rather, the special
training of a normal faculty, the imagination—to realize or
represent it. "A man born to and trained in the so-called
exact sciences, and fully matured in his powers of reason,"
Goethe noted, "will not find it easy to understand that there
is such a thing as an exact sensuous imagination—a faculty
without which art would not be conceivable." *An exact sensuous imagination*—there if anywhere you have Goethe's
definition of art, and both epithets, *exact* and *sensuous,* are
equally important.

Let us look a little more closely at this definition. What in
the first place did Goethe mean by using the word "exact" in
connection with art? We have seen that he did not mean
exactness in the sense of an exact reproduction. In the same
context he was fond of using two other words which give us
a clue—clearness and serenity. Further, he believed that these
qualities had been exemplified in classical art, and that they
were characteristics of a properly civilized epoch. "We are
in need of clearness and serenity," he said to Eckermann,
"and we should turn to those epochs in literature and art in
which men of quality attained to fully rounded *Bildung* and

D

45

lived serene lives and in time radiated the harmony of their culture to distant epochs."

The epochs to which we should turn for this conception of clearness and serenity were the classical epochs, more particularly Ancient Greece, and it is essential, before we can establish the real significance of Goethe's theory of art, to come to terms with his so-called *classicism*.

Goethe lived through a revaluation of classical culture—that revaluation we associate with the name of Winckelmann. For an appreciation of Winckelmann's significance we cannot do better than return to the essay on him by Walter Pater—himself, to an extent not often realized, a disciple of Goethe. Winckelmann was something more than a scholar and historian—he was one of the first of those philosophers of history that Germany has produced in such intoxicating quantity. It is not easy to reconstruct the pre-Winckelmann view of antiquity, but it is perhaps represented by the picturesque etchings of Piranesi. There was no precision in the outlines—rather the mossy be-whiskered ruins of an age that had completely vanished. Winckelmann scraped off the ivy and the weeds, revealed the ground-plan and true proportions underlying the desolate splendour. The past became at once more precise and more human, for it was possible for the first time to see how the Greeks and Romans had lived—to reconstruct their daily life in all its fascinating actuality. What then emerged, for the admiration of intelligent people like Goethe, was a way of life, a conception of culture, for which the Germans invented the untranslatable word *Bildung,* which has in it a suggestion of precise form and structure not rendered by English equivalents like education. *Bildung* is—or was, before it became a snob term in the hands of the German middle class—the "manners" that maketh man, the style of living; but style in the aesthetic sense, which we then call *grace,* and which the Greeks identified with nobility.

In so far as he admired the Greek or classical way of life, Goethe is rightly to be called a classicist. It was the ideal way of life, the only *healthy* way of life. And so we get that typically Goethean identification of health and classicism, weakness and romanticism. "What is sound [again he is talking to Eckermann] I call classical; and what is morbid I call romantic. And from this angle the Nibelungen are as classical as Homer, for both are sound and doughty. Most recent productions are romantic, not because they are modern but because they are weak, sickly and diseased; and the productions of older times are classical, not because they are old but because they are strong, fresh, tonic and sound. If we differentiate between classic and romantic on this basis, we shall avoid confusion."

Perhaps so; but Goethe himself did not always do so, either in theory or in practice. He claimed, for example, that in the earlier acts of *Faust,* Part II, classical as well as romantic notes are sounded in order to lead, as on rising ground, to the Helena act, where both of these political modes "assert their specific character and achieve a sort of synthesis". A synthesis of the diseased and the sound, of the sickly and the strong— that does not make sense. The real distinction is indicated in another statement to Eckermann. "The distinction of classical and romantic poetry, which now provokes so much discussion and dissension all the world over, originated with myself and Schiller. I held to the maxim of objective procedure in poetry and refused to admit of any other; Schiller, on the other hand, with his wholly subjective approach, regarded his way as the right one, and to defend himself against me he wrote *On Naïve and Sentimental Poetry.* He proved to me that I am romantic despite myself, and that my *Iphigenie*

47

is, by its preponderance of sentiment, not nearly so classical and in keeping with the ancients as you might be inclined to think."

Here we are on firmer ground. We have a psychological distinction—between the objective and subjective procedures in poetry—and an admission by Goethe himself that he was not always so objective in practice as he would like to be. On this psychological plane his talk of a synthesis begins to make sense.

Goethe refers to this psychological distinction between classical and romantic on several occasions. In his essay on Shakespeare he made a list of the opposed qualities which these terms cover—thus:

Ancient	Modern
Simple	Complex
Pagan	Christian
Heroic	Romantic
Real	Ideal
Necessity	Freedom
Obligation	Will

and he went on in particular to elaborate the distinction between obligation and will. "In the tragedy of the ancients [he pointed out] there is a sense of inescapable obligation bearing down on the individual, and the fact that the will tends in the opposite direction makes the pressure only so much the more acute. . . . All obligation has a despotic quality. . . . The will, by contrast, is free, or seems free, and gives leeway to the individual. There is something flattering about the assertion of will, and men were bound to come under its sway once they had become aware of this power. Will is the god of the modern age. Surrendering to it, we fear its opposite, and this opposition sharply divides our art and our outlook from those

48

of the ancients. Through the presence of obligation tragedy waxes great and strong, whereas the assertion of will makes it weak and small."

"Will is the god of the modern age." That pronouncement was made in 1813, in Weimar, with a young philosopher called Schopenhauer sitting at Goethe's feet. A few years later this young philosopher wrote *The World as Will and Idea*. Goethe had put his finger on the nerve of the age. After Schopenhauer came Nietzsche, Ibsen, Dostoevsky—the main current in modern literature. But it was Goethe who had released it, and *Faust* is the prototype—-the tragedy of the man who dares to assert his will.

There can be clearness or lucidity in such a work of art, but hardly serenity. The union of Faust and Helena gave birth to Euphorion, the new man, the synthesis of ancient and modern, of pagan and Christian, of necessity and freedom, of obligation and will; but the hero of Goethe's tragedy is Faust, not Euphorion, who remains a shadowy figure, never bodied forth in any realistic shape. Such a realization was perhaps only possible in another, more objective art—in sculpture; and only possible in one shape, the human form. Poetry is inspiration, conceived in the soul, inevitably subjective. One should call it neither art nor science, but genius. And genius, thought Goethe, is under the sway of man's daemons. Goethe was a great believer in the daemonic. "In poetry," he said to Eckermann, "there is something decidedly daemonic—especially in unconscious poetry, which fails to satisfy the intelligence and for that reason transcends everything conceptual in its appeal. It is the same with music, in the highest degree. Its loftiness is beyond the grasp of the understanding. It casts an all-powerful spell that defies rational analysis." Goethe was here approaching the hypothesis of the unconscious, even of a *collective* unconscious as it appears in the psychology of our contemporary, C. G. Jung. This seems to be the sense of the following passage from the *Autobiography*:

He [adolescent Goethe] fancied that in nature, animate as well as inanimate, he could perceive something manifesting itself only in contradictions and incapable for that reason of being reduced to a concept, much less to a word. It was not divine, for it seemed devoid of reason; not human, for it lacked intelligence; not diabolic, for it was benevolent; not angelic, for it often manifested malicious pleasure. It was like chance in being inconsistent. It resembled Providence, in suggesting a pattern. Everything that finds us blocked seemed penetrable to it. It seemed to manipulate the necessary elements of our life in arbitrary fashion. It controlled time and expanded space. It seemed to take pleasure only in the impossible and spurn the possible with disdain. This essence, that seemed to move in the midst of all others, uniting and separating them, I termed daemonic after the example of the ancients and those who had perceived something similar. . . .

Goethe recognized the presence of that daemonic energy in himself and in all great poets. He could not reconcile the creative powers of that energy with his classical ideals of harmony and serenity. He therefore tended to separate the arts into two categories—those that express this daemonic energy, the subjective arts of poetry and music; and those that transcend human feelings, projections into an ideal world of order, harmony and significance, the objective arts of sculpture and architecture. Sculpture in particular he thought of as in some sense an extension of natural evolution. Nature had produced, in man and woman at the moment of puberty, her finest and final achievement. *At this point* art takes over and attempts to go one step farther, in its representation of the *ideal* human form.

I think we might venture to express a doubt about this distinction of Goethe's. The daemonic forces in architecture are, in an obvious sense, subordinated to reason and utility. But the work of an artist like Rodin, or Henry Moore in our own time, shows that in sculpture too the daemonic unconscious insists on being expressed. We can only conclude that all artists, whether poets, musicians, architects or sculptors, are compelled in some sense to be interpreters of their time —"Our virtues," as Shakespeare's Coriolanus said, "lie in the interpretation of the time"—and as artists we cannot consciously mould the forces that unconsciously dominate the epoch. The corollary of this doctrine is the belief that the poet's exclusive concern is the effective artistic presentation of his subject. We are back at the point where we began —cultivating exact sensuous imagination, and we begin to see the importance of exactitude. The artist is a recording instrument, of value only if he is accurate.

There is another statement of Goethe's with which I would like to conclude, for it expresses the man and his attitude to life and art more adequately than anything I know, apart from his poetry. It is from a letter to Jacobi, dated January 13, 1813: "I for my part [wrote Goethe], drawn in many directions as I am, cannot content myself with one way of thinking. As poet and artist I am a polytheist; in my nature studies I am a pantheist—both in a very determined way. When I require one god for my personality, as an ethical being, this is provided for also. The things of heaven and earth contain such a wealth of value that only the organs of all beings jointly can encompass it."

6

Naum Gabo

THE CAREER of most artists of our time is punctuated by a series of unrealized "projects". Our age has not had the courage, nor the economic means, to realize the splendid visions of its architects, sculptors and painters. In this respect, Gabo's career is no exception—"Project for a Radio Station, 1919–20", "Monument for a Physics Laboratory, 1922", "Project for a Monument for the Institute of Physics and Mathematics, 1925", "Project for a Fête Lumière, 1929", "Project for the Palace of the Soviets, 1931", "Monument for an Airport, 1932"—so it continues until this year 1956, when the project initiated by Dr. Van der Wal for a monument to form part of the architectural design of the new Bijenkorf building will be realized in the city of Rotterdam. It is the culmination of a great artist's career.

Naum Gabo, who is the leading exponent of the movement in modern art known as Constructivism, was born in Russia in 1890 and had a scientific education. In further pursuit of that education he went in 1909 to Munich, a decisive step for at Munich were three teachers whose fundamental influence on the formation of the modern movement in art has never been adequately appreciated—Heinrich Wölfflin, Wilhelm Worringer and Wassily Kandinsky. Though Gabo did not have any direct contact with these animators of the modern movement, new interpretations of the history of art, new conceptions of its destiny, were being forged in that Bavarian city, and in this atmosphere Gabo became an artist, but an artist who did not renounce the scientific concepts

NAUM GABO: *Construction in Space with red* 1953

of a new era. But then in 1914 came the war, and the disruption of that nursery of genius. Gabo wandered through war-stricken Europe, but on the outbreak of the Russian Revolution he returned to Moscow where he joined a group of artists determined to give Russia a new art worthy of the ideals of a new society.

For three years this group worked passionately and experimentally, and by 1920 had formulated their famous manifesto: "We deny volume as an expression of space. . . . We reject physical mass as an element of plasticity. . . . We announce that the elements of art have their basis in a dynamic rhythm."

It was too much for the emergent Thermidorians of the Revolution, committed to the desperate task of maintaining power and defending doctrine. In this task too the artists were required to play a part, and that part, in terms of "socialist realism", could only be popular, illustrative, sentimental—a denial of all the principles of the Constructivist Manifesto. The breaking-point came in 1922. Gabo received permission to go abroad and made for Berlin; he never returned to Russia. He remained in Berlin for ten years, formed new friendships, and was then driven by the oncoming tragedy, first to Paris, then to England, where he remained until 1946, and finally to the United States, where he now lives and works.

It is not my purpose, in this brief Introduction, to trace Gabo's career in detail. I would rather concentrate on one more attempt at elucidating the principles which underlie his creative achievement.

Constructivism was an inevitable word for the movement founded by Gabo and his colleagues in Moscow between 1917 and 1920. Like most terms in the history of art, it was invented by the critics, not by the artists themselves (their first manifesto was actually called "Realistic"!). There was a good if superficial reason for such a name. We have developed a civilization that is predominantly mechanical, and for art to ignore the characteristics of such a civilization is a foolish form of conservatism. All stylistic periods in the history of art have made use of the characteristic techniques of the period—and just as we speak of Stone Age Art or Bronze Age art, and just as the Classical, Gothic and Renaissance periods made use of the prevailing materials and processes, so the Machine Age should naturally take advantage of the inspiring new materials and the fantastic extensions of constructive power brought into existence by the machine. That seems simple and logical enough, and already by 1909 the Italian Futurists had called on all artists to "take and glorify the life of today, incessantly and tumultuously transformed by the triumphs of science".

The Moscow group of artists were undoubtedly influenced by the manifestoes of Marinetti and by the violently original works produced by painters and sculptors like Boccioni, Severini and Balla. But as in naturalistic art, so in constructivist art: there is a fundamental difference between imitation and interpretation, between an art that follows and an art that leads. An awareness of this distinction gradually manifested itself within the Constructivist group itself; and from the beginning there was no doubt of Gabo's point of view. He has always affirmed the primacy of the creative will in art, the spontaneous nature of the artist's experience. "By means of constructive techniques," he declared on one occasion, "today we are able to light forces hidden in nature and to realize psychic events. . . . We do not turn away from nature, but, on the contrary, we penetrate her more profoundly than naturalistic art ever was able to do."

No word is more ambiguous than this word "nature". To one person it signifies the world of flowers and clouds, of beasts and birds, of man's sensuous experience. To another person it signifies the whole universe, with stars in their mathematical courses and atoms ordained in crystalline patterns. The poet and the philosopher will try to reconcile these two conceptions of nature, to see, as the poet Blake said, "a world in a grain of sand, And heaven in a wild flower". Gabo is a poet of this kind, a poet whose images are visual, and who seeks by means of the image to reconcile past, present and future; the many and the one, man and the universe. As he once wrote in a letter to me: "'Abstract' is not the core of the constructive idea I profess. The idea means more to me. It involves the whole complex of human relation to life. It is a mode of thinking, acting, perceiving and living. The Constructive philosophy recognizes only one stream in our existence—life (you call it creation, it is the same). Any thing or action which enhances life, propels it and adds to it something in the direction of growth, expansion and development, is Constructive."

In this philosophy Growth and Form are two inseparable concepts: there is no growth in nature that does not follow a principle of formation; no form that is not the result of a process of growth. The opposition of law and life, of science and art, is a false one; in general, in the words of a great natural philosopher,[1] "no organic forms exist save such as are in conformity with physical and mathematical laws". With equal authority it may be said that no aesthetic forms exist save such as are in conformity with physical and mathematical laws. And there are not two separate sets of laws, but only the one, the one universal tendency to the same

[1] Wentworth D'Arcy Thompson, in *Growth and Form* (Cambridge, 1942).

law of being, "the realization of unity of spatial form in the complex processes of physics, biology, psychology and art."[1] Gabo, and the group of artists of which he is the leader and prototype, are the first artists in our time (they had predecessors among the architects of Greece and Gothic Europe) to be animated by a more or less conscious realization of this fundamental unity of all visual form.

I say "more or less" conscious realization because the creative experience of art is never the result of calculation, but of what, for want of a better word, we call intuition or insight. The process of nature, we may believe, is entropic—it aims at economy of energy and *therefore* at perfection of form. The artist is intuitively aware of this natural process of development, and his work is an imaginative representation of it. He demonstrates these formative principles, for our enlightenment and pleasure, for our disinterested contemplation. He does more than abstract a static order from the modalities of natural phenomena: he constructs ideal representations (images) of the perfection towards which natural growth is striving—"I think [wrote Gabo in this same letter] that the image of my work is the image of good—not of evil; the image of order—not of chaos; the image of life—not of death."

Intimations of these images are everywhere in the world around us, so long as we look for the form of what we see. There is a formative principle in the act of perception: we focus the chaos of phenomena into a "field" of vision, a visually intelligible segment of reality. But there is another method of vision, which is better called contemplation, occlusive and penetrative, which reveals the wonders of the formative process—the supreme process, as Goethe called it, "indeed the only one, alike in nature and art". The Con-

[1] L. L. Whyte, in *Aspects of Form*. London, 1951.

NAUM GABO: *Construction* 1957

structive artist is dedicated to that vision, to that process of revelation.

When Gabo began to consider the Bijenkorf project, he first thought of the physical requirements, which were a sculptural image free-standing in space, of a scale of so many metres, strong in its material construction but light in its visual impact, and he came quite logically, quite inevitably, to the image of a tree. "The organic structure in the world of plants provided for me the solution for the new conception which I needed. There in the world of plants, in the structure of a tree—there lies a structural principle which . . . could be with great advantage applied to many a structural task. In particular, I felt it was there that I had to look for a solution of my structural problem and once this principle became evident to me, the image of the whole sculpture evolved out of it naturally."

In this manner a constructive image was created; and now this tree of steel rises from the Rotterdam pavement, like the poet Darley's

> blest unfabled Incense Tree,
> That burns in glorious Araby,
> With red scent chalicing the air,
> Till earth-life grow Elysian there!

But a better and more exact comparison is the constructive image first wrought into visible form by the Abbot Suger: the radiant, aspiring image of the Gothic cathedral, a constructive image if there ever was one, and which was wont to transport its creator into a higher world, *anagogicus mos,* by "the upward-leading method".[1] In this materialistic age of ours "a diversity of sacred virtues" has once again taken on

[1] I take the phrase from Erwin Panofsky's essay on "Abbot Suger of St.-Denis" (*Meaning in the Visual Arts.* New York, 1955), pp.108–45.

visible form, and is not to be ignored. People on their business will stop for a moment in the milling street to contemplate this image of universal beauty.

Naum Gabo is an artist who, in an age of confusion, of distraction and of despair, has remained faithful to a vision of transcendental order. His constructions are not *objets d'art* for the connoisseur—they do not belong in any sense to the bourgeois tradition of art. They are images of a tradition that has still to be established—prototypes of an art that is emerging to give expression to the unformulated ideals and blind aspirations of a new age. New materials, new processes, a new technology of unknown potentiality, are waiting to be fused by the imagination of a new breed of artists into the monuments of a new civilization. Of this breed of artists Naum Gabo is the forerunner.

7

Walter Pater

NO ENGLISH writer of the nineteenth century stands so much in need of rehabilitation as Walter Pater. Born in 1839, he lost his father at the age of five and his mother at the age of fifteen. Sensitive and reserved, he nevertheless won a scholarship to Queen's College, Oxford, and while there attracted the attention of that most formidable of all Oxonian pundits, Benjamin Jowett, Master of Balliol. "I think you have a mind which will come to great eminence," declared that ponderous professor. But it was not to be an eminence which Dr. Jowett could look upon with any satisfaction.

Indeed, there is evidence which suggests that once Pater began to show his independence and originality, Jowett moved into opposition. Appointed a Fellow of Brasenose in 1865, Pater was never, in spite of his brilliant gifts, to rise above this modest position. A. C. Benson, whose book on Pater is the best that has so far been written, says that "Jowett took up a line of definite opposition to Pater and used his influence to prevent his obtaining University work and appointments". Jowett was merely expressing the Oxford point of view, for to this point of view, in every aspect, Pater's philosophy was a scandalous obstruction.

This opposition was eventually to drive Pater out of Oxford—"there are in Oxford," he wrote, "some very objectionable people from whom I would gladly separate myself". But Pater had remained in Oxford long enough to become an influence, and even to found a movement, and this was to be the undoing of his subsequent reputation in the hands of a righteous and avenging puritanism. When Pater died in 1894 his reputation was firmly established, his influence was increasing, and continued to increase until the end of the century. But then came the trial of Oscar Wilde, and Oscar Wilde was his most brilliant pupil and follower, a living embodiment of his philosophy. Great was the rejoicing in the land of the Philistines; their worst enemy was down in the mud, and with him he had dragged his prophet Pater.

There is not, of course, the slightest excuse for involving Pater in Wilde's downfall. It is perhaps too optimistic to suppose that even an intelligent few would, in the face of such a moral outcry, attempt to save the good in Wilde's philosophy from the vindictive flames. His wit was not to be denied, and two of his plays and sundry aphorisms have been kept in circulation. But there is more in Wilde than that, as is perhaps now recognized; but that "more", apart from Wilde's socialism, is wholly contained in Pater. In any case, Pater is immensely wider in his scope and deeper in his philosophy, and the comparison is not worth making, except as a backward transition to the work of the master.

Mr. Richard Aldington, in a vigorous but petulant introduction which he contributed to an anthology of Pater's writings[1] seemed to doubt whether Pater could be appreciated by "a generation so sorely harassed" as ours, "warweary . . . scrambling on somehow from day to day". Instead of trying to show the relevance of Pater's philosophy to our present needs, he accuses the "intellectuals of this century" of setting out "to burlesque Pater's ideas by applying them too literally". Pater had said that we should "regard all things and principles of things as inconstant modes or fashions", and that we should be "for ever curiously testing new opinions and courting new impressions, never acquiescing in a facile orthodoxy". I believe that Pater meant what he said in such passages, and practised what he preached. But acting on these principles, says Mr. Aldington, we have "turned the palace of art into a giant Aesthetic Fun Fair, where newer and wilder exhibits vie with one another, and a jaded if impecunious public calls incessantly for bigger thrills and cleverer titters". Mr. Aldington then enjoys himself in giving us a long list of such thrills and titters, and while it includes items of a kind that would hardly have come within the range of Pater's observation, such as "Jellyroll Morton's Red Hot Peppers", there are others, not only "Japanese novels and Chinese poems", but even "Henry Moore's calamitous excrescences" and "the tortured pigs of Stravinsky's 'Sacre'", that would not, in my opinion, have been outside the range of Pater's sensibility. Pater had two

[1] London, 1948.

qualities that Mr. Aldington seems to lack: an instinctive sympathy for the struggles and aspirations of the artists of his own time, and a readiness to listen to "the note of revolt", as he called it, whenever and wherever sounded. There is a passage in the essay on "Coleridge" which well expresses his attitude, and since it is not included in Mr. Aldington's selection I would like to quote it:

Modern thought is distinguished from ancient by its cultivation of the "relative" spirit in place of the "absolute". Ancient philosophy sought to arrest every object in an eternal outline, to fix thought in a necessary formula, and the varieties of life in a classification by "kinds", or *genera*. To the modern spirit nothing is, or can be rightly known, except relatively and under conditions. The philosophical conception of the relative has been developed in modern times through the influence of the sciences of observation. Those sciences reveal types of life evanescing into each other by inexpressible refinements of change. Things pass into their opposites by accumulation of undefinable quantities. The growth of those sciences consists in a continual analysis of facts of rough and general observation into groups of facts more precise and minute. The faculty for truth is recognized as a power of distinguishing and fixing delicate and fugitive detail. The moral world is ever in contact with the physical, and the relative spirit has invaded moral philosophy from the ground of the inductive sciences. There it has started a new analysis of the relations of body and mind, good and evil, freedom and necessity. Hard and abstract moralities are yielding to a more exact estimate of the subtlety and complexity of our life. Always, as an organism increases in perfection, the conditions of its life become more complex. Man is the most complex of the products of nature. Character merges into temperament: the nervous system refines itself into intellect. Man's physical organism is played upon not only by the physical conditions about it, but by remote laws of inheritance, the vibration of long-past acts reaching him in the midst of the new order of things in which he lives. When we have estimated these conditions he is still not yet simple and isolated; for the mind of the race, the character of the age, sway him this way or that through the medium of language and current ideas. It seems as if the most opposite statements about him were alike true: he is so receptive, all the influences of nature and of society ceaselessly playing upon him, so that every hour in his life is unique, changed altogether by a stray word, or glance, or touch. It is the truth of these relations that experience gives us, not the truth of eternal outlines ascertained once for all, but a world of fine gradations and subtly linked conditions, shifting intricately as we ourselves change—and bids us, by a constant clearing of the organs of observation and perfecting of analysis, to make what we can of these. To the intellect, the critical spirit, just these subtleties of effect are more precious than anything else. What is lost in precision of form is gained in intricacy of expression.

Is it likely that a critic who could write in these terms *in 1865* would have been blind, as Mr. Aldington assumes, to the characteristic art of the period that followed—to Impressionism and Post-Impressionism, to Expressionism and Abstraction, to Proust and Kafka, to Bartok and Stravinsky, to Picasso and Moore. Mr. Aldington is entitled to his own opinion, but I would submit that a critic who could write with such prophetic foresight more than ninety years ago (he then being only twenty-six years old), and who could at the same time give Goethe as a true illustration of "the speculative temper"—as one "to whom every moment of life brought its contribution of experimental, individual knowledge; by whom no touch of the world of form, colour, and passion was disregarded"—such a spirit would not today be in the camp of reaction.

One might give many examples of the amazing modernity, the enduring validity, of Pater's criticism. I was particularly struck by this on re-reading the essay on Winckelmann, which was first published in 1867. It is not merely that Pater brings out clearly the significance of Winckelman's influence on Goethe (and indeed on the whole of the Romantic

Movement in Germany); he proceeds to define the limitations of Winckelmann's philosophy of art, and to show
how Goethe in particular surpassed it. This again has a
bearing on the point already discussed—Pater's "modern-
ism". "Breadth, centrality, with blitheness and repose, are
the marks of Hellenic culture"—so much had been revealed
by Winckelmann. "Certainly," observes Pater, "for us of
the modern world, with its conflicting claims, its entangled
interests, distracted by so many sorrows, with many preoccupations, so bewildering an experience [let us note,
incidentally, that they already said such things in 1867!], the
problem of unity with ourselves, in blitheness and repose,
is far harder than it was for the Greek, within the simple
terms of antique life. Yet, not less than ever, the intellect
demands completeness, centrality." But the problem could
not be solved in the Greek way—"by perfection of bodily
form, or any joyful union with the external world; the
shadows had grown too long, the light too solemn for that.
It could hardly be solved, as in Pericles or Pheidias, by the
direct exercise of any single talent; amid the manifold claims
of our modern intellectual life, that could only have ended
in a thin, one-sided growth. Goethe's Hellenism was of
another order, the *Allgemeinheit* and *Heiterkeit,* the completeness and serenity, of a watchful, exigent intellectualism".
But what did this imply for Goethe? Not, at any rate, to
indulge the commonplace metaphysical instinct. "A taste
for metaphysics may be one of the things which we must
renounce, if we mean to mould our lives to artistic perfection. Philosophy serves culture, not by the fancied gift of
absolute or transcendental knowledge, but by suggesting
questions which help one to detect the passion, and strangeness, and dramatic contrasts of life."

Few people now aspire to mould their lives to artistic

perfection, and "the relative spirit" has been somewhat crushed in these days of dogmatic politics and totalitarian states. All the more reason for returning to Pater, his wisdom, his poetry, his subtlety, his gentle humour. Humour is perhaps an unexpected word to apply to him, but he himself said that "a kind of humour is one of the conditions of the just mental attitude, in the criticism of by-past stages of thought"; and he charged Coleridge with "an excess of seriousness, a seriousness arising not from any moral principle, but from a misconception of the perfect manner. There is a certain shade of unconcern, the perfect manner of the eighteenth century, which may be thought to mark complete culture in the handling of abstract questions." Pater himself had this "shade of unconcern", and that is perhaps why he was not popular in Oxford, and why a suggestion that he was "superficial" still persists. It is a gross error. It is a common assumption that in order to be "profound" a writer must be pessimistic about nature and humanity—that a Pascal, therefore, is necessarily more profound than a Montaigne, a Kierkegaard than a Goethe. This is to confuse wisdom with metaphysics or mysticism. Pater quoted Montaigne with approval: "I love a gay and civil philosophy. There is nothing more *cheerful* than wisdom: I had like to have said more wanton." For Montaigne, said Pater, "to be in health was itself the sign, perhaps the essence, of wisdom—a wisdom rich in counsels regarding all one's contacts with the earthy side of existence". But health is not to be confused with heartiness, with mere grossness of appetite, with brutal affirmation. The governing method is ignorance—an ignorance "strong and generous, and that yields nothing in honour and courage to knowledge; an ignorance which to conceive requires no less knowledge than to conceive knowledge itself"—a sapient, instructed, shrewdly ascertained ignorance, suspended judgment, doubt, everywhere. Pater is speaking for Gaston (in *Gaston de Latour*): Gaston who is the final exponent of his philosophy and the pupil of Montaigne: "Balances, very delicate balances; he was partial to that image of equilibrium, or preponderance, in things. But was there, after all, so much as preponderance anywhere? To Gaston there was a kind of fascination, an actual aesthetic beauty, in the spectacle of that keen-edged intelligence, dividing evidence so finely, like some exquisite steel instrument with impeccable sufficiency, always leaving the last word loyally to the central intellectual faculty, in an entire disinterestedness." Mr. Aldington is right in regarding Pater as a bulwark resisting those world tendencies and pseudo-philosophies which "must result in a contemptuous repudiation of all that has for so many centuries formed the material of 'culture'". But the image is too negative, too static, for there is in Pater a positive philosophy, a philosophy which inspires and vitalizes the creative mind. He appreciated, none better, "the old, immemorial, well-recognized types in art and literature", but he was not so stupid as "to entertain no matter which will not go easily and flexibly into them". He was on the side of the progressive element in his own generation, one of those "born romanticists, who start with an original, untried *matter*, still in fusion; who conceive this vividly, and hold by it as the essence of their work; who, by the very vividness and heat of their conception, purge away, sooner or later, all that is not organically appropriate to it, till the whole effect adjusts itself in clear, orderly, proportionate form; which form, after a very little time, becomes classical in its turn".

Finally it is to be observed that Pater's work, critical and philosophical in intention, is nevertheless creative in its own kind. He believed that "imaginative prose" was "the special

art of the modern world", and he showed in all his work
how it should be written. We may have reservations about
his style—it is sometimes too coloured for its purpose, an
engraved scalpel; but at its best it is magnificent, and in certain of his *Imaginary Portraits,* in *The Renaissance* and in
certain chapters of *Marius,* one is aware that our language
is, perhaps for the first time, being used in the full measure
of its music and meaning.

8

The Writer and His Region

IN ENGLAND, broadcasting has made "region" a word of
daily usage, but has obscured its meaning. The region in
which I live, the Northern Region, is not a region in anything but an arbitrary geographical sense—its bounds determined partly by administrative convenience and partly by
the vagaries of electro-magnetic radiation. Lancashire is in
the north, but it has little in common with the county on
the east of the Pennines. Even in that county there are three
ridings, each with very distinct geographical and ethno-
graphical peculiarities. I doubt if we could isolate a distinctive
"northernness", getting more intense the farther north we
go. Indeed, beyond Northumberland we come to a region
called the Border, which is not a geometrical boundary, as
the name might indicate, but what might be called a buffer-
region, dividing incompatible realms. But the Border is
precisely one of the authentic regions, and the Border ballads
one of the best examples of great literature rooted in a

defined geographical space. Sir Walter Scott, collecting these ballads, gave his volume "the misleading and indeed mendacious title", as Swinburne called it, of *Minstrelsy of the Scottish Border*—Swinburne retaliated with a volume entitled *Ballads of the English Border*, and in a draft of a Preface to this volume he remarked rather bitterly that "it needs no more acquaintance with the Borderland than may be gathered from print by an English Cockney or a Scotch highlander, to verify, the palpable and indisputable fact that even if England can claim no greater share than Scotland in the splendid and incomparable ballad literature which is one of the crowning glories, historic and poetic, of either kingdom, Scotland can claim no greater share in it than England: and the blatant Caledonian boobies whose ignorance is impudent enough to question the claims of the English ballad—nay, even to deny its existence, and consequently the existence of any ballads dealing with any such unheard-of heroes as Robin Hood, Guy of Gisborne, Adam Bell, Clym o' the Clough, and William of Cloudesley—may be confuted and put to shame, if shame be possible for such thick-skinned audacity to feel or understand, by the veriest smatterer who has an honest and intelligent eye in his head". Swinburne was a Borderer himself, so his indignation is understandable. But the point he makes is also the first point I would like to make: that what we call regionalism in literature has nothing to do with nationalism in literature, which is usually a disguise for politics. Regionalism in literature (and in all the arts) is a product of historical tradition and geographical restrictions. The geographical factors come first, but geographical is not quite the right word for them. There is the basic factor of landscape—the actual conformation of the region—its hills and streams, its woods and buildings—all the surface appearances that make a familiar scene, loved for its own sake. But the buildings, as well as the fields and gardens, are themselves an expression of the people who generation after generation patiently and consistently created them. The people have a continuity of race—of intermarried families and accepted customs; and a continuity of language—and language which they may share for the most part with other regions, but which they speak with a special intonation and pronunciation. The dialect of a region, to those who live in the region, is an unconscious bond of feeling, and all these things—climate, landscape, buildings, speech and customs, make up an invisible matrix in which the minds of the people are moulded.

The Greeks had a word for this regional feeling—they called it *ethos*. This word generally signifies the prevailing spirit of a city, and we have derived our word *ethics* from this sense of the Greek word. But originally there was the idea that the ethos of a city was somehow dependent on its situation and physical characteristics, and the difference between the *ethos* of Athens, and that of Sparta, for example, was explained by the very different spirit bred in such distinct places. This, of course, was bound up with their mythology, which tended to localize the habitation of the gods. The gods, too, were part of the landscape.

The important distinction to make, in considering this question in its widest implications, is between this Greek sense of a prevailing spirit of a region and what I would venture to call the debased modern sense to which we might give the name *provincialism*. There is, of course, no clear distinction between a province and a region; but "provincial" has acquired a somewhat derogatory sense which fits certain characteristics in literature as in life and these are the characteristics which we must seek to dissociate from *regionalism* in life and literature.

If I proceeded to describe the characteristics of the provincial writer I shall inevitably offend some people, but it
is a risk I must run. The main distinction is that regionalism,
in spite of its local origins, is always universal—that is to
say, it appeals, not to the limited audience of the region in
which it is written, but to mankind everywhere and at all
time. Provincialism, however, is, like village gossip, of little
interest a mile beyond the village pump. It relies on local
knowledge of local types, and is inevitably petty and particu-
larising. A good test to distinguish the two types is that of
translatability. *Tristam Shandy* is a book wholly rooted, as
I shall argue presently, in the ethos of a particular countryside,
and yet it is universal. I cannot quote statistics about the
translations that have appeared in other countries, but I
know that it has had, and perhaps still has, a great vogue and
influence in Germany and France, where translations have
been current since the eighteenth century. In Russia it had
a decisive influence on two of her greatest writers, Pushkin
and Gogal. A Chinaman or a Mexican could enjoy its humour
and its style. Now take a book which in certain moods I
myself can enjoy, and which is not altogether dissimilar—
Handley Cross by Surtees. Jorrocks is, I suspect, a descendant
of Uncle Toby and Corporal Trim, but he lacks their universality. Sterne's characters are, like Bottom and that other
Toby, or Sir John Falstaff himself, larger than their local
life—they pluck at heart-strings wherever in this harsh world
the human breast is still equipped with such things.

Let us now turn to a different kind of book, though we
only pass from the North to the West Riding of Yorkshire
—Emily Brontë's novel *Wuthering Heights*. Here we have a
work of art comparable to the masterpiece of Greek drama,
and as those masterpieces had deep roots in the region of
Attica, so *Wuthering Heights* has its deep roots in the bleak

moorlands of Yorkshire: it could not have been written with its particular colour and intensity in any other region but the Yorkshire moors, and yet, like *The Oresteia* or *Antigone*, it is universal in its appeal.

Perhaps we shall get a little nearer to the secret of this intimate contract between the universal and the particular if we examine the example of *Wuthering Heights* a little more closely. Emily Brontë was a very strange genius, for out of nothing, it almost seems, she conjured a philosophy that has all the fortitude and grandeur of the philosophy of the Greek stoics—of Zeno and Cleanthes. But that "nothing", if we analyse it closely, resolves into the positive *ethos* of the Haworth moors. Charlotte, in her Preface to the 1850 edition of *Wuthering Heights,* admitted the presence of what she called a quality of "rusticity" in the book. "It is rustic all through," she said. "It is moorish, and wild, and knotty as the root of heath. Nor was it natural that it should be otherwise; the author being herself a native and nursling of the moors." Charlotte then went on to speculate on whether the case would have been different had Emily been born in a town. Different it would have been, assuming that she had written at all. The interpretation given to the tragedy by a lady of the world would have differed widely from that given by "the homebred country girl". It might have been more comprehensive—more "sophisticated", as we might nowadays say. But, said Charlotte, "as far as the scenery and locality are concerned, it could scarcely have been so sympathetic: Ellis Bell did not describe as one whose eye and taste alone found pleasure in the prospect; her native hills were far more to her than a spectacle; they were what she lived in, and by, as much as the wild birds, their tenants, or as the heather, their produce".

I remember, many years ago, while still a student in Leeds,

going for a walk over the Haworth moors and being awe-struck by what, in a poem I wrote at the time, I described as "the unheeding bleakness"; and I too called for a Stoic sacrifice of passion on the "black altars of rock" that lay strewn on those moors. There is only one other landscape that has given me a similar emotion—the bleak valley of Mycenae in Greece, where the tragedy of Agamemnon was enacted. I might have hesitated to put forward the notion that a region can directly inspire tragedy and tragic poetry, and even a characteristic philosophy, had I not had these personal experiences. But between the vague and numinous awareness of a region's *ethos* and the dramatic organization of a tragedy like *Wuthering Heights* there is, of course, all that the word "art" connotes. It is not sufficient to feel the *ethos* of a region: one must also *realize* it, and this is the artist's immediate concern. How it is done, no one knows—least of all, perhaps, the artist. There is the feeling, and there, after an exhausting wrestle with the angels of creation—*there* is the work of art.

I am not maintaining that all inspiration is of this immediate physical kind. Inspiration is a complicated relationship not only between the artist and his environment, but also between the artist and his material, and between the artist and tradition, by which I mean the technique of the art as handed down by previous generations of artists. But I believe that this quality in art which Charlotte Brontë called "power" is largely an unconscious communication from a region's *ethos*—from its physical physiognomy and racial collectivity. At the same time one must admit that not all works of art betray a regional origin. Some of the greatest, and Shakespeare immediately springs to mind, are not to be localized in any exact sense. Of course, Shakespeare had his roots deep in English soil. There is a profound and intensely felt Englishness in such works as *A Midsummer Night's Dream* and *The Merry Wives of Windsor,* and even *King Lear*, the most universal of Shakespeare's tragedies, is peculiarly British, and even anonymously local, in its atmosphere. *Macbeth,* too. Turgenev wrote a story called *A Lear of the Steppes*; another Russian writer, Leskov, wrote a story called *Lady Macbeth of the Mtensk District*; and what both writers succeeded in doing was to transpose a universal theme into a more familiar regional setting. But in doing so they were admitting that a tragedy gained something by such a transposition—and that something is the regional ethos. A tragedy that gains its force from a familiar ethos, gains an equivalent force from the ethos of another region.

So far I have perhaps confined myself too closely to tragedy, but the need for regional roots is not less evident in other forms of imaginative literature—notably in poetry. What better illustration is there than Wordsworth, a poet who was so conscious of this need that he deliberately planted himself in his native Lake District. His best poetry is intimately associated with the Lakeland ethos and takes its strength from that "primal sympathy, which having been must ever be". But I would like to return, for a less obvious and therefore more effective demonstration of my thesis, to Laurence Sterne. I happen to belong to Sterne's region myself, and though there have been many changes since he died in 1768 the changes have not been so drastic as in other parts of the country. Shandy Hall still stands, and the villages of Sutton, Stillington and Coxwold, where he lived or had a living, have not altered very much since the eighteenth century. I should get into trouble with my present neighbours if I said that their inhabitants too had not altered much since the eighteenth century, but though they may be eccentric characters, as indeed they were in Sterne's time, I

can meet any day the spit-and-image of Mr. Shandy and
Dr. Slop, of the widow Wadman and Uncle Toby. Such
characters have not changed, and never change, because
they are essentially human, and they are essentially human
because they are *native*. Here is Sterne's description of the
village midwife:

In the same village where my father and my mother dwelt, dwelt
also a thin, upright, motherly, notable, good old body of a midwife,
who with the help of a little plain good sense, and some years full employment in her business, in which she had all along trusted little to her
own efforts, and a great deal to those of Dame Nature—had acquired,
in her way, no small degree of reputation in the world—by which
word *world,* need I in this place inform your worship, that I would be
understood to mean no more of it, than a small circle described upon
the circle of the great world, of four *English* miles diameter, or there-
abouts, of which the cottage where the good old woman lived, is
supposed to be the centre?

There you have a very exact definition of the region, and
though only of four English miles diameter, it is large enough
to breed half a dozen immortal characters, and the man
that had the genius to depict them in immortal words. We
know that Dr. Slop was drawn from an original prototype
—a Dr. John Burton of York; and so with every character
in great fiction. Nothing is invented by the imagination:
the imagination discovers what has been created intensively
by the ethos of a small circle described upon the circle of
the great world. "The great Error of Life is," said Sterne
in one of his letters, "that we look too far. We scale the
Heavens—we dig down to the centre of the Earth, for
Systems—and we forget ourselves. Truth lies before us; it
is in the highway path; and the Ploughman treads on it
with his clouted Shoon" (Letter XVI, Coombe's collection,
1788).

It is this concentration of infinite time in a finite place that produces the intensities of great art. It is the finiteness of the region that makes the ethos that moulds the character that is copied by the dramatist or the novelist. As for the poet and the painter, the musician and the architect, they are in more direct contact with the same ethos—an epic, a folk-song, a lyric, even a house, these are emanations of the genius loci, which alone can give accent, colour and life itself to the universal prototypes of the mind.

I am not venturing as a paradox that the regional is universal, or that the particular is general. There is a sense in which the greatest artists transcend their origins. A Michelangelo, a Shakespeare, a Beethoven—they have been claimed by the world for qualities which are super-regional because they are in a sense super-human. I do not wish to end on a speculative note; I would rather confess that there is a supreme quality of greatness that eludes our critical faculties. But within the range of those faculties stand the shining lights that make our common glory, each in a local shrine.

9

Max Stirner

THERE ARE several reasons why the centenary of Max Stirner's *The Ego and His Own* should not pass without commemoration, the least important being the merely historical fact that it played a decisive part in the philosophical discussions out of which emerged Marxism. Marx devoted three-quarters of *Die Deutsche Ideologie,* an immense work, to a refutation of Stir-

ner's philosophy, and Marx was not given to wasting his time
on trivialities. Marx triumphed over Stirner as he triumphed
over Feuerbach and Bakunin: he had the last word and it is
still echoing in the political events of the present day. But
after a sleep of a hundred years the giants whom Marx thought
he had slain show signs of coming to life again. "The issues
which Stirner raised and Marx met," Sidney Hook observes
in a brilliant book which he devoted to the intellectual strife
of this period,[1] "have a definite relevance to the conflict of
ideas and attitudes in the contemporary world in Europe and
America today. Indeed, we might even say that this is due
to the fact that Stirner and Marx are here discussing the fundamental problems of any possible system of ethics or public
morality." That was written in 1936, and now, after a second
world war which has brought all these fundamental problems
into sharper focus, the relevance of Stirner's philosophy is all
the more apparent.

The clash of altruism and egoism is one of the commonplaces of ethics, and the issue is never in doubt. Stirner is
usually dismissed as the most extreme representative of the
philosophy of egoism known to history, and students in our
academies of learning only hear of him as a lost soul condemned to the lowest regions of limbo. His famous book was
originally published in Leipzig, ironically enough by the same
publisher who a few months later (in 1844) published Engels'
*Condition of the Working Classes in England. Der Einzige und sein
Eigentum* as Stirner's book was called, hardly survived Marx's
onslaught, but some mention of it is made in two books
which played a great part in the development of thought
during the second half of the nineteenth century—Lange's
History of Materialism (1866) and Eduard von Hartmann's
Philosophy of the Unconscious (1869). The references in Lange's

---

[1] *From Hegel to Marx.* London, 1936, p. 165.

book aroused the curiosity of John Henry Mackay, the German poet with a Scottish name, who then read *Der Einzige und sein Eigentum* and was so moved by it that he devoted a considerable part of his life to a rehabilitation of Stirner's name and work. His biography of the philosopher was published in Berlin in 1898. Later Victor Basch, who held the chair of aesthetics at the Sorbonne until quite recently, published an appreciative study of Stirner's philosophy. George Brandes also saw the importance of Stirner, and when, at the turn of the century, Nietzsche's philosophy became the vogue, Stirner was presented as one of his precursors. An English translation of Stirner's book was sponsored by the American anarchist, Benjamin Tucker, and excellently carried out by Steven T. Byington. This translation, with an Introduction by Dr. James L. Walker, another American anarchist, was published by A. C. Fifield in London in 1913. I bought my copy in 1915, and it is a book which I have never lost sight of—it is a book which once read is persistently recalled to memory. In America it has been re-issued as a popular classic in the Modern Library, but in England it remains unknown and unsolicited.

I have not read Stirner's original text, but its vitality survives translation, and it is easy to detect the influence it had on Nietzsche's *style* (its influence on his thought is still more obvious). Read the following passage (appropriate enough today for its content) and you hear the very voice of Zarathustra:

Listen, even as I am writing this, the bells begin to sound, that they may jingle in for tomorrow the festival of the thousand years' existence of our dear Germany. Sound, sound its knell! You do sound solemn enough, as if your tongue was moved by the presentiment that it is giving convoy to a corpse. The German people and German peoples have behind them a history of a thousand years: what a long life! O, go to rest, never to rise again—that all may become free whom you so long have held in fetters. The *people* is dead. *Up* with *me*!

O thou my much-tormented German people—what was thy torment? It was the torment of a thought that cannot create itself a body, the torment of a walking spirit that dissolves into nothing at every cock-crow and yet pines for deliverance and fulfilment. In me too thou hast lived long, thou dear—thought, thou dear—spook. Already I almost fancied I had found the word of thy deliverance, discovered flesh and bones for the wandering spirit; then I hear them sound, the bells that usher thee into eternal rest; then the last hope fades out, then the notes of the last love die away, then I depart from the desolate house of those who now are dead and enter at the door of the—living one:

For only he who is alive is in the right.

Farewell, thou dream of so many millions; farewell, thou who hast tyrannized over thy children for a thousand years!

Tomorrow they carry thee to the grave; soon thy sisters, the people will follow thee. But when they have all followed, then—mankind is buried, and I am my own, I am the laughing heir!

The whole of *The Ego and His Own* is not written in this exalted style—indeed, Stirner's style, for a German style, is unusually direct and clear, and not loaded with the symbolism so characteristic of Nietzsche. Some of his terminology is difficult to translate into English, for we have no exact equivalents for words like "Einzige", "Eigner", "Einzigkeit", "Eigenheit" and "Eigentum", but with the help of some footnotes Steven Byington successfully overcame these problems.

Stirner wrote his book at a decisive moment in the history of European thought—at a moment when the traditional dogmas of religion, politics and philosophy were being discarded, and people everywhere were adopting the new dogmas of socialism, communism, Hegelianism, materialism and many other "isms". It might be said that the whole purpose of Stirner was to show that these revolutionaries were merely jumping out of the frying-pan into the fire, throwing off one set of shackles merely to slip into another set. A man is only free, Stirner maintained, if he gets rid of *all* dogmas, renounces *all* "isms", and confronts the world as an "Eigner", a unique person existing in his own rights, self-determined and self-directed. "I am *my own* only when I am master of myself, instead of being mastered either by sensuality or by anything else (God, man, authority, law, State, Church, etc.); what is of use to me, this self-owned or self-appertaining one, *my selfishness* pursues."

In so far as this doctrine was applied to absolutism, to nationalism, to religious dogmatism, it was (and still is) acceptable enough to a large number of small-minded people. But Stirner carried his relentless analysis into the revolutionary camp, and showed that their ideals, called humanism, liberalism, communism or what not, were merely traps for the unwary. "The HUMAN *religion* is only the last metamorphosis of the Christian religion. For liberalism is a religion because it separates my essence from me and sets it above me, because it exalts 'Man' to the same extent as any other religion does its God or idol, because it makes what is mine into something otherworldly, because in general it makes out of what is mine, out of my qualities and my property, something alien—to wit, an 'essence'; in short, because it sets me beneath Man, and thereby creates for me a 'vocation'. But liberalism declares itself a religion in form too when it demands for this supreme being, Man, a zeal of faith, 'a faith that some day will at last prove its fiery zeal too, a zeal that will be invincible'."

That last phrase is quoted from Bruno Bauer, whose

uncritical idealism had been too much for Marx, When he comes to Stirner, Marx has to take a very different stand. Engels had already warned him (in a letter of November 19, 1844, quoted by Hook, p. 173*n.*) that "what is true in his principle, we, too, must accept. And what is true is that before we can be active in any cause we must make it our own, egoistic cause—and that in this sense, quite aside from any material expectations, we are communists in virtue of our egoism, and that out of egoism we want to be human beings and not merely individuals". That acute observation has been enormously reinforced since Engels' time by psychoanalysis, which has shown to what great extent our ideals, even when apparently most disinterested, are but rationalizations or sublimations of egoistic impulses or expressions of unconscious and yet selfish motives. Marx's criticism of Stirner's subjectivism would need drastic revision to be convincing today. But where Marx is on stronger ground is in showing that Stirner's "own" or "unique one" is a philosophical abstraction which one can divorce only in theory from the environmental influences which determine the nature of the individual personality.

At this point Stirner becomes relevant to the philosophy of personalism, and indeed Berdyaev has admitted that "in Max Stirner, in spite of the falsity of his philosophy, true personalism is to be found, but in a distorted form. In him a dialectic of the self-affirmation of the ego comes to light. The 'unique one' is not personality because personality disappears in the infinity of self-affirmation, in unwillingness to know another, and to achieve transcendence to the utmost. But in the 'unique one' there is a modicum of truth, for personality is a universe, a microcosm, and in a certain sense the whole world is its property and belongs to it; personality is not partial nor a particular nor subordinate to the whole and the common".[1] Stirner would have had his answer to Berdyaev—he would have found his surrender to "supra-personal values" nothing but the old slavery in a new form, and slavery not freedom in his mystical transcendentalism.

The most pertinent criticism of Stirner is that which is directed against his doctrine that freedom implies power, though it is not a criticism that a Marxist can make with any sincerity. Certainly some of Stirner's statements can be construed as a defence of the competitive spirit, and therefore as a defence of capitalism. But Stirner was really only con-cerned, as Erich Fromm has been in our time, to insist that freedom is a very ambiguous term—that there is all the difference between freedom *from* and freedom *for* something. "My freedom," wrote Stirner, "becomes complete only when it is my—*might*; but by this I cease to be a merely free man, and become an own man. Why is the freedom of the peoples a 'hollow word'? Because the peoples have no might! With a breath of the living ego I blow peoples over, be it the breath of a Nero, a Chinese emperor, or a poor writer." Marx, if not his followers, would have subscribed to this. And I think that most modern psychologists—cer-tainly Jung, Burrow, Rank and Fromm—would subscribe to what is the essence of Stirner's claim—that freedom, "in the full amplitude of the word" is "essentially self-liberation —i.e. that I can only have so much freedom as I procure for myself by my ownness". Stirner's doctrine is, in fact, a plea for the integration of the personality, and on that basis the charge of "selfishness" becomes somewhat naïve. As Fromm says, if an individual can only "love" others, he cannot love at all. "Selfishness is rooted in this very lack of fondness for oneself. The person who is not fond of himself, who does not approve of himself, is in constant anxiety concerning his own

[1] *Slavery and Freedom*. London, 1943, p. 34.

self. He has not the inner security which can exist only on the basis of genuine fondness and affirmation." But Stirner had said the same thing: "I love men too—not merely individuals, but every one. But I love them with the consciousness of egoism; I love them because love makes *me* happy, I love because loving is natural to me, because it pleases me. I know no 'commandment of love'. I have a *fellow-feeling* with every feeling being, and their torment torments, their refreshment refreshes me too; I can kill them, not torture them." Like Mencius and Chuang-tze, Stirner realized that "the feeling for right, virtue, etc., makes people hard-hearted and intolerant". The whole of Stirner's treatment of the subject of love is of great subtlety and profundity, and Marxian criticism does not touch it at all. So far as I know only Martin Buber, himself the most profound of modern philosophers of the self, has appreciated this aspect of Stirner's work and given some discussion of it.[1]

Finally I would like to suggest that the fashionable doctrine of existentialism must owe something to Stirner—the resemblances are too many and too close to be accidental. Sartre's philosophy is said to derive from Heidegger, a philosopher of whose work I have read very little, and Heidegger is said to derive from Kierkegaard, of whose work I have read a good deal. But I see no resemblance at all between the end-links of this chain, between Kierkegaard and Sartre. But the characters in Sartre's plays and novels are constructed round a philosophy which seems to me to be identical with Stirner's (plus a little American pragmatism). They are all busy discovering the illusory nature of freedom, the tyranny of "isms"; they are all resorting to a non-metaphysical, anti-hypothetical view of reality. Every Sartrean hero concludes much in the concluding words of

[1] *Between Man and Man.* London, 1947.

The Ego and His Own: "In the *unique one* the owner himself returns into his creative nothing, out of which he is born. Every higher essence above me, be it God, be it man, weakens the feeling of my uniqueness, and pales only before the sun of this consciousness. If I concern myself for myself, the unique one, then my concern rests on its transitory, mortal creator, who consumes himself, and I may say:

All things are nothing to me."

10

Frank Lloyd Wright

SOMEONE ONCE described Frank Lloyd Wright as a "provincial genius", as though genius could be qualified, and forgetting that geniuses are most often provincial, at any rate in their origins. In small countries they are drawn to the metropolis for economic reasons, especially if they are architects. But the United States has no metropolis in the Old World sense of the word, and a genius may alight, with equal propriety, in Wisconsin or Arizona, New York or Washington, D.C.

Mr. Wright cannot be so easily dismissed. His eccentricity is a positive quality, and is due to an obstinate holding on to certain truths from which others have diverged. Wright's early work was not particularly eccentric; apart from American exemplars, like Louis Sullivan, it seems to me to stem quite naturally from the European movement of the late nineteenth century, from Austrian and Dutch *Jugendstil*, from Macintosh and Voysey. There was still organic growth in that movement, but from the time of the building of the Crystal Palace the engineers began to declare their independence of the architects, and on their drawing-boards designed "structures" which were "erected". All they asked for was a clear space and a firm foundation, and their paper-work, their brain-work, could then be converted into terms of steel and concrete, into machines with various functions (to live in, to work in, to die in).

Wright's career has been a life-long protest against this betrayal of architecture—this substitution of construction for building. Building begins on the ground—and not in an office. It begins with something even more essential than a survey of the site. It begins with contemplation, with meditation, with an intuitive apprehension of the particular forms that will be "in harmony with" the site, and yet fulfil the functional purpose of the building. Mr. Wright has used the word "organic" to describe this kind of archi-tecture—an ambiguous word for which he is now prepared to substitute two or three others—integral, intrinsic, natural:

Organic means intrinsic—in the philosophic sense, entity—where-ever the whole is to the part as the part is to the whole and where the nature of the materials, the nature of the purpose, the *nature* of the entire performance becomes clear as a necessity. Out of that *nature* comes what character in any particular situation you can give to the building as a creative artist.

This might be called a romantic conception of archi-tecture—Wordsworth wrote an essay on the architecture appropriate to the landscape of the Lake District, and Mr. Wright is saying what Wordsworth said before him, and which all people of romantic sensibility have always felt. To live in unity with nature—it is not a sentimental idea: it is a philosophical idea, the philosophy of the Taoists, of the Stoics, and of the Romantic poets. But some of Mr. Wright's critics are sentimentalists, and think that to live in unity with nature means living in thatched cottages or log cabins.

That may be the way a stick-insect lives with nature, but it is not the way of man, who has developed a wonderful faculty for harmonization, which means the reconciliation or integration of disparate elements—the creation of a synthesis out of thesis and antithesis. That is the method of Frank Lloyd Wright. He was once asked how he came to relate Bear Run House to its site. He answered:

There in a beautiful forest was a solid high rock-ledge rising beside a waterfall and the natural thing seemed to be to cantilever the house from that rock-bank over the falling water. You see, in the Bear Run House, the first house where I came into possession of concrete and steel with which to build, of course the grammar of that house cleared up on that basis.

On the basis of reconciliation—the reconciliation of rigid steel and waving foliage, of smooth rectangular planes of concrete and rugged protruding rocks. Such a reconciliation is not achieved on the surface—it is part of the inner structure of the building, the use of principles of tenuity and flexibility, made possible by modern materials, which are actually the principles of organic growth. A Frank Lloyd Wright house grows like a tree rooted in the ground and spreading its branches to enfold a living-space. The machine-made, engineered house has no such organic conception, but is dumped inertly on the landscape, like a cardboard box. "I can see no evidence of integral method in their making," remarks Mr. Wright.

We should not be afraid to re-examine our principles, and it may be that we can convincingly demonstrate that for

84

the time in which we live, and under the economic conditions of our living, these principles are logical. But a revolt
may be directed against a prevailing dialectic: aesthetic
principles need not necessarily be logical—they can be
illogical, imaginatively irrational. It was not *reason* that
determined the architectural motive of the Gothic cathedral
or of the Baroque palace. It is not reason that has determined
the character of Frank Lloyd Wright's buildings. Another
reviewer of this book called Wright "the Father of the
Functionalists", but the truth is rather that Wright has been
a lonely giant battling against contemporary academicism:
a functionalist does not put carved larva peacocks over his
doorways, build dwellings over waterfalls, or erect above
a chapel a concrete tower-trellis for flowering vines.

Frank Lloyd Wright is, of course, a romantic—perhaps
the greatest romantic of our age. The mistake is to assume
that a romantic is a kind of village idiot with no interest in
science or "modern developments". On the contrary,
typical romantics like Goethe and Shelley had keen scientific
interests: a contempt for science is more characteristic of
the classicist. It is his romanticism which gives Wright's
Autobiography its typical flavour—it is an epic of self-absorp-
tion, of expansiveness, of quixotic idealism. It is a big book,
and it is all about the man himself, his notions and achievements, but never for a moment does it flag. And it is never
petty. Failures are accepted with courage, tragedy with
dignity. Call the man a charlatan if you feel that way about
him, but then recognize that his background is a continent
and that he fills it without strain, with ease and affluence.
If he is a charlatan, so was Whitman, so was Goethe, so was
Beethoven. "In Beethoven's music I sense the master mind,
fully conscious of the qualities of heartful soaring imagination that are god-like in a man. The striving for entity,

oneness in diversity, depth in design, repose in the final expression of the whole—all these are there in common pattern between architect and musician." The man is conscious of this kinship, and when we have measured his achievement, we are not disposed to deny his claim—though we might have doubts about the claims of the grandiose in general: doubts about Beethoven and Whitman no less than doubts about Frank Lloyd Wright.

In addition to the Man, there is in this book a philosophy and an architecture. The philosophy preaches "organic integration". It says that if you want to create a healthy civilization and a beautiful culture, man's artifacts must be in unison with the natural: there must be no hard and fast division between man and his environment. This is given a literal interpretation:

> In integral architecture the *room-space itself must come through*. The *room* must be seen as architecture, or we have no architecture. We have no longer an outside as outside. We have no longer an outside and an inside as two separate things. Now the outside may come inside and the inside may and does go outside. They are *of* each other.

This conception has a general application:

> Thus in this rise of organic-integration you see the means to end the petty agglomerations, miscalled civilization. By way of this old yet new and deeper sense of reality we may have a civilization. In this sense we now recognize and may declare by way of plan and building —the *natural*. Faith in the *natural* is the faith we now need to grow up on in this coming age of our culturally confused, backward twentieth century. But instead of "organic" we might well say "natural" building. Or we might say "integral" building.

Integral building includes "an awakened sense of Materials —their nature understood and revealed". Away with plaster and paint—let brick remain brick, stone stone, and wood an organic texture. But might not a painter claim that paint is also a material? And certainly a plasterer can go into raptures over *his* "textures". Wright extols glass, "a super-material", and textiles are admitted as "a beautiful overhead for space, the textile an attribute of genuine architecture instead of decoration by way of hangings and upholstery". There seems to be an unreasonable prejudice here: let us rather demand freedom to exploit the aesthetic potentialities of any and every material. This prejudice in favour of an arbitrary range of materials—brick, stone, glass and un-treated woods—might explain Wright's deficient sense of decoration. His interiors look bleak, his furniture is hard and angular, his ornament empty, and there is just no place at all for "art" (paintings, drawings, sculpture). Wright wishes to abolish the "cave" and restore "something of the freedom of our arboreal ancestors living in their trees". But in man's evolution the cave was a slight improvement on the tree-top, and for inhabitants of a temperate or arctic zone it was at any rate "cosier". Wright seems to be an enemy of *Gemüt-lichkeit*: his forefathers were Welsh Unitarians.

I speak without experience of living in a Frank Lloyd Wright house, and cosiness may be a prejudice. Alexander Woollcott found one of Wright's houses "exhilarating"— "just to be in that house uplifts the heart and refreshes the spirit. Most houses confine their occupants. Now I under-stand, where before I only dimly apprehended, that such a house as this can liberate the person who lives in it". We could do with a few more testimonies of this sort. If we can take the human aspect for granted, there is no denying the poetry. The houses are married to the landscape: there is lyricism in an office building, integrity in everything. No doubt inferior architects have built better houses—better in the sense that they will give satisfaction to dull-minded people for a century or two, and then pass into oblivion. But Wright's genius, always romantic, sometimes mad, hovers at the threshold of a new epoch, and no modern architect has offered so much inspiration, inspired so much hope. He is like his great painter-contemporary Picasso in that the fertility of his genius has given no excuse for the foundation of a new academicism.

I have not seen enough of Mr. Wright's architecture to venture any criticism, but I observe in what I have seen, and in all that I have seen illustrated—and what I have seen is supported by all that Mr. Wright says on the subject—a certain self-sufficiency and jealousy. Obviously, when the house is finished, he resents the intrusion of the client for whom he has built the house—the client with his furniture and knick-knacks, his all-too-human desire for comfort and cosiness. A Chinese screen is permissible; perhaps a few well-chosen pieces of Japanese pottery. Nature, in the form of drooping ferns or climbing ivies, may grace the natural background of wood or stone; and even a tree may, like a giraffe, thrust its head through the roof. Wright's architecture, no less than the severest functional architecture, predicts the end of all "cabinet" art—of the whole Renaissance tradition of bibelots and bric-à-brac, in which we must include the painted canvas and sculpture on its pedestal. The aesthetic impulse that proliferated such objects in the past five hundred years now seeks to inhabit other forms—the typical forms of our industrial civilization. The more sophisticated amenities of our civilization must, it would seem, be secreted in cupboards. Insofar as they have useful articles (and what, in this respect, is the difference between women's dresses and pictures, books and golf-clubs) there may be a certain logic in such austerity. But carried to its logical conclusion a sense of unity—"where the whole is to the part as the part is to the whole"—implies that every house Mr. Wright builds is his own house, and the people who live in them are not his clients, but his guests.

Every architect, inasmuch as he fulfils a social need (for housing) becomes a sociologist. You cannot build, on any considerable scale, without affecting the life of the community; and most communities exercise a strict control on building. In the course of a long experience Mr. Wright has acquired many definite ideas on social questions, and they are never far from the surface when he is writing about architecture. They constitute a devastating criticism of modern civilization. But it is always positive criticism. It is easy to trace most of our social ills to the big city, and to cry out for decentralization. But decentralization is a long word which means nothing unless you have a plan. Mr. Wright has a definite plan, an architect's plan, a plan for what he calls Broadacre City, a plan which we can criticize and try to improve. But he knows that a plan is useless unless there is the imagination to realize it, the vital creative impulse which is precisely the impulse that has been destroyed by modern civilization. So the fundamental problem is to restore this creative impulse, and this can only be done by a new kind of education—education through art.

I believe the time has come when art must take the lead in education because creative faculty is now, as ever, the birthright of man—the quality that has enabled him to distinguish himself from the brute. . . .

This creative faculty in man is that quality or faculty in him of getting himself born into whatever he does, and born again and again with fresh patterns as new problems arise . . . A false premium has been placed by education upon will and intellect. Imagination is the instrument by which the force in him works its miracles.[1]

[1] *The Future of Architecture.* New York, 1953.

Mr. Wright admits that creative art cannot be taught, but he has a practical suggestion to make—experimental centres endowed by industry where sensitive, unspoiled students ("and they may yet be found in this unqualified machine that America is becoming") may rediscover their creative talents—"where the creative endeavour of the whole youth is co-ordinated with the machinery, and where the technique of his time is visible at work, so that youth may win back again the creative factor as the needed vitalizing force in modern life".

II

Religion and Culture

THE AWARD of the Nobel Prize to Mr. T. S. Eliot in 1948 coincided with the publication of a new book by him—not a book of poems or of literary criticism, but of what would usually be called "sociology".[1] It is not the first book of this kind that Mr. Eliot has published—*Thoughts After Lambeth* and *The Idea of a Christian Society* also deal with social issues, and in general, even in his poetry, he is constantly aware of the problems that distress our age. His point of view is that of a Christian and a note of fervent apologetics underlies all his argument. But the pitch is always perfectly controlled—he believes, with Lord Acton whom he quotes to this effect, that our studies "want to be pursued with chastity, like mathematics".

The title of his new book is precise—*notes towards* the

[1] *Notes Towards the Definition of Culture*. London, 1948.

definition of culture; not a systematic treatise in the manner of a German or an American sociologist, not a claim to completeness or finality. Nevertheless, the argument is closely reasoned, and if we would understand it not one of its hundred pages can safely be omitted.

In a book whose whole purpose is to establish distinctions, to advance qualifications, we must not expect dogmatic conclusions. At the end of our reading we are more conscious of what culture is *not* rather than of what it is. It is, we are told, "a way of life of a particular people living in a particular place", a "peculiar way of thinking, feeling and behaving". It is the "pattern of the society as a whole" and it is "the creation of society as a whole". But not a conscious creation—it is in some sense unconscious and cannot be deliberately produced by education or political action.

Culture in this sense must be distinguished from the culture, or cultivated taste, of the individual, as well as from the culture of a group or class within a society. It is misleading to identify culture with any of its specific manifestations—it is a question of fine manners and good cooking no less than of great architecture and immortal poetry. But there is one general assertion which, in Mr. Eliot's opinion, can be made about all cultures—"no culture", he says, "has appeared or developed except together with a religion: according to the point of view of the observer, the culture will appear to be the product of the religion, or the religion the product of the culture".

Mr. Eliot takes great pains to define this "togetherness" of religion and culture. He warns us several times not to make Matthew Arnold's mistake of assuming that culture is something more comprehensive than religion. Equally we must avoid the error of regarding religion and culture as two separate things between which there is a *relation*; and further, it is an error to *identify* religion and culture. All these attempts at definition admittedly lack spiritual subtlety, and though he is "aware of the temerity of employing such an exalted term", Mr. Eliot cannot think of any other which would convey so well the intention to avoid *relation* on the one hand and *identification* on the other as the word *incarnation*: the culture of a society is the incarnation of its religion.

But there are further qualifications to make. There are religions "of partial truth" and people with "a truer light", "higher" religions and "lower" religions, and if we should be compelled by the objective evidence to admit that a religion of partial truth, such as Buddhism, is incarnated in a culture superior to our own, that is only because our culture is not really Christian. But surely the Buddhist might retort that if in some respect the culture of India or China is in our view inferior to our own, that is only because it is not "really" Buddhist. If we are to have what might be called a science of comparative culture, then we must also have a science of comparative religion; and all that the scientists will be able to conclude is that while culture is generally (not always) found in association with religion, there is no evidence to show that any one type of religion is "truer" than another. There is one way of life (comprising religion and art and every other kind of cultural manifestation) and there is another way of life, and the only *objective* test of their worth would seem to be the degree of happiness generated by each way of life—Bentham's sensible test of the greatest happiness of the greatest number.

I agree with Mr. Eliot on so many essential points that it is only with a feeling of hopeless bafflement that I find myself being sceptical on the issue which he obviously regards as the most important of all. I agree that culture is an indefinable way of life—that it cannot be potted or analysed or scientifically communicated in any effective way. "Culture can never be wholly conscious—there is always more to it than we are conscious of; and it cannot be planned because it is also the unconscious background of all our planning"—my own philosophy is embodied in that general statement of Mr. Eliot's. But even assuming that culture is the incarnation of religion, I cannot help observing that the flesh can be corrupted. How often in the history of mankind has a corrupted church been responsible for the disruption of a culture—for the destruction of a pattern of culture, for the distortion of a way of life! If you want the evidence, look round you at all the monuments defaced by a righteous spirit of asceticism.

If a sociologist allows himself to speak of "higher" and "lower" religions, of "truer" and less true lights, he is tacitly admitting an evolutionary order in religions. Whether this is or is not a correct interpretation of Mr. Eliot's meaning, the fact that societies have in historical times evolved from primitive to more elaborate or "civilized" patterns, taken together with the assertion that culture is the incarnation of religion, implies that religion itself has also evolved. But once we admit a principle of evolution in religion we are committed (as sociologists) to the prospect of a further stage in the evolution of religion. But that is not the underlying assumption of Mr. Eliot's thesis. If I do not misunderstand him, he assumes that our European destiny is to work out a pattern of culture ordained nearly two thousand years ago. I am genuinely anxious to understand the Christian sociologist on this point. I have always assumed that Christian culture reached its perfection in the Middle Ages—in the Christian society of Saint Louis, for example. It does not seem to me to be very realistic to suggest that we can re-establish the cultural pattern of the thirteenth century; and at the same time any incarnation of the Christian faith would seem to imply a society far more like the feudal societies of the Middle Ages than anything we have experienced in modern history. If that kind of medievalism is not in Mr. Eliot's mind, then he must envisage a very different kind of society—a society different from that of the thirteenth century no less than from the society of today. But a *different* society, on his own argument, would seem to imply the incarnation of a *different* religion. A different religion is precisely what I contemplate as the substance of any renewal of culture in the future, but from Mr. Eliot's point of view that is a gross heresy.

That Mr. Eliot seeks to restore a past order to correspond with a past stage of religious evolution is shown by his treatment of the question of *élites*. This fashionable word hides the social phenomenon more realistically known as a dominant or privileged class. Admittedly an élite can be cultured —it can encourage and protect artists and scholars and even to some extent assimilate such agents of culture into its own body. The fact that people are variously endowed at birth with genius or talent means that if a society is to benefit to the full from its humanity, it must allow its best brains, its wisest minds, to rise to positions of influence in the public service. It would seem, from a biological point of view, that the best system would be one that allowed this talent to rise freely to the top, like cream on milk. That is the policy known as "equality of opportunity". Mr. Eliot is opposed to it, with a somewhat surprising violence. He argues that it is "an ideal which can only be fully realized when the institution of the family is no longer respected, and when parental control and responsibility passes to the State. Any system which puts it into effect must see that no advantages of family fortune, no advantages due to the foresight, the self-sacrifice or the ambition of parents are allowed to obtain for any child or young person an education superior to that to which the system finds him to be entitled". I should have thought that the family, in Mr. Eliot's no less than in my own view, was bound together by something more spiritual than self-interest. But let us look for a moment at the consequences of an education depending on privilege.

In the administrative branches of the Civil Service, as well as in the Armed Forces, there is no doubt that a "career open to talents" has proved the only safe rule from the point of view of the efficiency of those services and the safety of our society. In the First World War the officers reared in privilege, trained in privilege and promoted by privilege proved a menace to our very existence, and had to be shed in their thousands and replaced by new blood drawn from the unprivileged classes before the war could be won. Even if this statement of facts is disputed, it cannot be questioned that the two world wars were organized and prosecuted not by a professional élite, nor by a class élite, but by an élite drawn by a selective process from the nation at large.

War, in my opinion, is not a cultural activity, but the position is not different in the peace-time cadres of our Civil Service, our county and borough services, and in the vast organization of our economic and industrial life. What is left? Mr. Eliot cannot reply: "All that we mean by the word culture", for he has already defined culture as an indivisible way of life. But religion, art, learning—these are left. Are we to assume that different rules apply to them—that in these spheres of life culture by exception must be formed and transmitted by a privileged class?—the privileges being exclusive property, exclusive schools, exclusive universities and exclusive clubs.

Levels of culture are inevitable; specialization of culture is desirable; but I am not convinced that these depend on an aristocratic organization of society. Mr. Eliot is contemptuous of the doctrine of egalitarianism; he thinks it leads to licentiousness and irresponsibility. I do not think he has given due consideration to what might be called the *mystique* of the doctrine. Some Christians argue that this mystique is implied in the Fatherhood of God, in the Brotherhood of Man—I am not in a position to substantiate their argument. I take my evidence from biology and history, and this evidence suggests to me that the highest achievements of man, moral and material, are due to the impulse of mutual aid. There is, of course, an individual one-way expression of this impulse— we then call it sympathy or charity. But the higher form of its expression is mutual, an "I-Thou" dialogue, a sinking of differences, an exercise of humility. To the extent that this relationship prevails in a society we have that social unity, that "peculiar way of thinking, feeling and behaving", which generates and transmits a culture.

I must confess that I have not given the whole of Mr. Eliot's argument at this point, but that is because it is not quite clear to me. He states that the primary vehicle for the transmission of culture is the family, and in that I agree. He then says that in a more highly civilized society there must be different levels of culture, and there too I agree, subject to my remarks about equality of opportunity. But he then concludes, from these two premises, that only by maintaining class privileges can culture be transmitted from generation to generation. Groups of families must persist each in the same way of life—the landed gentry, presumably, must remain landed gentry, the merchant adventurers must remain merchant adventurers (and not aspire to the House of Lords), and the poor must know their place and keep it.

Mr. Eliot recognizes the danger of *ossification*; he thinks that a modest flow of blood from one social level to another will prevent it. But that is not the lesson of history. Privilege does not necessarily lead to enlightenment, and only rarely to *noblesse oblige*. Rather it breeds a spirit of entrenchment, of pride, of infallibility; finally a tyranny against which the spirit of man again and again has risen in bloody revolt.

12

Michelangelo and Bernini

WHEN WE CRITICIZE great artists we have to take into account not only their personal achievements, but also their universal influence; and this is often an evil that "lives after them". Michelangelo is a particularly good example of this ambiguous fame—"a great fellow", as Ruskin said, "but the ruin of art". In Ruskin's earlier days Michelangelo had seemed to him the most sublime of all modern artists; but the more he considered the development of art after Michelangelo's death (which took place in 1564), the more convinced he became that Michelangelo had been responsible for its decline.

Ruskin felt that four great changes had been wrought by Michelangelo and they were all changes for the worse. They could be expressed in four terse phrases: Ill work for good; Tumult for Peace; The Flesh of Man for his Spirit; and the Curse of God for his Blessing. It will be useful to bear these criteria in mind in discussing two books which were published in the same year, 1955—one on Michelangelo, and one on the sculptures of Gian-Lorenzo Bernini, an artist

97

whom Ruskin would have considered a perfect illustration of Michelangelo's bad influence.

The book on Michelangelo is by Adrian Stokes,[1] a critic whose work is not so well known as it should be. He has written several books dealing with different aspects of Italian art, and in some of them he has written with especially subtle feeling and profound knowledge on the art of sculpture. He describes his book on Michelangelo as a "study in the nature of art", but though there is a whole section devoted to Michelangelo's poems, which are not often considered in relation to his visual works, sculpture is again uppermost in his mind. It is not a long book, but it is so tightly packed with meaning that it must be read more than once—I myself have read it three times, and with each reading have found increased understanding and pleasure.

Rudolf Wittkower's book on Bernini[2] is a work of great scholarship. Professor Wittkower has been studying Bernini for more than twenty years, and no one in the world writes upon this subject with so much authority. He also writes with feeling, and his introduction is, as he says, "an exposition of the principles of Bernini's art rather than . . . a biographical narrative".

Mr. Stokes's aim is similar: he says that his book is devoted to an "aesthetic appraisal" of "Michelangelo and humanist art, to an unique quality of humanist art". I think we might begin by asking what this unique quality is, and then we might ask if Bernini also possessed it, and finally whether we can use this quality as a criterion of greatness in art.

Let me first reveal the fact, which I hope will not prejudice the reader, that Mr. Stokes is a Freudian. But let me hasten to add that his book is not one of those crude psycho-analytical

[1] *Michelangelo: a Study in the Nature of Art.* London, 1955.

[2] *The Sculptures of Bernini.* London, 1955.

approaches that reduce the work of art to a sexual symbol and the artist himself to a sexual pervert. His book is an attempt "to substantiate, in the person of Michelangelo, the distinctive character of art as self-expression or catharsis, what is called the Form, the mode of treating each subject-matter". Michelangelo suffered from periods of acute anxiety and depression; he was testy and, in spite of his great fame, always felt persecuted. He never married, and an element of bi-sexuality is clearly discernible in his work. It is the aim of Mr. Stokes to show that the very greatness of Michelangelo's art is due to a superhuman effort to repair this tormented psyche: "I live on my death," wrote Michelangelo . . . "And he who does not know how to live on anxiety and death, let him come into the fire in which I am consumed." This gives us some inkling of his inner suffering, and Mr. Stokes's thesis, that Michelangelo "projected into art a heroic, constant movement that overcomes, or rather absorbs, depression and the state of being overpowered", becomes entirely convincing.

Let me take this opportunity to quote, because it is relevant, a paragraph from Mr. Stokes's book which is an illustration of the occasional magnificence of his prose style. He is discussing the statues of Night and Dawn in the Medici chapel:

They are carvings that make of depression itself, rather than of the defences against it, a heroic cycle; a statuary less of uneasy grandeur than of grandeur in unease, yet figuring an anguish not unreconciled with the formula of an antique river god's vegetative settlement. The women are inactive; there is no expressionist thrust beyond the material, nothing pointed; on the contrary, a great deal to distract us momentarily, sleep, fatigue, surfeit, a relaxed and slow awakening upon the perilous incline, fruitful images that soon broaden to an universal recognition, undisturbed by the intensity that provokes rejoinder, of profound unrest. This feeling is unescapable: it comes to

99

us through the sense of touch and the consuming eyes, from a hundred sources that interweave, monumental composition, modelling, movement, directional contrast and the rest. It finds the hidden depressive centre in ourselves, but even did we not possess it, we should be aware that here are great works of art, here an eloquence of substances that is read by the tactile element inseparable from vision, by the wordless Braille of undimmed eyes. On the other hand such clamant evocations of hidden depression could not reach us—our minds would be closed—were it not that they are conveyed in the reparative, reposeful terms of art.

"The reparative, reposeful terms of art"—there you have the guiding idea of this book—the idea that an artist like Michelangelo can live on anxiety and death because he can transmute such themes into the sublime forms of his art.

It is part of Mr. Stokes's thesis that such ideal relationships of form can be expressed only by means of images of the human body, and he goes so far as to say that "it is likely that images of the body belong to the aesthetic relationship with every object; emotive conceptions of physique are ancient in us; awareness of our own identity has always been based upon the flesh". It almost seems as if he would explain even the aesthetic appeal of abstract art as in some sense related to the body image. And here we come to the possible source of Michelangelo's fatal influence.

One of the charges brought by Ruskin against Michelangelo was that he had substituted the Flesh of Man for his Spirit. Although Ruskin is usually considered a Romantic, he had strong classical prejudices, and one of these was that the human body should be idealized, made androgynous or sexless, and that the face should be the principal feature, and should express perfect serenity, free from either vice or passion. I will not go into the personal psychology of Ruskin that pre-disposed him to such a view, and certainly it is not an eccentric view, but one that has been held by many people, and by whole civilizations. The consequence of such a view is that the forms of painting and sculpture should be severely restrained, clear and compact. As an artist profoundly influenced by classical models, and by Italian predecessors like Donatello who held this same view, Michelangelo at first kept his forms closely packed. But we are always conscious of a tremendous power trying to break the bonds of form. As Wölfflin says, "every turn, every bend of a limb, has a latent power—quite trivial displacements have an incomprehensibly powerful effect and the impression so produced can be so great that one forgets to seek the motives behind the movement". And then Wölfflin—I am quoting from his book *Classic Art: an Introduction to the Italian Renaissance*[1]—points to the fatal weakness in Michelangelo's style:

It is characteristic of Michelangelo that he forced his means relentlessly to gain the utmost possible effect so that he enriched art with new effects hitherto undreamed-of, but he also impoverished it by taking away all joy in simple, everyday things; it was he who brought disharmony into the Renaissance and prepared the ground for a new style—the Baroque—by his deliberate use of dissonance.

The great interest of Adrian Stokes's book is that it shows with great subtlety how this formal dissonance is related to the inner conflicts of the artist—how Michelangelo forged beauty out of conflict itself, and thereby resolved the conflict. What he calls the "rational" nude was necessary for this process—"a man's predicament, conflict, are not only explored but embodied by means of the 'rational' nude in rivalry, as it were, with the precise actuality, separateness, solidity, of another human being or of ourselves".

The means to this end were complex—a spiritual contest

[1] London, 1952. Trans. M. D. Hottinger.

with brute matter in which even the material itself, in its uncouthness, must collaborate—the block must bear witness to the emotional process of searching for that ideal form— "add to depth and vivification; allow the worked forms to suggest both emergence and shelter, a slow uncoiling that borrows from the block the ideal oneness, timelessness, single-ness of pristine states". This is beautifully said, but it also makes it clear why Ruskin called Michelangelo one of "the leading athletes in the gymnasium of the arts" (the other is Raphael). Great art might be described as strong passions firmly contained. When the passions are weak or common-place, and the bonds themselves are feeble, then we get the decadence of art, and that is the charge we must bring against the whole of the Mannerist style that Michelangelo inspired. Bernini began his career about fifty years after Michelangelo's death. The Mannerist style had had time to run its course, and it is Professor Wittkower's contention that Bernini repre-sents a return to strength and discipline, to Michelangelo's "dynamic vigour". To Ruskin, and I confess to me also, any comparison of Bernini to Michelangelo is almost blasphemous. I would like to explain why.

Professor Wittkower thinks that Bernini is still suffering from comparative neglect, but that "his fortunes seem to be changing". It is true that there is now in this country a wider appreciation of Baroque art in general, and of Bernini in par-ticular, than existed twenty years ago. This I suspect is in a large measure due to the advocacy of foreign scholars who were brought up in a Baroque atmosphere and came to England as refugees. It is significant that the six columns of Professor Wittkower's bibliography contain only one item by a British scholar, and this is a reference to a magazine article. There is some quality in Baroque art to which people like myself do not respond. The usual assumption is that our attitude is a religious or a moral one. We do not like Baroque art because it is the art of the Counter-Reformation; it offends our ingrained Protestantism. But this is not true. The revulsion I experience when I enter St. Peter's in Rome is not moral—it is physical, even visceral. It is literally an aesthetic reaction, and it is not confined to Protestants—I have met many Catholics who agree with me. Fundamentally we are agreeing with that great Catholic, St. Bernard, who reacted against similar tendencies in the art of the twelfth century. The Cistercian order which he founded perfected an architecture that is at the opposite extreme to Baroque—instead of richness, austerity; instead of agitation, stillness; instead of emotional expressionism, ideal harmony. These dissident Benedictines were instrumental in spreading the serene Cistercian style throughout northern Europe, and there can be no doubt that it corresponded, and still corresponds, to something more universal than sectarian prejudice: the longing to contrast the futile indulgences of the flesh with an order that is perfect in its proportions, at once objective and absolute, superhuman and serene.

Bernini's personality is somewhat elusive. He was a devout Catholic, and, as Professor Wittkower tells us, "remained to the end of his life an ardent follower of Jesuit teaching". He does not seem to have been tortured by any of the doubts and despairs that made Michelangelo's life such a misery; and he does not seem to have felt the need to cast his broken mind into the reparative mould of a perfected form. On the contrary, his impulse was to break all bonds, to escape from a confining mould, and to use the utmost freedom of gesture— to be rhetorical rather than restrained. His particular type of Catholicism encouraged him in this. As Professor Wittkower says, the *Spiritual Exercises* of St. Ignatius which he practised "were designed to stimulate a vivid apprehension of any given subject for meditation through an extremely vivid appeal to the senses". The religious imagery which he was called upon to create had to fulfil precisely the same purpose as the *Spiritual Exercises*. Professor Wittkower then gives the statue of St. Bibiana (in the church in Rome dedicated to her) as an example of this achievement; he says that

the beholder finds himself face to face with the gnosis of an individual rather than with a supra-personal cult image. His sympathy is roused, he feels with her and tries to identify himself with her experience. He receives even more than he is immediately aware of, for with her he shares emotions of universal significance. Herein seems to lie the secret of Bernini's spectacular success: it is through emotional identification with the mood symbolized in a figure that the faithful are led to submit to the ethos of the triumphant Counter-Reformation.

We turn to the illustration of this statue and find all that is so artificial and repellent in this type of art: "the prevalent prototype of female saints", as Professor Wittkower incautiously calls it—a calculated pose, a languid hand uplifted in benediction, a head inclined sentimentally, and sweet empty features whose stereotyped details—half-open mouth and upturned eyes—are a kind of rubber-stamp of piety. Bernini certainly has finer conceptions to his credit, but this statue is nevertheless representative of all he stands for in the history of art: for a pictorial conception of the art of sculpture (sculpture seen from a single viewpoint, and not as a rounded palpable mass), for emotional involvement rather than timeless contemplation; for tumult rather than peace; for conscious conceit rather than naïvety.

The notion that sculpture should be a plastic three-dimensional composition rather than a pictorial composition—that it should appeal to our tactile sensations as well as to our visual sensations, that it should be read, as Mr. Stokes says, "by the wordless Braille of undimmed eyes"—this is perhaps a modern prejudice, but if one has become accustomed to this full range of sculptural effect, then Bernini's work must seem shallow and relatively ineffective. As for its dramatic effect, which might be thought to compensate for this lack of tactile palpability, again a confusion of medium seems to be involved. I confess that I am subdued by the theatrical brilliance of Bernini's St. Teresa group in the church of St. Maria della Vittoria, but only by forgetting (or not noticing) that I am looking at sculpture. I am penetrated by a dramatic vision, by a dream-like illusion; and if art is a form of illusionism, then Bernini is a great artist for whom sculpture is a means, not an end. That perhaps explains why, following Baudelaire, I attach so much importance to naïvety in art. To use art is to abuse art. In true art there is no interval between intuition and execution, between vision and design: everything is immediate and spontaneous, and even the sculptor, who labours against time, seeks always to retain the unity of feeling and form.

It may be that in expressing a preference for such qualities in art as unity, objectivity, serenity, and simplicity, we are merely revealing our own psychological type, and I have no wish to dismiss Bernini dogmatically. Obviously he was a genius—his architecture alone is sufficient evidence of that. But the corruption that was inherent in Michelangelo's later work is blatant in the whole of Bernini's sculpture, and it springs, in my view, from a corruption of consciousness itself, whereby what should be direct and unique in feeling and expression becomes stereotyped and calculated.

13

The Limits of Logic

PROFESSOR AYER suggests that his book[1] may be of interest to the general reader, and it is as a general reader that I presume to comment on it. There is, indeed, much in his closely reasoned argument of general application; to follow it is a profitable mental discipline; and I can imagine no intelligence that would not benefit from its clear presentation of certain basic problems of philosophy. It is as a general reader that I am immediately held up by the first sentence of the first page: "It is by its methods rather than its subject-matter that philosophy is to be distinguished from other arts or sciences."

The five chapters that follow are confined to a consideration of method. The problem is not to make a valid statement (about being or existence, truth or beauty), but to discover how a statement of any kind can be made. "Knowing as having the right to be sure", "How do we know?", "The justification of statements about physical objects", "The analysis and justification of statements about other minds" —such sectional headings will indicate the kind of question that is discussed. But is this philosophy in any traditional or complete sense? Most philosophers have attempted to solve such epistemological problems, but very few would have regarded them as the be-all and end-all of philosophy. Hume and Locke, who may be regarded as the father and grandfather of the empirical tradition to which Professor Ayer belongs, treated these questions of method as prolegomena to the more weighty problems of morals and politics. Contemporary analytical philosophy never seems to advance

[1] *The Problem of Knowledge.* London, 1956.

beyond its prolegomena and this is due to its exclusive reliance on linguistic logic or "scientific method".

The general reader is not likely to be in a position to question any of Professor Ayer's propositions. Apart from the fact that they are usually in support of a commonsense view, which he is likely to share, they are presented with a dialectical brilliance which only a logician of equal skill could counter. But while agreeing that there is more to it than "running hard in order to stay in the same place", it is possible to question the general utility of some of these logical exercises. "Why cannot cause succeed effect?" The general reader might feel that the answer to such a question is precluded by the agreed usage and function of the words "cause" and "effect", and if this is nevertheless Professor Ayer's own conclusion, one can still wonder whether the question need ever have been raised. But apparently contemporary philosophers love to conduct long arguments on such subjects, and to conclude that indeed cause cannot succeed effect. We knew it, but our knowledge is confirmed. Of most propositions it could be said that it is *logically* conceivable that they are false; but human discourse has to ignore logic, or there would be no art and no invention, no spring of action whatever, but only universal scepticism. The conduct of life is not logical, but pragmatic.

Logic is a necessary science because language is an imprecise instrument of communication, and the average mind uses it bluntly. But there is an opposite error based on the assumption that language can be scientific, and that meaningful discourse is only possible in so far as this ideal of scientific method is achieved. The truth is rather that human beings communicate with each other by various and devious methods, from grunts and gestures to mathematical symbols and works of art. Several of these methods dispense with language altogether, and yet communicate the structure of feelings with great precision. Admittedly the knowledge thus communicated is not infallible; but Professor Ayer admits that empirical statements are in no better position—there are very few of them which are in any important sense indubitable.

Plato believed that it was possible to have innate knowledge of universal ideas—that is, of truth. Knowledge of truth, he would have said, is acquired by metaphysical intuition, and the function of logic or scientific method is then deductive. This kind of philosophy has been discredited in our time because all manner of religious or mystical statements that have no basis in experience are then open to discussion, and they tend to clog the dialectical machine. All modern philosophers, except perhaps certain Catholics like Gilson and Maritain, would claim to be empirical in some sense, but there is no agreement as to what constitutes experience; or, since we are here concerned with a theory of knowledge, as to what constitutes cognition.

Professor Ayer does not like the word "intuition" ("Words like 'intuition' and 'telepathy' are brought in just to disguise the fact that no explanation has been found"), and though I have noted the word "unconscious" two or three times, it is not used to imply any theory of access to hermetic levels of knowledge, such as Freud's "archaic heritage" or Jung's "collective unconscious". Nor does Professor Ayer presumably admit the existence of two distinct types of cognition— discursive (logical) and presentational (symbolic). I would not venture to take up a dogmatic position in such matters, but I do in my amateurish way feel as I read *The Problem oj Knowledge* that the problem of knowledge is either more complicated than Professor Ayer suggests, or that it is possibly much simpler.

I can only very tentatively, and surely revealing my ignorance of places where these questions have been definitely settled by Professor Ayer and his followers, ask certain questions. For example, while duly qualifying his defence of "naïve realism", Professor Ayer seems to treat all perception as mirror-like. How the perceptual apparatus functions is an extremely complicated problem, for which the neurologists have no simple explanation. "When we perceive a two-dimensional circle," Sir Russell Brain has pointed out, "we do so by means of an activity in the brain which is halved, reduplicated, transposed, inverted, distorted, and three-dimensional." But more significantly, there is in perception itself (if I have understood the Gestalt psychologists) a selective and formative element. It has even been called an aesthetic element. That is to say, if perception were direct, it would be formless, confused and confusing. As the mind perceives, it automatically selects and organizes the field of perception.

To this modern psychological observation corresponds Kant's fundamental notion that "experience is without doubt the first product which our understanding brings forth". This means, as Professor Charles Hendel has observed (in his Introduction to Cassirer's *Philosophy of Symbolic Forms*), that "in knowledge truth is whatever is in accordance with the form of understanding. . . . Whatever human consciousness appropriates for any purpose whatsoever, whether to gain knowledge or to handle imaginatively in art, is already possessed of form at the very taking". It is on such grounds that Cassirer rejected positivism.

The Gestalt psychologists have demonstrated that in the act of perception a "segregation of wholes" takes place in the nervous system. We see the external world through a shape-giving filter. It is no longer possible, as Rudolf Arnheim

said in *Art and Visual Perception*,[1] to think of vision as proceeding from the particulars to the general—"vision is not a
mechanical recording of events but the grasping of significant
structural patterns", and these patterns are the primary data
of perception. We have to think of perception as a creative
activity that achieves at the sensory level a form of knowledge
(symbolic cognition or "perceptual concepts") independent
of the processes of logical reasoning. This fact, if fact it be,
would have considerable significance for the problem of
memory, to which Professor Ayer devotes one of his most
interesting chapters. He argues very convincingly that
memory is not necessarily based on image recollection. He
even suggests that memory perhaps functions best when no
images intervene. But granted that the senses work through
significant patterns, one can imagine an almost mechanical
process of sorting that has no reference to concrete visual
particulars. It will still seem true that "where one remembers
something that one has seen, there need not always be a
present image". But this is a limited, figurative or representational, notion of an image. There may be a shadow-play
of imageless "Gestalten".

This is pursuing the argument into the psychological sphere,
which Professor Ayer seems studiously to avoid. But again
the general reader in his ignorance might ask whether the
problems of perception and memory can be realistically
discussed apart from psychology, or even apart from physi-
ology. If one reads a neurobiologist such as J. R. Smythies[2]
one has the feeling, perhaps deceptive, that the problems
discussed by Professor Ayer are being discussed more realistically.

The closest correspondence in my limited reading of

[1] London, 1956.

[2] *Analysis of Perception*. London, 1956.

philosophy to the kind of reasoning pursued by Professor Ayer is not in neurobiology, and not even in Locke or Hume, but in St. Thomas Aquinas. Logic can function with a certain sublime disregard of facts: it is happiest when dealing with abstract categories. St. Thomas, for example, discusses whether the intelligence can know the indivisible before the divisible (*Summa Theologica* I, Qu. 85, Art. 8), which corresponds to Professor Ayer's discussion of whether the effect can come before the cause. St. Thomas and Professor Ayer even discuss an identical problem—e.g. can we have any knowledge of the future (*Summa*, I, Qu. 86, Art. 4: *Utrum intellectus noster cognoscat futura*).

The remoteness of logic is due to a limited and frustrating notion of cognition: not only the denial of intuition as a mode of knowledge, but also, and more seriously, the contemptful neglect of symbolic modes of communication. Symbolism has, unfortunately, a traditional aura of superstition, but what symbols communicate is not necessarily irrational or even numinous, but concrete and positive—a pattern of feeling, for example. Symbolic modes of communication are non-verbal, and a symbol that is non-verbal, say a painting by Cézanne, can be as positive a contribution to knowledge as any statement verified by scientific method. Symbolic statements can be elaborated or extended: it is possible to communicate by means of "the language of art", and by means of this language convey a knowledge of reality.

Cassirer's hypothesis of "mythical thinking", for which he gives the empirical evidence, Susan Langer's "symbolic discourse", extend the idea of such a language and suggest several modes of mental experience that function on a non-verbal level. Even behaviouristic semanticists like Charles W. Morris admit that "such arts as music and painting may signify in any of the modes of signifying". The arts are languages and their logic is *sui generis*. The statements they make are meant to be true, and refer to the same probable truths as philosophy.

It is possible that Professor Ayer presupposes a distinction between philosophy and metaphysics, and that he would dismiss all metaphysics as outmoded Platonism. But finally, as Kant held, the intellect is incapable of anything but platonising. What we hanker after is some form of integral experience: a mode of knowledge that is not partial or exclusive, but in our human degree, absolute. Philosophy, said Whitehead, "is akin to poetry, and both of them seek to express that ultimate good sense which we term civilization". There is neither religiosity nor sentimentality in such an ideal; even Hume would have accepted it.

It is not for a general reader to pronounce on the validity of any particular system of philosophy—he lacks the technical equipment. He must modestly decline to enter into an argument with a professional philosopher. It is not that he is afraid of finding himself in error. He is merely less ambitious. In the past philosophy has been more than a theory of knowledge or a clear understanding of the dimensions of language. It has been an adventure of ideas, and if this phrase of Whitehead's now seems too corny, let Cassirer express the same thought with his subdued eloquence:

Every authentic function of the human spirit has this decisive characteristic in common with cognition: it does not merely copy but rather embodies an original, formative power. It does not express passively the mere fact that something is present but contains an independent energy of the human spirit through which the simple presence of the phenomenon assumes a definite "meaning", a particular ideational content. This is as true of art as it is of cognition; it is as true of myth as of religion. All live in particular image-worlds, which do not merely reflect the empirically given, but which rather produce it in accordance with an independent principle. Each of these functions creates its own symbolic forms which, if not similar to the intellectual symbols, enjoy equal rank as products of the human spirit.[1]

14

Baudelaire as Art Critic

IT IS OFTEN said that no form of writing is so ephemeral as art criticism; and one has to be careful, in writing about contemporary art, not to be dominated by a sense of ultimate futility. But such despair is not justified, and I know of no better proof of this than Baudelaire's art criticism, written about a hundred years ago, but only recently adequately presented in an English edition.[2] It will be said that Baudelaire is unique—that he was a poet who abolished the distinction between creation and criticism, and who knew (he alone) how to transform his *volupté* into *connaissance*. Baudelaire is certainly unique, but not in this respect—in France Gautier and Mérimée had the same faculty, in England Ruskin (and if we no longer read Ruskin, it is a reflection on our own dullness of sensibility, and not on his continuing vitality). Baudelaire's uniqueness consists not in his method, but in certain *idées fixes* to which he returned in almost every article he wrote. "We are living in an age in which it is necessary to go on respecting certain platitudes," he wrote, "in an

[1] *The Philosophy of Symbolic Forms.* Vol. I: *Language.* Trans. by Ralph Manheim. Yale University Press, 1953, p. 78.

[2] *The Mirror of Art.* Translated and edited with Notes and Illustrations by Jonathan Mayne. London, 1955.

arrogant age which believes itself to be above the misadventures of Greece and Rome. We may not now be so confident of ourselves, but we still live in the same age—the age of "steam, electricity and gas—miracles unknown to the Romans—whose discovery bears full witness to our superiority over the ancients".

Of the informing ideas that still give Baudelaire's criticism such vitality, three seem to stand out as still immediately relevant. The first is his rejection of the concept of progress—"this gloomy beacon, invention of present-day philosophizing licensed without guarantee of Nature or of God—this modern lantern throws a stream of darkness upon all the objects of knowledge; liberty melts away, discipline vanishes. Anyone who wants to see his way clear through history must first and foremost extinguish this treacherous beacon. This grotesque idea, which has flowered upon the rotten soil of modern fatuity, has discharged each man from his duty, has delivered each soul from its responsibility and has released the will from all the bonds imposed upon it by the love of the Beautiful". The idea of progress was based on the achievements of nineteenth-century science and industry—already associated by Baudelaire with America—and even for this material notion of progress there is no guarantee—it is a form of credulity. But transported into the sphere of the imagination the idea of progress "takes the stage with a gigantic absurdity, a grotesqueness which reaches nightmare heights". And then Baudelaire goes on to point out, what is always so evident to any student of the history of art, that genius is not governed by any laws of progress. "Every efflorescence is spontaneous, individual . . . The artist stems only from himself."

Baudelaire did not deny the existence of development within the individual artist—on the contrary, he was much concerned to trace such a development in the case of a painter like Delacroix. Nor did Baudelaire deny the existence of "the laws which shift artistic vitality". He was well aware of "that curious law which presides over the destinies of great artists, and which wills it that, as life and understanding follow opposing principles of development, so they should win on the swings what they lose on the roundabouts, and thus should tread a path of progressive youth and go on renewing and reinvigorating themselves, growing in boldness to the very brink of the grave". Baudelaire was, of course, anything but a reactionary. He explained and defended the most experimental art of his day, and was content to leave the final judgment to Time.

The most experimental art of his day was Romanticism —it still is. "To say the word Romanticism is to say modern art—that is, intimacy, spirituality, colour, aspiration towards the infinite, expressed by every means available to the arts." Baudelaire is nowhere more vital, and nowhere more relevant to our present preoccupations, than in his attack on realist art. Mr. Mayne, in his introduction to the English translation, says that "Realism (associated by him with Positivism) was for Baudelaire a flat negation of the Imagination—it was little less than a blasphemy; hence his somewhat curious coupling of the names of Ingres and Courbet, both of whom he regarded as having sacrificed the imaginative faculty on the altars of other gods—'the great tradition' and 'external nature', respectively". Painting for Baudelaire was above all *evocation*—"a magical operation (if only we could consult the hearts of children on the subject!), and when the evoked character, when the re-animated idea has stood forth and looked us in the face, we have no right— at least it would be the acme of imbecility—to discuss the magician's formulae of evocation". Baudelaire, as Mr. Mayne points out, comes very near to the doctrine of the creative imagination as developed by Coleridge in the *Biographia Literaria,* and Coleridge in England and Baudelaire in France (Schelling in Germany)—these are the prime sources of a romantic philosophy. For Baudelaire imagination is a *cardinal* faculty, "the queen of truth". "It is both analysis and synthesis... It is sensitivity.... It is Imagination that first taught men the moral meaning of colour, of contour, of sound and of scent. In the beginning of the world it created analogy and metaphor. It decomposes all creation, and with the raw materials accumulated and disposed in accordance with rules whose origins one cannot find save in the farthest depths of the soul, it produces the sensation of newness. As it has created the world (so much can be said, I think, even in a religious sense), it is proper that it should govern it."

I must neglect the practical application of this doctrine (though briefly one might say it involved the rejection of Ingres and the praise of Delacroix) in favour of a brief reference to the third and perhaps the most neglected of Baudelaire's informing ideas—his doctrine of *naïveté.* This crops up in almost everything he wrote—on poetry no less than on painting. *Naïveté* for Baudelaire means "the dominion of temperament within manner", "knowledge modestly surrendering the leading role to temperament", and it is "a divine privilege which almost all are without". I would say that it is closely related to Keats's conception of "negative capability". It does *not* mean leaving things to chance— there is no pure chance in art, any more than in mechanics. A picture is a machine, whose systems of construction are intelligible to the practised eye; in which every element justifies its existence, if the picture functions well; where one tone is always geared to engage another; and where an occasional fault in drawing is sometimes necessary, so as to avoid sacrificing something more important. That something more important—it may be "truth of movement", fidelity to feeling, but is perhaps that "absolute emptiness" of which the Zen Buddhists speak. "Thus, mastery in ink-painting is only attained when the hand, exercising perfect control over technique, executes what hovers before the mind's eye as the mind begins to form it, without there being a hair's-breadth betwĕen them. Painting then becomes spontaneous calligraphy. Here again the painter's instructions might be: spend ten years observing bamboos, become a bamboo yourself, then forget everything and—paint."[1] The opposite to *naïveté* is the *poncif*—"The *poncif* in conduct and behaviour, which creeps into the life of artists as into their works." The *poncif* is the studied effect, the knowing gesture, all that is academic and self-conscious—corrupt consciousness, we might call it. It is the absence of faith and spontaneity, and in it Baudelaire saw the subtle symptom of our decadence.

15

The Image in Modern English Poetry

WE ARE NOW sufficiently advanced into the twentieth century to ask whether the poetry of our period has acquired any significant character. Its achievement, in a quantitative sense, is impressive: we should have to go back to the Elizabethan period for any comparable efflorescence. But we must not forget that English is now the native language of at least two hundred and fifty million people, most of them acquiring

[1] *Zen in the Art of Archery,* by Eugen Herrigel. London, 1953, p. 102.

some standard of literacy as a birthright, whereas the great wealth of Elizabethan poetry was created by a small society not numbering, on its literate level, more than a few thousands. If averages were of any account in this connection, our present rating would be miserably low.

The truth is that both numbers and literacy have been handicaps to poetry in our time. If we suppose that a law of probability would allow one genuine poet to every thousand children born, then twenty poets would stand a better chance of being listened to in a population of twenty thousand, than would a hundred and fifty thousand poets in a population of a hundred and fifty million. Some principle of diminishing returns operates in literature no less than in economics. Indeed, our civilization is so organized that the larger it grows and the more literate it is made, the more uniform it becomes in its opinions and the more liable to irrational hero-worship. It prefers to be represented by *one* great man, to crowd to the concerts of *one* great conductor, to the performances of *one* leading actor, and finally, to recognize *one* great poet as the representative of its collective taste. A critical discrimination that would estimate particular merits and give due attention to individual qualities is nowadays more often to be found on the racecourse than on the campus, and even there the public, left to itself, will select a favourite upon whom it will lavish irrational odds. The Elizabethans had their favourite poets, but each was held to be as good as the other until proved a failure, and competition was encouraged. The apotheosis of a poet like Shakespeare was the work of later ages, and chiefly of our own.

My intention is not to deflate any of the great reputations of our own century, but if we are to arrive at an estimate of general characteristics we must take care not to be dazzled by particular glories. No poet has dominated our age, in the sense of giving to it a uniform direction or a uniform technique. If uniformity exists, it is in public opinion and not in poetic style. We might use the word *drift* to describe our course, a derogatory word no doubt, but one exactly descriptive of the tides and currents of poetic expression in our time. The so-called "age of Johnson" was an age rich in dogmatism, but poor in invention, the least *original* age in our literary history. If our age has not been dominated by a single poet, much less has it submitted to a single critic, though there are plenty who wish it had been, and some who would dearly love to occupy the throne of the Great Cham. But we are now a literate democracy, and what we have to deplore is the dictatorship, not of an individual, whether poet or critic, but of a uniformly educated taste.

In such circumstances the critic finds himself in a dilemma. Confronted by a uniformity of taste, he ought to encourage diversity: to insist on the unique achievement of individual poets. But he has an even more insistent duty, which is to free a poetic essence from all the accretions of the Zeitgeist— from fashionable causes, political ideologies, philosophical crazes, and all the social and commercial rackets under which that essence is buried. But this is to insist on the singleness of poetry rather than on its diversity. I do not claim to have any touchstone for testing the poetry of our century, but by confining myself to certain technical matters I hope to be able to show in what respects we have kept faith with essential poetry.

I shall confine myself to English poetry, but English poetry is the poetry of the English language, and I hold any attempt to distinguish a specifically British, or a specifically American poetry to be a vulgar heresy, inspired by motives which may be worthy in themselves—nationalistic or patriotic motives —but have nothing to do with literature. The attempt is shown to be absurd in practice, for we find the bodies of poets like Eliot and Auden hung, drawn and quartered by the rival factions. This might be an amusing spectacle did not the heresy in question stem from a fundamental misunderstanding of the nature of poetry. Poetry is a linguistic art, an art which is a fusion of image and utterance. Utterance is instinctive—a mode of symbolic discourse which the child absorbs from the community within which he is born and bred; even the art of rhetoric is only an elaboration of this biological heritage. Now it is true that certain linguistic differences have grown up between England and America. Billy Potts's shoulders

> were wide, and his gut stuck out
> Like a croker of nubbins and his holler and shout
> Made the bob-cat shiver and the black-jack leaves shake . . .

It is expressive language, but the average British reader is left guessing. He reads such lines (they are Robert Penn Warren's) as he reads equivalent lines in French or German poetry, perhaps guessing the meaning correctly, but only pretending to be emotionally affected by the sound. But such lines are rare even in American poetry, and they never amount to the degree of dialectical obscurity presented by an English poet like Chaucer, or even, occasionally, Shakespeare; and certainly never to the degree of obscurity represented by a poet writing in the Scots dialect, such as Burns. If no meaning is conveyed, no poetry is conveyed, but we can exaggerate the disadvantages of obscurity. Even nonsense poetry has its nonsensical meaning. If I hear an expressive line like:

> The robin chirps in the chinaberry tree

my poetic reaction is not impeded by the fact that I have no botanically *precise* visual image of a chinaberry tree. Indeed, the word perhaps conveys to me a more beautiful and phantastic image than it would if I were actually familiar with a botanical specimen. In other words, the imagination sometimes works more effectively, and more poetically, if it is left guessing.

When, therefore, I speak of twentieth-century poetry I mean, not British or American poetry, which are non-essential categories, but the poetry of the English language in all its variability—the poetry of Frost, Yeats, Bridges, of Eliot, Pound or Dylan Thomas, the poetry that exists in our common language, uncontaminated by ideas of race or place.

The poetry of our century began on a soft and sensuous note, as if tired of its inheritance, timid to advance into new estates. The Victorian energy—the exuberance of a Browning or a Swinburne—had been expended. We listen to the weary voice of Arthur Symons' "Absinthe Drinker":

> Gently I wave the visible world away.
> Far off I hear a roar, afar yet near,
> Far off and strange, a voice is in my ear,
> And is the voice my own? The words I say
> Fall strangely, like a dream, across the day;
> And the dim sunshine is a dream. How clear,
> New as the world to lovers' eyes, appear
> The men and women passing on their way!
>
> The world is very fair. The hours are all
> Linked in a dance of mere forgetfulness.
> I am at peace with God and man. O glide,
> Sands of the hour-glass that I count not, fall
> Serenely: scarce I feel your soft caress,
> Rocked on this dreamy and indifferent tide.

This *fin de siécle* mood, with its concordant diction, dominated the first decade of the century. The visible world was alien. It may be objected that there were exceptions—the pessimistic poetry of Hardy, the realism of Kipling, the social protest of John Davidson. But these were particular sentiments, individual opinions, not part of the poetical essence of the period. Even in Hardy we find the same tired rhythms:

> I idly cut a parsley stalk,
> And blew therein towards the moon;
> I had not thought what ghosts would walk
> With shivering footsteps to my tune.
>
> I went, and knelt, and scooped my hand
> As if to drink, into the brook,
> And a faint figure seemed to stand
> Above me, with the bygone look.
>
> I lipped rough rhymes of chance, not choice,
> I thought not what my words might be;
> There came into my ear a voice
> That turned a tenderer verse for me.

The lassitude is in that tenderer verse, in moods of regret that inevitably fall into accents of the whispering gallery, ghostly echoes of the past. The only alternative for Hardy is an awkward artificiality—the artificiality of those lines on the loss of the *Titanic*, where the "steel chambers" of the modern ocean liner are seen as "stilly couching" "in a solitude of the sea", "the pyres" of "salamandrine fires". The image of "this creature of cleaving wing" fatefully converging on "a Shape of Ice" is well conceived, well realized, but the accompanying machinery of an Immunent Will and a Spinner of the Years is a creaking structure copied from Schopenhauer, who designed it after a Greek model. It is not poetic—rather, it is rhetorical, and like all rhetoric, a corruption of the poetic consciousness.

This same corruption of consciousness exists in two further figures who survived well into our century—Housman and Kipling. The tragic sense is keen in each, and when the war came, their poetic interventions did not strike the participant as too unreal. But nevertheless, there is a factitiousness in both. Blood and sweat, spade and hearse, lad and lass, life and death—the antitheses are too easy, semantic marriages, not made in any passionate heaven or hell. True poetry is not so coldly perfect, so immaculate in diction. It is concentrated; it is crystalline; but its edges are sharp and cutting. Kipling knew this, and when he wasn't, as Henry James said, telling a story in the Smoke Room, his metaphysical awareness was condensed into perfect images.

> If any God should give
> Us leave to fly
> These present deaths we live
> And safely die
> In those last lives we lived ere we were born—
> What man but would not laugh the excuse to scorn?
>
> For we are what we are—
> So broke to blood
> And the strict works of war—
> So long subdued
> To sacrifice, that threadbare Death commands
> Hardly observance at our busier hands.
>
> Yet we were what we were,
> And, fashioned so,
> It pleases us to stare
> At the far show
> Of unbelievable years and shapes that flit,
> In our own likeness, on the edge of it.

Such a poem is not of our century, in any specific sense: in form it might belong to the seventeenth century. But the difficult thought is realized in a clear image, and the rhythm winds round the thought with geometrical exactitude. Such an achievement belongs to the universal types of poetry, and is exempt from the limitations of the *Zeitgeist*, which are our particular concern on this occasion.

There exist archetypal images which belong to all time, and which may be transferred from language to language without undue loss. If Kipling's poem were to be skilfully translated into Greek or Latin, French or German, it would not lose its poetic effect, because that effect is metaphysical, idea realized in image, thought felt. The thought process is primary, not in the sense that the poet thinks and then seeks a poetic form of expression for his thought (which is the recipe for bad poetry) but in the sense that the particular poet is a thinker, a philosopher, and his thought takes poetic form in the act of expression. This is a rare combination, for the poet is more usually a sensationalist, or possibly an intuitionist, and reacts directly through his imagination—he uses a symbolic rather than a conceptual form of discourse. His activity, we say, is lyrical. Now, though many images are archetypal, or universal, and reappear repeatedly throughout the course of world literature, the characteristic images of any age are more immediate and sensuous, a direct reaction to individual experience. The archetypal images are not individual in this sense—they are at once collective and unconscious, and any conscious attempt to tap them is apt to produce an effect of banality. The ship of death, for example, is an archetypal image—it occurs in the myths of several cultures, and is particularly familiar to our own cultural tradition in the form of Charon's boat. When, therefore, D. H. Lawrence takes this image as the basis of one of his most ambitious poems, he is under the necessity of reanimating it if he is to avoid the effect of banality. He tries to do this by combining his main universal image with subsidiary and more personal images: the image of the falling apple, that falls to bruise itself an exit from itself—a metaphor for the bruised body, from whose bruised exit the soul oozes. It is doubtful if he is entirely successful —the new and personal image might have been more effective if it had not been associated with an old and familiar image.

The borrowed images in modern poetry are not always so familiar as Lawrence's Ship of Death. One of the most consistent features of the whole period is its eclecticism— its willingness to search out and incorporate the symbols and myths of past ages. Some degree of eclecticism is characteristic of all historic cultures—distance lends enchantment to the past, and the enchantment is all the stronger the more distant the time. All the poets of our English tradition, from Chaucer to Eliot, have freely borrowed the forms and figures of other cultures. But there is an important distinction to be made at this point, a distinction between assimilation and accretion. When a Shakespeare takes a plot of even a metaphor from Plutarch or Ovid, he absorbs it into his own poetic system, and reproduces it in the terms of his own poetic essence. It is not merely a question of playing Julius Caesar in Elizabethan costume: Julius Casesar *is* an Elizabethan—more than that: he is a projection of Shakespeare's own multiple personality. But when Pound and Eliot take the structures of Greek drama as a framework for their poetic sentiments, they are avoiding the problem of creating a contemporary structure. *Hamlet* is a significant play, not because it relates the tragedy of a Danish prince of the Middle Ages, but because it uses this dim figment of the chronicles as an excuse to present the doubts and indecisions of a humanistic age.

The Waste Land, the most eclectic of Eliot's works, is a mythical landscape, a landscape of broken columns and discarded masks, into which no hero intrudes. Pound's *Cantos* are cluttered with literary stage-props. All this is academic vanity. The poet claims that it is not vanity

> To have gathered from the air a live tradition
>   or from a fine old eye the unconquered flame
> This is not vanity.
> Here error is all in the not done,
>   all in the diffidence that faltered.

But the diffidence faltered because it could not fuse the tradition to a modern sensibility—to a consciousness of the modern dilemma. Eliot became aware of that necessity and in the *Four Quartets* redeemed his eclecticism, not in a new myth, but in "aftersight and foresight", in metaphysics, like Kipling (a comparison he would not find objectionable). Again, the words caress the contour of the thought—

> . . . words I never thought to speak
> In streets I never thought I should revisit
> When I left my body on a distant shore.

Our eclecticism has been part of a deliberate attempt to provide the twentieth century with mythical poetry, ignoring the fact that a myth cannot be consciously imported into a culture, but must emerge gradually from the collective unconscious. When I am informed that Ezra Pound's *Cantos* repeat the pattern of Homer's *Iliad,* or that *The Cocktail Party* has the same dramatic pattern as some play by Euripides, I refuse to be intimidated. All that is merely in line, it seems to me, with the repetition, on some American campus, of the architecture of an Oxford college. From this point of view

Yeats proceeded more intelligently than any of our major poets, for though the cosmography of *The Vision* is deliberately worked out, and to that extent personal, it is a serious attempt to submit the imagination to trance-like inspiration: to follow certain mystical disciplines in the hope that they will lead to illumination. Yeats did not succeed in creating an impersonal myth—he did not even establish a cult. But his heresy has consistency: it is not fragmentary, except in the sense that all personal philosophies are fragments of the truth.

We may conclude that there is no characteristic myth of our age, and that we are not likely to find one where we are looking—in the overt attempts of the poets to create one. We must therefore look for the peculiar virtues of our poetry in its poetic structure—in its diction, idiom and imagery. We shall at once be aware of a difference from the poetry of other ages.

Let us begin with the image, for that is the original sensational experience of the poet. He is original in that he sees things for the first time in a metaphorical relation, either to other things, or to his own feelings. But admittedly it is very difficult to isolate the image as a visual event: it is inevitably expressed in words and we are immediately in doubt about the visuality of the image. In Hardy's poem, which I quoted, you may have been struck by the unusual image of a parsley stalk. No poet of the classical age would have given such prominence to such a humble plant. Did Hardy depart from poetic usage because his discerning eye had selected the parsley stalk as an object of visual beauty or formal significance, and as such apt for the desired effect of his poem? Or did the phrase, "a parsley stalk", strike his aural sensibility as poetically forceful and expressive? Did eye or ear dictate the image? Impossible to say, but in any case a new image had been introduced into English poetry, and it is an image characteristic of a certain phase of twentieth-century poetry—the phase we call "Georgian" in England.

> . . . the yellow flavorous coat
> Of an apple wasps had undermined. . . .
>
> EDWARD THOMAS

> Soft as a bubble sung
> Out of a linnet's lung
>
> RALPH HODGSON

Robert Frost will perhaps serve as the transatlantic equivalent:

> . . . ploughing the grain
> With a thick thumbnail to show how it ran
> Across the handle's long drawn serpentine,
> Like the two strokes across a dollar sign.

It is true that one may find visual acuity of the same kind in earlier poets—in Marvell, Cotton, Wordsworth, Hopkins —but the objects or actions observed are more conventional, less violent. Wordsworth's acuity is exercised on common objects—on daisies and daffodils—and I doubt if he would have thought a wasp-eaten apple or a bubble or a dollar sign as images worthy of his poetry. His aim was to endow earthly objects with a celestial light: to transfuse matter and spirit: to identify his sensational vision with his mystical vision. But the Nature poets of the twentieth century are not idealists in this sense, but empiricists. They are satisfied —in so far as they are typical of their time—with the sensational effects of the image, though such an image may be used in a descriptive or sentimental poem where it lies embedded like a barbaric stone in a circlet of gold. It was probably the contrast between the sensational *image* and a traditional *diction* that first suggested to T. E. Hulme the isolation of the image. If the image could be identified as the only poetic force within a poem, why not proceed to identify poem and image, as had been the common practice in China or Japan? To cut the cackle—that was to be the first aim of a modern poetry.

But Hulme discovered—as certain French poets had discovered before him—that the cackle could not be cut without a fundamental change of diction. An image is always jealous of words—that is to say, it is most effective when conveyed in a minimum of words. It proved very difficult to reconcile this minimum with any regular metrical structure, for metre is basically aural and quite independent of imagery. Free verse was not, of course, invented by Hulme, or by anyone else in our century—in some sense it has existed for many centuries, as in Hebrew poetry. Modern experiments began in France about 1880, but these earlier experiments in free verse had been in the interest of rhythm—the desire had been to get away from the monotonous regularity of traditional metres and create new rhythms—rhythms directly expressive of emotional experience. The free verse of Whitman and Henley is of this kind, and is not necessarily accompanied by any particularly vivid imagery.

When therefore Hulme

> saw the ruddy moon lean over a hedge
> like a red-faced farmer

he was not merely introducing a sensational image into a poem, but seeking a verse-form that would effectively convey the image. Actually, within the limits of seven lines, he found a verse-form for a number of images—all images of "Autumn":

> A touch of cold in the Autumn night—
> I walked abroad,
> And saw the ruddy moon lean over a hedge
> Like a red-faced farmer.
> I did not stop to speak, but nodded.
> And round about were the wistful stars
> With white faces like town children.

The diction of such a poem is best described as laconic—that is to say, it is just adequate for the occasion. The poetry is in the image, or images, and that, for some time, was to be the distinctive characteristic of twentieth-century poetry. No other English poetry—no other poetry of the Western World —had hitherto been based so strictly on visual appeal.

The School of Imagists, which included at one time or another poets like Lawrence and Pound, as well as self-styled Imagists like Aldington and Flint, H.D., Amy Lowell and John Gould Fletcher, was not destined to survive the interruption and dispersal of the First World War, but its influence on poetic diction was decisive for a whole generation. Even Yeats, through the direct mediation of Ezra Pound, was influenced, and influenced for the better. His diction from 1914 onwards is lean, his imagery precise:

> That girls at puberty may find
> The first Adam in their thought
> Shut the door of the Pope's chapel,
> Keep those children out.
> There on that scaffolding reclines
> Michael Angelo
> With no more sound than the mice make
> His hand moves to and fro.
> Like a long-legged fly upon the stream
> His mind moves upon silence.

Such images, of mice and long-legged flies, will not be found in Yeats's earlier poetry. But it is the substance of Pound's poetry and Eliot's: it is the new imagery of the twentieth century. There is no longer an undertone of verbal music, or naturalistic sentiment, as in Hardy's parsley stalk, but a direct sensationalism, without benefit of sweet sound—Eliot's patient etherised upon a table, crabs scuttling across the floors of silent seas, newspapers blowing through vacant lots, rats, broken glass; Pound's full and fascinating junk-shop.

But such imagery, which might be called Homeric in its directness if it were consistent, is, in these two cases, contaminated, as it were, by a very un-Homeric eclecticism—by a very unrealistic romanticism, the Classicist and Medievalist romanticism of Eliot, the Troubadour and Orientalist romanticism of Pound. But "eclecticism" is too superficial in its implications to describe a process that is not deliberate, but rather an automatic release of imagery from what would technically be known as the pre-conscious—that level of the mind just below conscious memory, from which images can be drawn more or less pell-mell in a state of poetic excitement.

> The word within a word, unable to speak a word,
> Swaddled with darkness. In the juvescence of the year
> Came Christ the tiger
>
> In depraved May, dogwood and chestnut, flowering judas,
> To be eaten, to be divided, to be drunk
> Among whispers; by Mr. Silvero
> With caressing hands, at Limoges
> Who walked all night in the next room;
> By Hakagawa, bowing among the Titians;
> By Madame de Tornquist, in the dark room
> Shifting the candles; Fräulein von Kulp
> Who turned in the hall, one hand on the door. Vacant shuttles
> Weave the wind. I have no ghosts,
> An old man in a draughty house
> Under a windy knob.

These are personal memory-images, and the odd thing is that they should be transferable, to constitute indubitable poetry. We do not know, and need not ask, who were Mr. Silvero and Hakagawa, Madame de Tornquist and Fräulein von Kulp; any explanation would render them less effective, less poetic. They sit under a chinaberry tree, in poetic obscurity.

Effective as these automatic images are when personal to the poet, nothing is so ineffective as a conscious imitation of them: the introduction into verse of arbitrary images, not preceding from whatever depths the poet's mind possesses, but consciously invented to produce a similar effect. One might even go farther and say, that even when such images are projected automatically, nothing proves to be so dreary as the furniture of an inferior mind. The surrealist movement was responsible for much forced imagery of this kind, and the process itself, which had been so effective in the case of Eliot (and in the case of certain contemporary French poets) was eventually discredited by abuse. The spontaneous memory-image remains, however, a characteristic feature of modern English poetry, and Eliot's significant role in the technical development of modern verse is largely due to his masterly use of the invention. Pound, of course, has been no less energetic in this exploitation of the spontaneous memory-image, and these two poets have made the device an integral part of modern poetic diction.

Imagist development in our period does not end with Pound or even with William Carlos Williams, a poet who has sustained the experimental verve of the early days of the movement. The visual image in his verse is always conveyed without obscuring rhetoric, nakedly:

> (the
> grapes still hanging to
> the vines . . .

> like broken
> teeth in the head of an
> old man)

which, incidentally, is an excellent example of the reversed metaphor so popular with modern poets—the inhuman illuminated by reference to the human. Williams's use and presentation of the image is in the tradition of the Imagist School, but his poetry is not exclusively imagist—he might, indeed, be called a moralist—a laconic commentator on the contemporary American scene. He is exceptional in that he has transferred to a conceptual type of verse ideals of economy and precision that were evolved for a perceptual type of verse. To the visual clarity of the image corresponds a logical definition that takes an aphoristic form.

It might be possible to trace the imagist influence into wider fields and even to find it in unexpected places, but it gradually became merged in that efflorescence of metaphor which I believe is predominantly Celtic in its origins. Hopkins, who was partly responsible for it, was strongly influenced by Welsh poetry, and the chief representative of this metaphorical school has been a Welshman, Dylan Thomas. But we must not forget the influence on Thomas of surrealism, and, indirectly through surrealism, of the new significance which began to be attached to the dream image and to automatic projections of the symbols of the unconscious. All those influences created a metaphorical ferment in the mind of this young poet which at first was too private in its references to convey any emotion:

> Joy is no knocking nation, sir and madam,
> The cancer's fusion, or the summer feather
> Lit on the cuddled tree, the cross of fever,
> Nor city tar and subway bored to foster
> Man through macadam.

Rimbaud wrote such poetry, and it is not surprising to find it transubstantiated in English words. But the reader cannot endure the blind fury of it for more than the course of a few stanzas, and Thomas soon realized the limitations of this method. He worked towards simplicity and clarity, without sacrificing any of the force of the far-fetched image. I give as an example an extract from his lines in memory of Ann Jones:

> Her flesh was meek as milk, but this skyward statue
> With the wild beast and blessed and giant skull
> Is carved from her in a room with a wet window
> In a fiercely mourning house in a crooked year.
> I know her scrubbed and sour humble hands
> Lie with religion in their cramp, her threadbare
> Whisper in a damp word, her wits drilled hollow,
> Her fist of a face died clenched on a round pain;
> And sculptured Ann is seventy years of stone.
> These cloud-sopped, marble hands, this monumental
> Argument of the hewn voice, gesture and psalm,
> Storm me for ever over her grave until
> The stuffed lung of the fox twitch and cry Love
> And the strutting fern lay seeds on the black sill.

There are images here that are specifically modern, in the sense already discussed. "Her fist of a face clenched on a round pain"—I do not think an image like that would have occurred to a poet writing before 1910; though if we skip the centuries we shall find an analogue in Shakespeare's description of the death of Falstaff; and there is Anglo-Saxon sparseness and dinned anvil-clangour in the concentrated mono-syllabic words:

> . . . her death was a still drop;
> She would not have me sink in the holy
> Flood of her heart's fame; she would lie dumb and deep
> And need no druid of her broken body . . .

That is the elemental simplicity of our unrivalled English music.

Dylan Thomas's images were threaded to coherent themes of birth and death, of love and sorrow—human, universal themes, to which he gave a fresh, contemporary expression. But these few ideas were intuitive—static convictions rather than the products of a philosophical activity. Dylan Thomas is not singular in this respect. It is, indeed, difficult to discern in twentieth-century poetry any common ideological trend, such as we find in the Romantic Movement from, say, 1780–1830. We have had ideological poets—Mr. Eliot is one, Mr. Pound has a political philosophy and Mr. Auden is dogmatic in an off hand way. But these three typical poets of the period have nothing in common, ideologically speaking, and certainly have no common philosophy of art, such as the Romantics had. Each poet expresses, in a personal way, his private philosophy, and in an age such as ours, when there is no integral social consciousness, we need not pay any particular respect to a philosophy that pretends to be universal. Catholic philosophy, for example, is universal for those who have made a personal choice to be Catholics. It was different in the Middle Ages, or in Dante's time, when no personal choice was involved. Catholicism was then an expression of the social consciousness, and the individual was dissolved in that consciousness, and did not assert a separate and personal consciousness. We, who have no integral social consciousness, have only a Zeitgeist to substitute for it, and this super-individual manifestation, of which we are rarely conscious, is historical, not universal. It is a product of a particular environment—of economic and social conditions—and after the passage of a generation or two, is seen as a deception.

Romanticism, in its most general sense, is the only attempt since the end of the Middle Ages to construct a universal philosophy. Hegel, in this sense, is a romantic philosopher. Romanticism is essentially a philosophy of immanence, as

Catholicism had been a philosophy of transcendence; it remains a philosophy of immanence when allied to poetry. Poetry, indeed, is an essential instrument of this philosophy, for, as Schelling claimed, the immanent spirit of the universe is manifested through poetry, including the plastic arts and music. Poetry has thus the role of revelation in this immanent religion, and the only universal philosophy of poetry, since the Middle Ages, gives to the poet the priest-like function of mediation.

The Romantic poets of 1780–1830 accepted this role. Goethe and Schiller, Hoelderlin and Novalis, Wordsworth and Coleridge, saw themselves as performing a priest-like task, and they sought for the best method of ensuring the immediate communication of their vision. The triumph of materialism in the nineteenth century brought discredit or ridicule on this romantic philosophy, but only at the cost of a further and more drastic disintegration of social consciousness. Nietzsche, the last of the great romantic philosophers, proclaimed the death of God; Marx substituted the vision of a society integrated on a basis of common wealth. But poetry, in any universal sense, had died with God, and all our efforts to revive it, since the middle of the nineteenth century, have been fragmentary and individualistic.

Some of us attempt to recover the universal philosophy of the Middle Ages—to resurrect the transcendental God; others seek to revive the universal philosophy of Romanticism—to recover the pantheistic intuitions of the Romantic poets. But the Romantic poets realized that the act of mediation was a poetic act, and not an intellectual effort. Revelation was made evident in the structure and imagery of poetry. For a short time in our century—the time between the birth of Imagism and the return to traditional forms in the "thirties"—it seemed as though an effort would be made to recover this immediacy of inspiration, but there was no supporting ethos: what ethos there was came from revolutionary politics, and was essentially anti-poetic; it acted on the false assumption that society could be unified on a materialistic basis. It is too early to proclaim the failure of the new Romanticism—has it not, in Dylan Thomas, produced a poet who continues the tradition on its highest level? But Thomas, though he has a following, is nevertheless an isolated figure—he has no significance for our materialistic civilization. He wrote "for the love of man and in praise of God", but he wrote in subjective solitude.

Yeats was probably the only poet of our age who had some understanding of the poet's predicament. He has been ridiculed for trying to find a substitute religion in astrology and spiritualism, but his naïve effort is not necessarily more absurd than the attempt to revive a medieval thearchy. He dared, until he was disillusioned, to believe in a rebirth of Gaelic Ireland—free from commercialism and materialism. He may have underestimated the difficulty of effecting any correspondence between a practical level of experience and a symbolic level of experience—between act and grace, achievement and glory, ceremony and innocence. But in the end Yeats knew that just as

> twenty centuries of stony sleep
> Were vexed to nightmare by a rocking cradle

So we must await, and might expect, in our darkness, a Second Coming—

> And what rough beast, its hour come round at last
> Slouches towards Bethlehem to be born

I have been sparing of names in this survey of the drift of twentieth-century poetry, but let us look back across the chart for a moment. There was one clear line of progress—the isolation and clarification of the image, and the perfecting of a diction that would leave the image unclouded by rhetoric or sentiment. To that task our greatest poets—Yeats, Pound, Eliot and Thomas—devoted their best energies. But now there is a failure of nerve: eyes are dazzled, diffidence falters, and once again a veil of rhetoric is drawn over the vision of the poet. Sentiment supersedes sensation, the poetic consciousness is corrupted. Many individual voices rise again in the dusk. Yeats dead, Pound silenced, Eliot lost to the theatre, Thomas gone before his time—it is the hour of the twittering machines. We listen to them as we drink our martinis or smoke a cigarette, and for an hour or two we feel content. Then the night comes and there is no voice to fill the silence. That is not as it used to be. Poetry used to be in speech, in transaction, in worship; at the banquet, before the battle, in the moment of birth and burial. Why is poetry no longer our daily bread? We have to search for an answer to this question, and the search leads us to the foundations of our society. We have the poetry we deserve, just as we have the painting we deserve, the music we deserve; and if it is fragmented, personal, spasmodic, we have only to look around us to see the satanic chaos through which nevertheless a few voices have penetrated. The voices are pitched high and may sometimes sound discordant; but the image they convey has a crystalline brightness and hardness, and cannot be shrouded.

16

De Tocqueville on Art in America

TRIBUTE HAS often been paid to the amazing percipience of De Tocqueville's *Democracy in America*, but this tribute has usually referred to the political and sociological sections of that great book. It is not until one has been to the United States, and *then* read De Tocqueville, that one realizes how completely he covered every aspect of American life, and always with the same realistic insight and prophetic vision. I read his book on the way back from my first visit to that country, and its immediate effect was to deprive me of any desire I might have had to write about my own experiences or to record my own impressions. Every detail seemed to have been anticipated by De Tocqueville. It is not merely a book about America: it is a work of universal significance, ranking to my mind with Plato's *Republic* and *Laws*, and much more relevant to our present needs than books like the *Leviathan* and the *Esprit des Lois*.

Democracy in America was based on observations made in the years 1831 and 1832, when the author was in his twenty-sixth year: it was written, and the first volume published, before the author was thirty. The second volume, which is the one I am mainly concerned with here, appeared in 1840. It has often been quoted before, but for my particular purpose I would like once more to draw attention to the conclusion of the first volume, which is a remarkable example of De Tocqueville's political vision:

There are at the present time (i.e. 1834) two great nations in the world, which started from different points, but seem to tend towards the same end. I allude to the Russians and the Americans. Both of them have grown up unnoticed; and while the attention of mankind was directed elsewhere, they have suddenly placed themselves in the front rank among the nations, and the world learned their existence and their greatness at almost the same time.

All other nations seem to have nearly reached their natural limits, and they have only to maintain their power; but these are still in the act of growth. All the others have stopped, or continue to advance with extreme difficulty; these alone are proceeding with ease and celerity along a path to which no limit can be perceived. The American struggles against the obstacles that nature opposes to him; the adversaries of the Russians are men. The former combats the wilderness and savage life; the latter, civilization with all its arms. The conquests of the American are therefore gained by the plowshare; those of the Russians by the sword. The Anglo-American relies upon personal interest to accomplish his ends and gives free scope to the unguided strength and common sense of the people; the Russian centres all the authority of society in a single arm. The principal instrument of the former is freedom; of the latter, servitude. Their starting-point is different and their courses are not the same; yet each of them seems marked out by the will of Heaven to sway the destinies of half the globe.

There is one phrase in this passage, "the Anglo-American", which indicates a development De Tocqueville did not foresee —the drastic redistribution of racial elements which has taken place in the United States during the past thirty or forty years. To speak of Anglo-Americans is an anachronism now: in most parts of the country, the Anglo-Saxon strain is now a tiny minority, far outnumbered by the Irish, Polish, German, Jewish or even Scandinavian strains. This nullifies a few of De Tocqueville's generalizations: but still more remarkable is the fact, demonstrable in any sphere of American life, that environment is stronger than race, education more radical than heritage.

De Tocqueville takes the aristocratic view of art. Art is a product of leisure, and leisure the attribute of wealth. Democratic nations will "cultivate the arts that serve to render life easy in preference to those whose object is to adorn it. They will habitually prefer the useful to the beautiful, and they will require that the beautiful should be useful". But in aristocratic nations the ruling class "derive from their superior and hereditary position a taste for what is extremely well made and lasting. This affects the general way of thinking of the nation in relation to the arts. It often occurs among such a people that even the peasant will rather go without the objects he covets than procure them in a state of imperfection". De Tocqueville was writing before the industrial revolution had got into top gear, but he already foresaw the doom of craftsmanship in America:

There are only two ways of lowering the price of commodities. The first is to discover some better, shorter, and more ingenious method of producing them; the second is to manufacture a larger quantity of goods, nearly similar, but of less value. Among a democratic population all the intellectual faculties of the workman are directed to these two objects: he strives to invent methods that may enable him not only to work better, but more quickly and more cheaply; or if he cannot succeed in that, to diminish the intrinsic quality of the thing he makes, without rendering it wholly unfit for the use for which it is intended. When none but the wealthy had watches, they were almost all very good ones; few are now made that are worth much, but everybody has one in his pocket. Thus the democratic principle not only tends to direct the human mind to the useful arts, but it produces with great rapidity many imperfect commodities, and the consumer has to content himself with these commodities.

It is not possible to appreciate the full force of these remarks until one has been to America. In Europe we still have the remnants of a tradition of craftsmanship, and when a thing can still best be made by hand, we make it by hand and pay more for it. Hence the superiority of our leather goods, our tailoring, our jewellery. The richer Americans are willing to pay very high prices for these products of an "aristocratic" society, which is very good for our export balance. But apart from these imported articles, it is impossible to find, even in the most luxurious shops of New York or Chicago, ordinary objects of utility which have any beauty of finish. A lady's handbag, for example, will be spoilt by a hideous machine-punched clasp. There is no *love* in any workmanship: no *time*. But where the product is wholly inhuman, devoid of hand-work, as in the innumerable gadgets, machines, household equipment, plumbing, then of course the democratic prin-ciple triumphs. But even then no time, no material, nothing is, sacrificed: the appeal is on the surface, everything is thin, streamlined and synthetic. De Tocqueville anticipated even this characteristic: "The handicraftsmen of democratic ages not only endeavour to bring their useful productions within the reach of the whole community, but strive to give to all their commodities attractive qualities that they do not in reality possess."

When De Tocqueville passes to the consideration of the fine arts, he finds the same tendencies—"the productions of artists are more numerous, but the merit of each production is dimin-ished". "In aristocracies a few great pictures are produced; in democracies countries a vast number of insignificant ones." We must recall once again the period at which De Tocqueville was writing. American painting was represented by West, Copley and Stuart. He might possibly have seen the work of Washington Allston (1779–1843), but apart from him, all that we now regard as distinctively American painting was un-conceived. Winslow Homer, Eakins, Ryder, Whistler, Mary Cassatt and Sargent were not yet born. But De Tocqueville could observe: "The social condition and the institutions of democracy impart certain peculiar tendencies to all the imitative arts, which it is easy to point out. They frequently withdraw them from the delineation of the soul to fix them exclusively on that of the body, and they substitute the representation of motion and sensation for that of sentiment and thought; in a word, they put the real in the place of the ideal." That observation does not quite fit painters like Allston and Ryder, who might be said to represent a hangover of European idealism and romanticism, but it looks forward to Homer and Eakins, to Sargent and still farther on to Grant Wood and Charles Sheeler. It is true that more recently the mass immigration of Jewish and German artists has made Expressionism a noticeable feature of contemporary American art, but it remains to be seen whether it too will not be assimilated to "the social condition and the institutions of democracy".

There were no skyscrapers in De Tocqueville's time—only "little palaces" of "whitewashed brick . . . columns of painted wood". Yet from the tendencies inherent in a democratic way of life (where "the imagination is compressed when men consider themselves: it expands indefinitely when they think of the state") he could predict that "the same men who live on a small scale in cramped dwellings" would "aspire to gigantic splendour in the erection of their public monuments". He could even suggest that between these two extremes there would be a blank—which is the first thing that strikes a visitor to New York or Chicago—the abrupt transition between palatial skyscrapers and the modest brownstone or even clapboard house.

On "the literary characteristics" of the United States De Tocqueville was no less perceptive and prophetic. Once again let us remember what American literature then consisted of— Cotton Mather and Jonathan Edwards, Franklin and Hamilton, Washington Irving and Fenimore Cooper. Poe was not yet known, nor Melville; Emerson, Hawthorne, Longfellow, Thoreau and Whitman, though born, had not yet published anything. Looking into that future De Tocqueville could prophesy:

Taken as a whole, literature in democratic ages can never present, as it does in the periods of aristocracy, an aspect of order, regularity, science, and art; its form, on the contrary, will ordinarily be slighted, sometimes despised. Style will frequently be fantastic, incorrect, over-burdened, and loose, almost always vehement and bold. Authors will aim at rapidity of execution more than at perfection of detail. Small productions will be more common than bulky books; there will be more wit than erudition, more imagination than profundity; and literary performances will bear marks of an untutored and rude vigour of thought, frequently of great variety and singular fecundity. The object of authors will be to astonish rather than to please, and to stir the passions more than to charm the taste.

That prophecy looks beyond the New England school, to Faulkner and Hemingway rather than to Emerson and Haw-thorne. But even the New Englanders are provided for: "I have just depicted two extreme conditions," writes De Toc-queville, "but nations never leap from the first to the second; they reach it only by stages and through infinite gradation. In the progress that an educated people makes from the one to the other, there is almost always a moment when the literary genius of democratic nations coinciding with that of aristocratic nations, both seek to establish their sway jointly over the human mind. Such epochs are transient, but very brilliant; they are fertile without exuberance, and animated without confusion." This is precisely the transient epoch of Emerson, from which Whitman emerged as representative of a different, a democratic vista.

Some further observations might pass without comment. "Democratic literature is always infested with a tribe of writers who look upon letters as a mere trade; and for some few great authors who adorn it, you may reckon thousands of idea-mongers", "Democracy not only infuses a taste for letters among the trading classes, but introduces a trading spirit into literature". "The most common expedient em-ployed by democratic nations to make an innovation in language consists in giving an unwonted meaning to an expression already in use."

De Tocqueville approaches the art of poetry as a confessed Idealist. He did not therefore have much hope of a democratic poetry, for "in democracies the love of physical gratification, the notion of bettering one's condition, the excitement of competition, the charm of anticipated success, are so many spurs to urge men onward in the active professions they have embraced, without allowing them to deviate for an instant from the track. The main stress of the faculties is to this point. The imagination is not extinct, but its chief function is to devise what may be useful and to represent what is real. The principle of equality not only diverts men from the description of ideal beauty; it also diminishes the number of objects to be described". That "democracy gives men a sort of instinctive distaste for what is ancient" has hardly proved true, for nothing is more popular in the United States than the tawdry historical romance, and American cities abound in "antique" shops. There is, indeed, a deep-seated nostalgia for the past in America, but this is a product of the raw physical environment rather than of any specifically democratic institutions. In poetry, however, it remains true that "among a democratic people poetry will not be fed with legends or the memorials of old traditions. The poet will not attempt to people the universe with supernatural beings, in whom his readers and his own fancy have ceased to believe; nor will he coldly personify virtues and vices, which are better received under their own features. All these resources fail him; but Man remains, and the poet needs no more. The destinies of mankind, man himself . . . with his passions, his doubts, his rare propensities and inconceivable wretchedness, will become the chief, if not the sole, theme of poetry . . ."

That song is now attenuated, but American poetry is still

essentially a song of the self, of the separate but no longer simple person.

When these words were being written, the poet who was to fulfil the prophecy was in a Brooklyn printing office, learning the trade. When he came to describe his mission as a poet, it was in words which echo De Tocqueville's:

> One's-self I sing, a simple separate person,
> Yet utter the word Democratic, the word En-Masse.

> Of physiology from top to toe I sing,
> Not physiognomy alone nor brain alone is worthy for the
>   Muse, I say the Form complete is worthier far,
> The Female equally with the Male I sing.

> Of Life immense in passion, pulse, and power,
> Cheerful, for freest action form'd under the laws divine,
> The Modern Man I sing.

17

Sotto Voce: A Plea for Intimacy

A NEW art generally inherits an old aesthetic. The first picture-houses were an offshoot of the fun fair; photography has only with difficulty emancipated itself from the ideals of painting. Broadcasting was at first treated as merely the diffusion of what already existed: it was a wonderful invention, like the telephone, which enabled you to overhear what was being said or sung in some distant place. What was overheard was not designed to be overheard: it was a normal noise of some kind.

Broadcasting still remains largely on that level. If I turn to the day's programme I find orchestras playing as they played before broadcasting was invented, lectures which might have been delivered to a learned society fifty years ago, talks about gardening or agriculture which might have been given in the village hall just as long ago, and the Black Dyke Mills Band playing as it might have played in the Crystal Palace in 1851.

If we turn to the physical shape of things, we find at one end, the recording end, anything from a theatre to a "studio". The theatre may be as large as Covent Garden or the Albert Hall; the studio may be as small as a normal living-room. At the other end, the receiving end, there may be a workshop or a canteen, but the vast majority of licences are for receivers placed in a normal living-room. Into this room—into this space of some 1,600 cubic feet—issues the voice of the lecture-room, the ranting of the stage, the blare of the brass band, the concentrated blast of a hundred female voices, the shattering crescendoes of some famous symphony. What is the aesthetic effect?

I know there are "knobs". There are knobs in Broadcasting House which control the volume before it escapes into the ether (much to the distress of musical purists); there are knobs on the receiver marked "Volume" or "Tone". You turn them and the voices are stifled, the brass bands are muffled; we hear the lecture as from the corridor. Our nerves are spared, but our enjoyment is not intensified. A "reduced" reception of a Beethoven symphony is like a "reduced" reproduction of a Rubens painting: it only gives one a vague idea of the original.

All this could probably be expressed in scientific terms—the ratio of sound vibrations to cubic volumes. The aesthetic canon would insist on an optimum relationship between the two. It is not merely a question of frequency, but of complexity.

Let us imagine that the three existing programmes were rearranged with this aesthetic principle in mind. Instead of Home, Light and Third Programmes we would have Theatre, Hall and Room Programmes. To the Theatre Programme we would give all concerts and music-hall shows, all operas and most plays. To the Hall Programme we would give chamber music and lectures. Finally, we would begin to design a new style of broadcasting for "homes" in the real sense of the word—for the sitting-room and study, the bedroom and the nursery. The aesthetic principle underlying this new style might be indicated by the word *Intimacy*.

Admittedly a few broadcasters have already cultivated this style—Max Beerbohm was a master of it. In talks it can easily degenerate into a mannerism, but essentially I do not mean any "heart-to-heart" business, nor even necessarily a languid conversational tone. But gentleness is essential—no blustering, no talking *at*, no conventional "volume". Considering how much care is taken not to broadcast a rustling page or a shortness of breath, the broadcaster might be allowed a much lower range of modulation. A *whisper* is perfectly audible under normal conditions. Much poetry should be whispered; and many scenes in drama *could* be whispered.

Obviously we need an Intimate Art. It has not yet been realized that broadcasting has created new physical determinants of art. There is a form of art called "drawing-room comedy", but it is comedy *about* drawing-rooms, not comedy *for* drawing-rooms. But that is what we want—plays of a new kind for an auditorium of 1,500–2,000 cubic feet. I think they would necessarily be plays with a limited cast—it is difficult to receive more than four or five *distinct* voices. They would also have a limited duration—an hour is about the maximum limit. They would have a new kind of content—being utterly independent of action, they would develop compensations in

148

pyschological tension, in mood and in intensity of expression (they could afford to be more poetic). But most of all they would require a completely new type of actor.

I must confess that at present I find it almost impossible to listen to a radio play. Again and again I make the effort, but I find the normal actor's voice, divorced from the stage and the *Raum* of the theatre, excruciating. It is not merely horrible to listen to: it also completely destroys (for me) the felicity of the words, should that exist. But a voice *can* be modulated to the right relationship between recording and room-reception. Twenty years ago I heard Moissi reciting Shakespeare, and I can still hear him—it was little louder than a whisper, but all Shakespeare's poetry was in it. Some years ago I overheard a woman's voice broadcasting "physical jerks" at some very early hour. I was staying with a friend who indulged in this form of masochism, and I, who have quite different ways of torturing myself, was on this occasion compelled to grip the sides of my bed, so sweetly persuasive was that voice.

I have never been inside a dramatic academy and the mysteries of voice production are unknown to me. But as a lecturer I have often received "tips"—about pitching my voice against the back of the hall, keeping my lungs inflated, breathing rhythmically, holding the audience in photographic focus, etc. (all of which I either forget, or practice unconsciously). But I suppose that a dramatic academy, like academies in the other arts, teaches a convention, a tradition, and supports it with all kinds of technical tricks. Such teaching is no doubt directed towards a certain ideal—a grand manner (shades of Irving, Forbes Robertson, Sarah Bernhardt). Whatever it is (and it is no doubt much more streamlined nowadays than I have imagined), it is almost certainly a "theatre" style —that is all that dramatic art can mean under present conventions. In any case, the products of such academies are of the stage, stagey; and when they are invited to broadcast they bring their best stage manners to the studio. I realize that the distinction I am making is a commonplace among the intelligent producers in Broadcasting House, and that they do their best to restrain their actors, to make them shed their stage voices as well as their stage costumes. But what is needed is not restraint, not a negation of any kind, but the elaboration and projection of an entirely new technique. I don't know what to call it, but it is an art of "suggesting" rather than acting. In stage acting there is a correlation of voice and action; abolish the possibility of seeing the action and a new situation arises. The correlation is destroyed for the listener; and if it persists in the actor, what goes across is a limping affair, a voice without its physical crutches. The listener is painfully conscious of the missing crutches.

(Incidentally, I fancy that the practice of having studio audiences in Broadcasting House for certain programmes [mainly music-hall] is a thoroughly bad one. It encourages the actors to act, to rely on their theatrical tricks. They should be compelled to develop compensations for these tricks—to broadcast to the imagined, the invisible listener. It is said that the listener likes to hear the audience—to imagine himself part of that audience. This merely shows that the broadcast does not satisfy the intimate needs of the fireside. A theatre audience should not invade the home, either physically or audibly.)

The question I am raising is mainly one of interpretation, and there is certainly much material already written that would lend itself to an intimate style. The blustering chronicles of Shakespeare will never do, and a *Bartholomew Fair* is a Babel; but I can imagine an intimate *Hamlet* and even an intimate *Lear*. (The soliloquy, so artificial on the stage, is the very idiom of intimate broadcasting.) I can imagine an intimate Congreve, for the spatial scale is that of the drawing-room, and Millamant should certainly speak to Mirabell in natural tones, not much above a whisper. Ibsen and Chekov are suitable—especially Chekov: all his life he was trying to subdue the theatre, to reduce it to some intimate, human scale. Maeterlinck is another dramatist who had the same desire for intimacy. Most of his plays are perhaps too languid and etherial for present tastes, but if they are even revived for broadcasting, they will require a very subtle range of voices. One of his one-act dramas (*Les Aveugles*—"The Sightless") calls out for a radio interpretation in this intimate style—it is a play *about listening*! Another lyrical dramatist who has never, so far as I remember, been adapted to broadcasting is Hugo von Hofmannsthal. Yet his "lyrische Dramen" are perfect in scale—*Der Tod des Tizian*, *Der Tor und der Tod*, *Der weisse Fächer*, *Die Frau im Fenster*. They demand a translator of genius, but at least they give us the form and style of an intimate *poetic* drama.

And then there is Yeats. It is a pity that Yeats did not live to write especially for an intimate radio drama, for I am sure that the qualities he was seeking on the stage, and never succeeded in finding, could have been realized in broadcasting. His definition of "tragic art" is so exactly what I would give as a definition of intimate broadcasting art that I must quote it (from his Preface to *Plays for an Irish Theatre*, 1913):

Tragic art, passionate art, the drowner of dykes, the confounder of understanding, moves us by setting us to reverie, by alluring us almost to the intensity of trance. The persons upon the stage, let us say, greaten till they are humanity itself. We feel our minds expand convulsively or spread out slowly like some moon-brightened image-crowded sea. That which is before our eyes perpetually vanishes and returns again in the midst of the excitement it creates, and the more enthralling it is the more do we forget it. When I am watching my own *Deirdre* I am content with the players and with myself, if I am moved for a while not by the contrasted sorrows of Deirdre and Naisi, but because the words have called up before me the image of the sea-born woman so distinctly that Deirdre seems by contrast to those unshaken eyelids that had but the sea's cold blood what I had wished her to seem, a wild bird in a cage.

It was only by watching my own plays that I came to understand that this reverie, this twilight between sleep and waking, this bout of fencing, alike on the stage and in the mind, between man and phantom, this perilous path as on the edge of a sword, is the condition of tragic pleasure, and to understand why it is so rare and so brief. If an actor becomes over emphatic, picking out what he believes to be the important words with violence, and running up and down the scale, or if he stresses his lines in wrong places, or even if an electric lamp that should have cast but a reflected light from sky or sea, shows from behind the post of a door, I discover at once the proud fragility of dreams.

At first I was driven into teaching too statuesque a pose, too monotonous a delivery, that I might not put "vitality" in the place of the sleepwalking of passion, and for the rest became a little deaf and blind.

But alas! it is often my own words that break the dream. Then I take the play from the stage and write it over again, perhaps many times. At first I always believed it must be something in the management of events, in all that is the same in prose or verse, that was wrong, but after I had reconstructed a scene with the messenger in *Deirdre* in many ways, I discovered that my language must keep at all times a certain even richness. I had used "traitor", "sword", "suborned", words of a too traditional usage, without plunging them into personal thought and metaphor, and I had forgotten in a moment of melodrama that tragic drama must be carved out of speech as a statue is out of stone.

There are one or two definitions in this passage which I would like to emphasize. First, the mood to be induced in the listener to intimate broadcasting—*reverie*, the intensity of the trance. That, Yeats realized, is a question of words, of words so spoken that there is no danger of waking us out of that trance, once it has been induced. Yeats goes so far as to ask his theatre audiences to shut out the visible stage, to retreat into a stage in the mind. That effort is no longer required in broadcasting—as we sit listening to the disembodied voices that come across the ether, we should have no difficulty in maintaining that perilous path which is the condition of tragic pleasure, provided the words are appropriate and the voices convey them in their objective purity. The words can only be created by the poet, but the method of delivery is defined—a delivery without undue emphasis, within a natural vocal scale, and with a natural stress, not monotonous, not too statuesque—yet carved out of living speech.

Yeats probably considered himself as primarily a dramatist, and he would not admit the qualification, a *poetic* dramatist, for he did not agree that an antithesis exists between drama and lyric poetry. The matter is argued out in the Preface to the 1911 edition of *Plays for an Irish Theatre*, and on the acceptance of Yeats's argument depends the kind of valuation we are likely to give to his dramatic work as a whole. He held that "character" (which his plays conspicuously lack) belongs to comedy alone. In great tragedy, that of Corneille, Racine, the tragedy of Greece and Rome, the place of character is taken by passions and motives, "one person being jealous, another full of love or remorse or pride or anger". He was faced by the exception of Shakespeare, but Shakespeare, he pointed out, is always a writer of tragi-comedy, and "there is indeed character, but we notice that it is in the moments of comedy that character is defined, in Hamlet's gaiety let us say; while amid the great moments . . . all is lyricism, unmixed passion, 'the integrity of fire'". In tragedy it is always ourselves that we see upon the stage, ourselves in the living symbols of our passions and desires. "Tragic art, passionate art, the drowner of dykes, the confounder of understanding, moves us by setting us to reverie, by alluring us almost to the intensity of trance. The persons upon the stage . . . greaten till they are humanity itself."

I am not suggesting that because he had such a perfect understanding of the requirements of intimate drama, that Yeats's own plays are models for broadcast drama. But they should be tried in the style Yeats indicated—beginning, perhaps, with the acting version of *The Shadowy Waters*. There is a short play in his last volume called *The Death of Cuchulain* that might be very successful, if broadcast in this intimate manner.

Between the first play (*The Countess Cathleen*, 1892) and the last play (*The Death of Cuchulain*, 1939), there is not so much difference of form or diction as the passage of nearly half a century might have brought about in a poet less sure of his mission. The tragic feeling becomes harsher, the line tends to become shorter, the lyric element detaches itself into song, becomes a crystallization of the action. But there is no compromise with realism (for even *The Words Upon the Window-pane* is merely grand-guignol realism); there is no compromise with that commercial slickness known as "theatre". The poetic diction is perfected, especially in *Purgatory* (1939). But was the poetic diction of *The Countess Cathleen* so much in need of improvement?

> Come, sit beside the fire.
> What matter if your head's below your arms
> Or you've a horse's tail to whip your flank,
> Feathers instead of hair, that's all but nothing.
> Come, share what bread and meat is in the house,
> And stretch your heels and warm them in the ashes.
> And after that, let's share and share alike
> And curse all men and women. Come in, come in
> What, is there no one there?

There are a few recent plays which have been broadcast and which undoubtedly gained from the intimacy possible in radio production. One was Eliot's *Family Reunion*; another was Sartre's *Huis Clos*, which is one of the few radio plays I have been able to listen to without discomfort. But even in these cases the voices were too insistent, nagging away at our aural nerves instead of falling on them softly, insidiously.

I believe that a new style of production, involving a new school of actors never trained for the stage, is the first necessity of intimate drama. There is enough material of the kind I have indicated to practise on, but eventually our poets and dramatists must support this development with appropriate creative work. It need not necessarily be dramatic. The imaginary conversation, as Rayner Heppenstall has shown in his productions, offers great possibilities, not so much for intimate drama (for then it is no longer a separate category) but for the presentation and broadcasting of ideas—it should be a variation on the talk rather than on the drama. "Features", too, can be devised for the intimate scale. Music already has its intimate forms—thanks, not to broadcasting, but to the habit in earlier ages of performing appropriate music in intimate circles.

I have discussed this problem of scale in spatial terms, but to some extent time also is involved. I wonder how many people really enjoy a full-length drama or opera, cutting across meal-times and children's bed-times, incoming telephone-calls and outgoing fires. It is different in the theatre—one has left these interruptions behind, and there is the excitement of mutual participation in an event. But in the home? There is a wealth of works of appropriate length, even in opera. The limit of sustained attention, without visual aids, is about an hour. I do not wish to exclude the possibility of longer broadcasts; but if we are reaching after perfection, in broadcasting

as in any other art, we must consider every aspect of this
question of scale.

18

George Lukács

ONE OF the most prominent figures in the Hungarian Revolution was George Lukács, Minister of Education in Nagy's
second, short-lived government. But Lukács is more than
a Hungarian politician. Thomas Mann called him "the most
important literary critic of today", and though Mann was
no doubt influenced by the attention which Lukács had
paid to his own work, I myself, who disagree profoundly with
some of Lukács's doctrines, would not dissent from this
opinion. His importance as a critic was first made clear to me
by the late Karl Mannheim, who had known him well in
Hungary, and who again did not agree with the Marxist
basis of Lukács's criticism. What one was made to realize
after the reading of a single essay by this critic (and to envy),
was the formidable superiority of any polemicist who com-
bines dogma with sensibility. It is the same kind of for-
midability that one finds in certain Catholic writers (such
as Jacques Maritain), and it makes one realize, rather ruefully, that sensibility is not enough: our humanist or
libertarian criticism must have an equally strong foundation
in faith.

Lukács was born in Budapest in 1885, the son of a wealthy
bank director (and such an origin was bound always to inspire
distrust among his more proletarian comrades). His intelli-

gence was of a prodigious kind, and while still in his teens he won a literary prize with a two-volume study on *The Evolution of Modern Drama*, which I am told is still worth reading today. Other early works, which he later repudiated, include *The Theory of the Novel* and a volume of essays on such writers as Hoffmansthal, Stefan George and Rilke. I have not read any of these early works, and I must confess that I find Lukács's German very rebarbative—the syntax of his thought is presumably Hungarian, and in transposition to another language every sentence becomes a tangled nest of subsidiary clauses. All the more credit, therefore, to Dr. Edith Bone, who in 1950 produced a very readable English version of *Studies in European Realism*.

But this is to anticipate. In 1918 Lukács was converted to Communism and was a member of Bela Kun's revolutionary government. After the fall of Bela Kun he went into exile and spent most of his time in Berlin. When the Nazis made that refuge too uncomfortable for him, he went to Moscow, where he spent twelve fruitful years. When Hungary was liberated by the Russian army at the end of the war, he immediately returned to Budapest, and has since that time been the intellectual leader of the Communist party in Hungary, exercising a supreme influence over the intellectual development of the country. He occupied the chair of Aesthetics in the University of Budapest, and when the inner history of the recent revolt comes to be written I suspect that it will be found that Lukács was its main inspiration. He had a great following among the students and was closely connected with the Petőfi Society which set off the revolt.

Lukács's first important publication after his conversion to Communism was *Geschichte und Klassenbewusstsein*—History and Class Consciousness—and this no doubt remains the most complete statement of his philosophical point of view. Its

L   157

purpose is described by Professor Roy Pascal (in his Foreword to *Studies in European Realism*) as:

> to analyse the real constituents of the ideological world, that is, to show the process of literary and ideological production as part of the general social process; and thereby to point out the practical task of our own time, the rejection of an oppressive society and a culture grown sterile, and the building of a classless society and a new humanity in which the tensions between man and nature, art and science, subjective "freedom" and social necessity, theory and practice become fruitful relations, stimulating men to productive communal labour, and in which art and poetry focus and intensify men's powers and joy.

One recognizes the jargon, and the "objective" has produced the dreariest mass of doctrinaire literature since the Age of Scholasticism. But Lukács is different. He is saved, not only by his innate sensibility, which leads him to respect those elements of form and style so often contemptuously dismissed by Marxist critics, but also by his passionate humanism, which leads him to concentrate on Balzac and Tolstoy and to present their essentially humanitarian ideals with sympathy. All this leads, as I said in a review of *Studies in European Realism*, to a certain amount of "doublethink"; but how refreshing, for example, to find a Marxian critic expatiating on "the extraordinary concreteness of poetic vision" in Tolstoy, or, more generally, seeing in romanticism, not one more form of bourgeois escapism, but "the expression of a deep and spontaneous revolt against rapidly developing capitalism".

Lukács's work on Balzac and Tolstoy is perhaps his most important contribution to literary criticism—certainly the most readable part of it—but there are other books of importance—*German Literature in the Age of Imperialism* (1946), *Goethe and his Time* (1947), *The Young Hegel* (1948), *In Search of the Bourgeois* (1945—the work on Thomas Mann).

There can be no question of the acuteness of Lukács's intelligence—he is by far the most formidable exponent of the Marxist point of view in literary criticism that has yet appeared anywhere in the world. Like most Marxist critics in whatever sphere, Lukács begins with claims that are merely pretentious. "Marxism," he said in *Studies in European Realism*, "searches for the material roots of each phenomenon, regards them in their historical connections and movement, ascertains the laws of such movement and demonstrates their development from root to flower, and in so doing lifts every phenomenon out of a merely emotional, irrational, mystic fog and brings it to the bright light of understanding." This is to ascribe to "Marxism" what is merely the agreed practice of all critics who have any claim to be regarded as "scientific", and one could mention a hundred names from Taine to Sartre, from Lessing to Schücking, from Dr. Johnson to Dr. Leavis, who have had the same ideal of scientific method. What distinguishes Marxist criticism is not its scientific method (for when it comes to the point it disclaims any notion of "objectivity"), but certain *a priori* assumptions—for example, the assumption that realism is the highest type of art. Realism is defined as "the adequate presentation of the complete human personality" and its "central category and criterion" is "the type, a peculiar synthesis which organically binds together the general and particular both in characters and situations".

This use of the word "type" is peculiar to Lukács, or perhaps to Marxist criticism, but as it runs throughout the book, the reader has to understand that "what makes a type a type is not its average quality, nor its mere individual being, however profoundly conceived; what makes it a type is that in it all the humanly and socially essential determinants are present on their highest level of development, in the ultimate unfolding of the possibilities latent in them, in extreme presentation of their extremes, rendering concrete the peaks and limits of men and epochs". All that realism opposes is "the destruction of the completeness of the human personality and of the objective typicality of men and situations through an excessive cult of the momentary mood".

It is necessary to come to terms with this idea and the jargon in which it is wrapped before reading the particular studies on Balzac, Stendhal, Zola, Tolstoy and Gorki which follow—otherwise much that Professor Lukács has to say will seem like arbitrary nonsense. In a short essay it is only possible to point out that this conception of art is indeed arbitrary. It is equally possible to hold what might be called the heiratic or anti-humanistic view of art, one that T. E. Hulme developed on the basis of Byzantine art. There is also a rhetorical conception of literature, according to which art is a game whose only use is to develop the skill and sensibility of its practitioners. There is also a pragmatic or pluralistic view of art, according to which any poem or novel, painting or sonata which happens to give pleasure to a few people needs no further justification. But all these theories of art, in so far as he admits them into his consciousness, are dismissed by Lukács as bourgeois, reactionary, fascist, etc. A simple, sensuous enjoyment of beauty seems to be the worst sin, for what matters in art is "an ardent love of the people, a deep hatred of the people's enemies and the people's own errors [note that!], the inexorable uncovering of truth and reality, together with an unshakable faith in the march of mankind and their own people towards a better future".

Loving and hating in this manner, Lukács proceeds to the analysis of his chosen authors. The essays on Balzac and Tolstoy are the most interesting. There is no doubt that Lukács has revealed new aspects of these great novelists, and brought into clear focus certain elements that explain their enduring appeal. But in the end the bourgeois reader is likely to get most pleasure from observing that process which Orwell has satirized as "doublethink". Lukács is too honest, too sensitive, to question the greatness of Balzac and Tolstoy—they are for him the incomparably greatest artists of their epochs. But the awkward facts are, that Balzac was a reactionary royalist and Tolstoy a utopian anarchist. Doublethink is a little difficult to follow—it is meant to be. But the passionately held views of Tolstoy, for example, which to him were implicit in all his work and life, become "historically necessary illusions", and it has to be admitted that "a great artist creates immortal masterpieces on the basis of an entirely false philosophy". It is even admitted that this "swimming-against-the-current" was a necessary element in Tolstoy's development to greatness. His bourgeois freedom was essential to his "specific manner of concentration". But then doublethink takes another twist, for it is nowhere implied that such freedom would be permitted to a writer in the Marxist paradise. On the contrary, Gorki is extolled for his perfect conformity, and this somewhat dreary writer (admittedly a fine "fighting humanist") is invested with Tolstoy's mantle. It is a sorry spectacle. Subject to a few evasions, the integrity of the critic can be maintained so long as his subject is *in the past*, but it abdicates entirely to the exigences of a contemporary tyranny. For it has to be demonstrated "concretely" (i.e., at all costs) that "the contradictions of bourgeois art can be overcome in Socialist practice".

19

The Romantic Revolution

WITHIN THE past two hundred years the literature of the Western World has undergone many changes of style and direction, but this time-span begins with one great revolution that dominates them all. I refer, of course, to the Romantic Movement, which was more than a change of style: it was a sudden expansion of consciousness—an expansion into realms of sensibility not previously accessible to the human imagination. I believe that we are still living within the mental reverberations of that great event; I believe that the way then opened still presents itself as a challenge to the human mind. Our duty at the moment, as creative writers and as critics, is to maintain the impetus of that revolution.

It was a great, but perverse American critic of the last generation, Irving Babbitt, who first specifically associated the Romantic Movement with the name of Rousseau. Let that name stand as representative. I would add the names of only two other men, Denis Diderot and Laurence Sterne. All three men were born within a few months of each other, in the years 1712 and 1713, and all had reached the age of forty before they began to write anything significant.

Our attitude to romanticism is likely to be determined by the predominance in us of either an ethical or an aesthetic standard of judgment. Babbitt was a moralist, and it was as a moralist that he attacked, not only the ethics of romantic writers, but also their achievements in literature. But from the aesthetic point of view the literary achievements of the period are so great that the moral egotism they exhibit seems a relatively unimportant fact. It is not impossible for a moralist to

condemn romantic morality and at the same time admit his
admiration of the poetry; and the enthusiast of romantic
literature may freely condemn the morals of romantic writers.
But a real dilemma does exist, as we shall see. It was first
clearly realized by the great Danish romantic, Søren Kierkegaard.

What was the revolutionary idea that first came into the
world in the seventeen-fifties? It would be tedious to pass in
review all the various and often inconsistent definitions that
have been given of romanticism, but I think everyone would
agree that it is the expression of a certain kind of sensibility,
and that what was revolutionary in its character was the recognition of sensibility itself, as the raw material of literature and
painting. One cannot suppose that before 1750 men had no
sensibility: human nature does not change from one year to
the next. Rather we must assume that the human disposition
itself did not change at all, but that certain sentiments which
are always ready to overflow from the heart had hitherto been
suppressed. That is, indeed, the true and obvious explanation,
but we shall not understand *what* happened unless we realize
how it happened. For what is essential to romanticism is not
its content, but its form.

One might quickly retort that this distinction is unreal:
form does not exist in the abstract, to be filled by some fluid
substance of the soul—it is the crystallization of this substance
as it cools in the mind of the poet. But to think in this way is
already to think romantically. To identify form with substance—that is precisely the romantic revolution. The essential
notion is that literature—creative writing whether in verse or
prose—is a *formative activity*. Form emerges spontaneously
from the poet's intuitive apprehension of the thought: or, if
he is a painter, from his plastic realization of the image present
to his mind. But when the Romantic Revolution acquired its

full momentum, towards the end of the eighteenth century, there was the further suggestion, for which the German philosopher Schelling was responsible, that artistic creation is one with natural creation. "Yes," said Coleridge, echoing Schelling, "not to acquire cold notions—lifeless technical rules—but living and life-producing ideas, which shall contain their own evidence, the certainty that they are essentially one with nature . . ."—such was the profoundest, the most daring claim of the Romantics.

It will now be seen that sensibility, in the romantic sense of the word, is something more than the crude emotionalism which is all that a critic like Irving Babbitt sees in it. One may perhaps call it subjectivism, but I think that would be merely to substitute one word for another, without any essential change of meaning. I would prefer to pause a moment on the word *spontaneity*, for that is the active, the kinetic aspect of romanticism—spontaneity instead of cold notions, or lifeless technical rules.

It is at this point that I would like to insist a little on the importance of Laurence Sterne. In one sense Sterne was not an original writer—he continues the humorous tradition of Lucian, Rabelais and Cervantes. His ideas he owes to Locke, Montaigne and Burton. He plagiarized right and left, and his work is full of an impudence that spoils him for some serious people. But he is completely *spontaneous*—that is his distinction and his originality. He became a writer by accident, being provoked to compose and print a satirical account of a local ecclesiastical quarrel. He continued to write by instinct, free from "lifeless technical rules". The result was a style which is the style peculiar to romantic prose—the interior monologue. It begins with Sterne and it ends, for the moment, with the latest disciple of James Joyce or William Faulkner. The monologue is not always in the Shandean form—loose, syncopated,

maze-like; it can be confessional or confidential, clear or obscure, emotive or rhetorical: the style, not only of Sterne, but
of Jean Paul; of Charles Dickens and Henry James—the style
of all the great romanticists: Emily Brontë, Chateaubriand,
Tolstoy, Dostoevsky, Proust and Kafka. It may be objected
that these are all prose writers, but romantic poetry, the poetry
of Wordsworth and Coleridge, of Shelley and Browning, of
Swinburne and Yeats, of Rilke and Eliot—is, in a sense which
I shall now explain, the poetry of the interior monologue, the
whispered secrets of the self.

I have said that the Romantic Revolution began with
Rousseau, Diderot and Sterne. That is true so long as we
confine ourselves to literature, but the literary revolution had
been preceded by the philosophical revolution that began
with Descartes and his basic principle, *cogito, ergo sum*: I think,
therefore I am. This philosophical slogan had been given out
more than a century before, but Sterne was the first author to
apply it to literature and to act on the principle: I think,
therefore I write. There had, of course, been much introspec-
tive writing in previous ages, but if we examine, say, St.
Augustine's *Confessions*, or the poems of Petrarch, we see that
they are all governed by the rules of rhetoric. Augustine had
been "a prime fellow in the Rhetoric Schools", and "joyed
in it very pertly"; he was at one time "a rhetoric reader in
Carthage", and later in Rome and Milan. His confessions are
full of the most intimate and moving detail, but the book is
composed, and artful. He examines his own soul, but as an
object: he sees his past, but as a picture. He writes, above all,
not from the love of Self, but of God.

Petrarch has been called "the founder of the modern spirit
in literature" (by Renan); incidentally, he was a favourite
poet of Rousseau. Petrarch is famous for something other
than his poetry—for being the first man to climb a mountain

for the sake of seeing the view. But when he got to the top of Mount Ventoux he recalled a passage from St. Augustine's *Confessions*—a passage which says that "men go abroad to wonder at the heights of mountains, the lofty billows of the sea, the long courses of rivers, the vast compass of the ocean, and the circular motions of the stars, and yet pass themselves by"; and Augustine goes on to discourse on the wonders of memory and imagination. He even discusses man's unique faculty of cogitation, which he defines as the drawing together of dispersed or suppressed memories; and it seems likely that Descartes had this passage in mind when he formulated his famous principle.

Thus, though one might say that the principle of romanticism was latent in such writers as Augustine and Petrarch, yet it was never a principle of writing until Sterne stumbled on the technique of it, and Rousseau consciously affirmed it. At the beginning of the latter's *Confessions* is one of the shortest and proudest sentences in literature: *Moi seul*—only myself, nothing but myself, the self in which you will recognize *your* self. St. Augustine began his *Confessions* on a very different note, admiring God's majesty, desirous to praise him, but feeling that he carried about a burden of testimony which he must unload in order to praise God with a pure heart. Rousseau, too, mentions God on his first page, but only to present him with his confessions and to claim that at the Last Judgment they would be found to be uniquely sincere: that no other being would be found capable of displaying man's nature with such complete truth.

Rousseau has had plenty of emulators, and if none has exceeded his sincerity, some, such as a French writer of our own time, Jean Gênet, have had worse things to confess. But again, from our present point of view, it is the manner and not the matter of the confession that matters: it is the fact

that, in a work of romantic literature, we are in contact with
a naked heart, or, to put it more abstractly, with a state of
pure subjectivity, Kierkegaard called it the archimedean
point: "The reason why I cannot really say that I definitely
enjoy *nature*," he once wrote, "is because I am unable to
understand clearly *what* I enjoy. A work of art, on the other
hand, I can understand; I can—if I may so express it—find
the archimedean point, and once I have found that, everything
easily becomes clear to me. I can then follow the one great
thought and see how all the details serve to throw light upon
it. I can see, as it were, the author's whole individuality like a
sea in which every detail is reflected. The author's mind is
related to mine, it may well be far superior to mine, but like
mine it is circumscribed. The works of God are too great for
me; I inevitably lose myself in the details. That is also why
people's expressions when they look at nature—it is lovely,
magnificent, etc.—are so insipid, for they are all too anthropo-
morphic, they stay at the outside; they cannot express the
depths within." (*Journals*, 1834, trans. A. Dru, p. 1.)

"The depths within"—there lies the unique scope of
modern literature. The depths within the self, "true inward-
ness", "at the maximum proving to be objectivity once
again". Reason itself is found to be part of that true inward-
ness, and to those critics who assert that modern literature
is irrational, and therefore to be condemned, the romantic
replies, not only that the heart has its own reasons which
Reason does not know (which is Pascal's answer), but also
that there is no true reasoning that does not take the heart
into account.

Such is the inescapable paradox of romanticism—it can only
find an archimedean point, a sense of objectivity, within the
self. But as Sartre has said, "the subjectivity we thus postulate
as the standard of truth is no narrowly individual subjectivism,

for . . . it is not only one's self that one discovers in the *cogito*, but the self of others too. . . . When we say 'I think' we are attaining to ourselves in the presence of others and we are just as certain of the other as we are of ourselves". (*Existentialism and Humanism*, p. 45.)

That is the existentialist dogma, but it is also the romantic dogma, and existentialism is nowadays the philosophical aspect of romanticism. "Before there can be any truth whatever," says the romantic philosopher, "there must be an absolute truth, and there is such a truth which is simple, easily attained, and within the reach of everybody; it consists in one's immediate sense of one's Self." (*Ibid.*, p. 44.) But the romantic poet says exactly the same in language which is scarcely distinguishable. "One realm we have never conquered," wrote D. H. Lawrence, "the pure present. One great mystery of time is *terra incognita* to us: the instant. The most superb mystery we have hardly recognized: the immediate, instant self. The quick of all time is the instant. The quick of all the universe, of all creation, is the incarnate, carnal self. Poetry gave us the clue." (*Phoenix*, p. 222.)

The critical Babbitts of our time—and they include some very distinguished minds—have never been able to understand this affirmation of self-consciousness as the truth, because in their hearts they have never accepted the Cartesian logic. I know that Descartes has had and still has formidable opponents; but since his time (he died in 1650) this opposed faith in the authority of impersonal values has not inspired any imaginative literature. The poet does not need to be convinced of the truth of Descartes' proposition for the simple but sufficient reason that he knows that his own creative activity is based on it; and he knows further that the literature which has been inspired by an immediate sense of one's self opens up a completely new range of human consciousness.

The Romantic does not claim that the subjective poetry of Goethe, Wordsworth, Hölderlin, Shelley, Baudelaire or Rilke is necessarily greater than the objective poetry of Homer, Virgil, Dante, Milton, Racine or Pope. But he does claim that it is a different kind of poetry, and he is fairly confident in his assertion that it has widened the sphere of human sensibility; and to have done that, Wordsworth said, is the only infallible sign of genius in the fine arts. That is why we claim that the Romantic Revolution is more than a change of fashion or of style; it is the discovery of a New World, and as a consequence the Old World can never be the same, can never return to its former limits. Romantic literature is a "sentimental journey" into this new world of the Self, and it is possible that the discovery of a geographical New World was the inspiring archetype for the poet's voyage of discovery.

The new world of the Self still has large areas which we must mark *terra incognita*, in spite of the explorations that we associate with names like Balzac and Stendhal, Dostoevsky and Tolstoy, Henry James and Proust, Kafka and Joyce. The point I wish to emphasize is that this new world would never have been discovered but for the invention of new vessels of exploration—new forms of literature like the novel and the short story, new techniques like free verse and the interior monologue. Even now further progress awaits new inventions. But what is still more important to emphasize is the continuing need for a prevailing spirit of freedom. Many of our pioneers found themselves in conflict with authority. Sometimes it was because, as in the case of Dostoevsky, their human sympathies had drawn them into political action, for there is a natural sympathy between the artist and the politician when liberty is in question. But for another and perhaps a narrower reason the freedom of the artist must be guaranteed by liberal institutions. The very fact that he is engaged in widening the sphere of human sensibility means that the artist will inevitably outrage an older and more restricted range of sensibility. Every innovating artist encounters this often insensate and brutal opposition—in our own time we have seen with what difficulty writers like Lawrence and Joyce established their right to be read and freely circulated. Their greatness is now generally acknowledged, but during their lives they suffered, not merely the negative punishment of neglect, but also the positive persecution of ignorant authorities.

Modern literature can exhibit many botched experiments, and its pioneers often got lost in the desert, became mad like Nietzsche, or were suddenly silent, like Rimbaud. But its achievement is immense: there is no comparable wealth of creative literature in any other period of the world's history. Perhaps I am putting undue stress on the word "creative", but the guiding motive, throughout the Romantic Revolution, has been to live life more abundantly. "It seems a strange thing," said D. H. Lawrence, "that men, the mass of men, cannot understand that *life* is the great reality, that true living fills us with vivid life, 'the heavenly bread', and earthly bread merely supports this. No, men cannot understand, never have understood that simple fact. They cannot see the distinction between bread, or property, money, and vivid life. They think that property and money are the same thing as vivid life. Only the few, the potential heroes or the 'elect', can see the simple distinction." (*Phoenix*, pp. 285–6.)

These heroes in our time have been the poets and novelists, the imaginative artists of all kinds, who have sought inwardly for the heavenly bread, and have found it in their own vital sensibility. The great paean, the great lyrical celebration of this inward-turning, was written in a new-found land, in America, just a hundred years ago. At the end of his *Song of Myself* Whitman spoke for all modern poets. "There is that in me," he said, "I do not know what it is—but I know it is in me.

> Do you see O my brothers and sisters?
> It is not chaos or death—it is form, union, plan—it is
>   eternal life—it is Happiness."

20

The Sustaining Myth

IT IS curious that we should return, after two hundred years, to a discussion of the problem that Lessing made the subject of his *Laokoon*. To read that essay now is to plunge into a philosophical sea in which all our values sail upside down. Lessing set out to separate the spheres of painting and poetry. The false criticism of his time, he felt, had confused the categories. "It has produced the love of description in poetry, and of allegory in painting: while the critics strove to reduce poetry to a speaking painting, without properly knowing what it could and ought to paint; and painting to a dumb poem, without having considered in what degree it could express general ideas, without alienating itself from its destiny, and degenerating into an arbitrary method of writing."

Hand in hand with Herr Winckelmann and Count Caylus, Lessing turns to the past. Painting, at Breslau in 1760, did not exist. Shakespeare and Pope might be good for a passing reference, but the debate was more logically confined to the paragons of Greece and Rome. Homer and Virgil still remain, moving exemplars of the poetic virtues; but it was unfortunate for posterity that Lessing should have chosen as the

171

marble support of his logic, a Hellenistic work of the first century B.C. which now evokes more astonishment than admiration. Alas, that it should have been recovered from the palace of Titus in time for Michelangelo to see it! But it will still serve as an allegory, for the figure in the toils of the serpent is Lessing himself, and the serpent is that theory of *mimesis* which for centuries held art in its suffocating coils. It is fascinating, though perhaps a little indulgent to one's sadistic sensations, to watch this German dramaturgist struggling with a theory which condemned all art to the imitation of nature, while his sensibility told him that the mirrors held by the poet and the painter had very different powers of reflection. The machinery of German metaphysics must be brought into action—space must be separated from time, the whole from its constituent parts! "Subjects whose wholes or parts exist in juxtaposition are called bodies. Consequently, bodies with their visible properties are the peculiar subjects of painting. Subjects whose wholes or parts are consecutive are called actions. Consequently, actions are the peculiar subject of poetry." A neat dichotomy, only complicated by the categories of space and time. But the two arts were divinely ordained to solve the difficulty, for poetry can describe "progressive" actions, canto after canto, to the end of the epic; painting or sculpture can immobilize all action into a plastic instant, a "pregnant" instant, "from which what precedes and what follows can be most easily gathered".

Transposed to the modern technique of photography, Lessing's argument makes perfect sense: he describes with acuteness precisely those qualities which should distinguish the camera "still" from the "moving" picture.

But of the fruitful relation that should exist between painting and poetry, and had existed in examples not so far-fetched as the *Laokoon* (not a mention of Poussin or Claude), Lessing seems to have no inkling. If art is imitation, and each artist imitates the same model (nature), then logically artists can only imitate each other, and the relation between the poet and the painter can only be one of theft. And theft, even in the arts, is not ethical!

The lack in all this logomachy is an overriding theory of the imagination, which was not to be provided until the Romantic philosophers came along: Herder, Schelling, the Schlegels. The imagination was then conceived as a common source of all creativity: as indeed it still is. These hidden springs now have a name: the Unconscious. From that seething cauldron (the metaphor is Freud's) come the impulses that move the painter no less than the poet; and whether their realization is achieved in the plastic media of the painter or sculptor, or in the images of the poet, does not greatly matter from a philosophical point of view. We have learned to abolish the shackles of space and time, and bodies and actions no longer seem to be so independent. Picasso presents us with a multiple vision of subjects; and the poetry of Eluard is immobilized in the pregnant image. But vitalizing all the arts (even when most abstract) is the sustaining myth of the unconscious. The mirror has been shattered, and behind it we have found the ear of Dionysius, a cave of inexhaustible wonders.

21

On First Reading Nietzsche

IF AS ON THIS occasion one is invited to describe the impact of some work of art—a poem, a book, a painting, any aesthetic experience which produced a crisis in one's mental development—then I have no doubt what, in my own case, I must choose. It will necessarily be a book, for much as I have loved and served the visual arts, I must confess that their impact on my sensibility cannot compare in strength with that of certain works of literature. If my assignment were to describe those poems, dramas, or works of philosophy which . have enlarged my experience, or merely hastened a development already in progress, then I might well hesitate between various possibilities. I can think of many books that had an effect—a deep emotional effect—on my nascent mind. The first reading of Blake's poems, for example, was a revelation, producing an ecstatic mood of long duration. But I cannot describe that experience as a CRISIS, because no *conflict* was involved. I absorbed Blake—his strange beauty, his profound message, his miraculous technique—and to emulate Blake was to be my ambition and my despair. But there was no crisis— only a joyous acceptance. I could say the same of other poets —Wordsworth and Donne; and of certain philosophers and mystics, such as Bergson and Traherne. But the crisis, distinct in its impact, decisive in its outcome, was to take place, at the age of nineteen, when I first opened a book by the German philosopher, Friederich Nietzsche.

This is a confession, and if you are to understand the force and the excitement of this experience, I must describe to you in a little detail my circumstances at the time. Of my life of nineteen years, ten had been spent on a remote Yorkshire farm, utterly removed from any intellectual influences. The next five years had been spent in the almost monastic seclusion of an orphanage. In both these phases of my childhood I had been subject to a strict and unquestioned Christian upbringing. When I opened that first volume of Nietszche, I had lived for barely four years in the outer world—the world of business, of traffic, of newspapers, of theatres, of bookshops, of men and women. And then I had found myself—it was my own design—a student in one of our provincial universities. Every day, every hour, almost, my horizon was widening, my immature mind struggling with thousands of new ideas, new impressions, new sensations and experiences.

It was in that condition of rapid mental expansion—and, I would, add, of complete intellectual innocence—that I discovered Nietzsche. I will not say that I discovered him by accident—his name was being bruited abroad in those years—1911, 12 and 13—and no doubt it had floated past my reading eyes on many an occasion, with some suggestion of challenge. But now I had a university library at my service, and there just waiting to be picked up, I found the works of Nietzsche—a whole row of new and shining volumes in the authorized translation then being edited by Oscar Levy.

I cannot remember which volume I read first—I think it was the one I should have read last, his masterpiece, *Thus Spake Zarathustra*. But I read them all, or all that were then available—there were eventually eighteen volumes. Undoubtedly, two volumes of the series produced the deepest effect—two related volumes: the one already mentioned, *Thus Spake Zarathustra*, and the book which comes immediately after it in chronological sequence—*Beyond Good and Evil*. These two volumes contain the essence of Nietzsche's philosophy and the reading of them produced a decisive crisis in my intellectual development.

I find it difficult now to reconstruct my pre-Nietzschean state of mind. But it was a simple state of mind, a very naïve state of mind. I was pious, I was loyal, I was conventional—though I doubt whether I was destined to remain in that estate of innocence even without the influence of Nietzsche.

What I found in Nietzsche, of course, was the complete destruction of all my ancestral gods, the deriding of all my cherished illusions, an iconoclasm verging on blasphemy. All of that I might have found elsewhere—there were plenty of strident atheists and persuasive rationalists about in those days. But I found something more in Nietzsche—a poetic force that survived translation into another language, an imagination that soared into the future, a mind of apparently universal comprehension. Something still more: something which I can only call prophetic fire. My youthful intelligence was tinder to such electric flashes: my stock of immature ideas, my Sunday-school piety and priggish morality—all were utterly consumed in that mental conflagration.

My study was an attic, with no other illumination than a skylight. I would take one of the precious volumes home to this retreat, and read secretly, solitarily, long into the night. I would prop up *Zarathustra* on an improvised lectern, between two candles, and declaim its heady rhetoric aloud, to a distant audience of stars.

Did I fully comprehend what I was reading? Perhaps not, but then (and this is perhaps the important point) I did not take it wholly on trust. Nietzsche was writing about ideas I might not understand, criticizing philosophers I had never read. But I made it my business—no, that is not the right phrase—I was *incited* to reconstruct the idols that Nietzsche had demolished. These charred remains of Kant, this bruised image of Schopenhauer, the dissected corpse of Wagner— these pitiable sights did not satisfy me. I went back to find what these philosophers had been like before they came into the hands of Nietzsche, and in that manner I gradually explored a wide range of philosophy and literature—it was Nietzsche who first drew me to Pascal and Stendhal, and many others. If he had done nothing else for me, Nietzsche would have remained in my memory as the prime educative inspiration of my life.

Some notebooks which I kept at the time have survived, and I can see, sometimes with astonishment, sometimes with amusement, the thoughts which I abstracted from Nietzsche's works, and sometimes wrote out in emphatic capitals. They are not always thoughts that I still find appealing or profound. I also have copies of *Zarathustra* and *Beyond Good and Evil* which I acquired at this time, and they too bear evidence of what then appealed to me, and some rarer marginal notes which express disagreement. Here are some of the aphorisms which I copied out with evident approval:

Rebellion is the superiority of the slave.

Brave, unconcerned, scornful, violent—thus wisdom would have us be; she is a woman and ever loveth the warrior only.

Throw not away the hero in thy soul.

Dead are all Gods: now we will that Beyond-man live.

One should not go into churches if one wishes to breathe *pure* air.

By one's own pain one's knowledge increaseth.

The secret of a joyful life is to live dangerously.

Aphorisms, we might agree, such as *would* appeal to a lonely ambitious youth! But among the aphorisms I find in these notebooks, and the passages I have marked in the two volumes I then possessed, there are many which I still find profoundly significant. In fact, now that I have been led back to Nietzsche, I am amazed to find how much I owe to him—how much I have unconsciously absorbed; and in this "much" there is a considerable amount which, a few days ago, I would either have attributed to some other source, or credited to my own originality. Take these short passages from *Beyond Good and Evil*:

As little as the act of birth comes into consideration in the whole process and procedure of heredity, just as little is "being conscious" *opposed* to the instinctive in any decisive sense; the greater part of the conscious thinking of a philosopher is secretly influenced by his instincts, and forced into definite channels.

And this passage:

What we experience in dreams, provided we experience it often, pertains at last just as much to the general belongings of our soul as anything "actually" experienced; by virtue thereof we are richer or poorer, we have a requirement more or less, and finally, in broad daylight, and even in the brightest moments of our waking life, we are ruled to some extent by the nature of our dreams.

I read and marked these passages long before I had even heard the name of Freud, but the substance of what I was to find most valuable in Freud, for my particular purposes, is clearly expressed in these sentences of Nietzsche's.

Or take this passage from *Zarathustra*, which I can still declaim with zest and full approval:

The State? What is that? Give ear to me now, for now will I speak to you of the death of peoples.
The State is the coldest of all cold monsters. Coldly it uttereth its lies; and this is the lie that creepeth out of its mouth: "I, the State, am the people."
It is a lie! Creators were they which created the peoples and imposed on them one faith and one love: thus they served life.
Destroyers are they which lay snares for the many and call them States: they impose on them a sword and an hundred lusts.
Where there remaineth a people it understandeth not the State but hateth it even as the evil eye and as a sin against customs and rights.
But the State lieth in all the languages of good and evil: whatsoever it saith, it lieth; whatsoever it hath, it hath stolen.
False is it wholly; it is a biter which biteth with stolen teeth. False are its very bowels.

There are the seeds of my philosophy of anarchism, though at the same time I was reading Tolstoy, William Morris,

Kropotkin and Edward Carpenter. From such sources, which were fundamentally Christian or humanitarian in their inspiration, arose a counter-influence which turned the impact of Nietzsche into a crisis—a mental conflict which had to be solved.

How it was solved is another story, and I would be deceiving you if I suggested that there was, or is, any easy solution of what is, indeed, an eternal inescapable dilemma. This dilemma had received its perfect expression, a year or two before Nietzsche wrote *Zarathustra*, in Dostoevsky's "Legend of the Grand Inquisitor", but I think it was not until sometime later that I read this wonderful chapter in the *Brothers Karamazov*. What I did seize on, so many years ago, was a passage in *Beyond Good and Evil*, marking it with triple-lines: and I would like to think that it has never, since then, been absent from my consciousness. Here it is:

Everything in the nature of freedom, elegance, boldness, dance, and masterly certainty, which exists or has existed, whether it be in thought itself, or in administration, or in speaking and persuading, in art as in conduct, has only developed by means of the tyranny of arbitrary law . . . Every artist knows how different from the state of letting oneself go, is his "most natural" condition, the free arranging, locating, disposing, and constructing in the moments of "inspiration"—and how strictly and delicately he then obeys a thousand laws, which by their very rigidness and precision, defy all formulation by means of ideas . . . The essential thing "in heaven and in earth" is, apparently . . . that there should be long *obedience* in the same direction; and thereby results, and always has resulted in the long run, something which has made life worth living; for instance, virtue, art, music, dancing, reason, spirituality—anything whatever that is transfiguring, refined, foolish or divine.

This is the essential message of Nietzsche's philosophy, and though since I first came across it I have read much and travelled far, I still know none finer. But it is not an easy doctrine. Indeed, it is a doctrine of *hardness*. Become hard, cried Nietzsche, but he did not mean become hard towards other people. This is what he meant: "The discipline of suffering, of *great* suffering—know ye not that it is only *this* discipline that has produced all the elevations of humanity hitherto? The tension of soul in misfortune which communicates to it its energy, its shuddering in view of rack and ruin, its inventiveness and bravery in undergoing, enduring, interpreting and exploiting misfortune, and whatever depth, mystery, disguise, spirit, artifice, or greatness has been bestowed upon the soul—has it not been bestowed through suffering? In man *creature* and *creator* are united: in man there is not only matter, shred, excess, clay, mire, folly, chaos; but there is also the creator, the sculptor, the hardness of the hammer, the divinity of the spectator, and the seventh day—do ye understand this contrast?"

Since I first read and was moved to the bottom of my being by these and other words of Nietzsche's, there have been two wars against Germany; and Nietzsche was a German. As a consequence he has been reviled, spat upon, misinterpreted and distorted in a thousand ways, and by both camps. But wars and their pestilential hatreds pass, and they cannot destroy the greatness of a great soul. Nietzsche and his philosophy will return, justly criticized, deeply modified, but still unmistakably Nietzschean. One aspect of that philosophy has already been revived under the name of Existentialism. The existentialists acknowledge their debt to Nietzsche, but I find nothing of value in Sartre, in Jaspers, in Heidegger, which is not expressed more forcibly, more beautifully, and more completely, in the works of Nietzsche. I think that Nietzsche anticipated the existentialists and condemned their shortcomings when he wrote: "Was it not necessary in the end for men to sacrifice everything comfortable, holy, healing, all hope, all faith in hidden harmonies, in future blessedness and justice? Was it not necessary to sacrifice God Himself, and out of cruelty to themselves to worship stone, stupidity, gravity, fate, nothingness? To sacrifice God for nothingness —this paradoxical mystery of the ultimate cruelty has been reserved for the rising generation . . .''

22

The Drama and the Theatre

The Complete Plays of Henry James have been awaited with some impatience by the devotees of the Master, and now that we have them we see that there is some excuse for the delay. Together they constitute the most spectacular failure that a major literary artist has ever encountered. In his disillusion, late in life, Henry James could hardly have been brought to look at the typescripts again; but Mr. Edel, who has edited them, is probably right in assuming that he would not have objected to their eventual publication. In 1913, answering a critic who had asked for a sight of the plays in order to write an article about them, James said:

While they were being played they of course came in for whatever attention the Press was paying to the actual and current theatre. They were inevitably then Theatre-stuff, and as such took their chance; but they are now, enjoying complete immunity from performance as they do, Drama-stuff—which is quite a different matter. It is only as Drama-stuff that I recognize their exposure to any public remark that doesn't consist simply of the critic's personal remembrance of them as played things . . . When my Plays, such as they have been, *are* published, then of course the gentleman you mention will enjoy all aid to his examination.

There is present, in this statement, a distinction which is at the root of the whole problem of drama, and which makes this volume, as a classical demonstration of the issue, of importance for all who are interested in the craft of writing.

For many years there has existed a certain antagonism between the imaginative writer and the professional stage (it has now extended to the film). The producer, and the actor, are firmly convinced that there is some sixth sense, a feeling for what is possible in the theatre, a "stage-sense", which they possess and which the writer lacks. In the past two hundred years the overwhelming majority of successful plays have been written by "playwrights" (an odious word to indicate the singularity of the tribe), and what they wrote, once the stage had finished with it, is as dead as an old newspaper. In certain cases it is obvious that the writers were at fault—they simply refused to conform to the limitations of the stage. The plays of Tennyson, Browning and Swinburne are either inordinately long or massively static. But this divorce between the writer and the stage did not always exist, and the plays of Shakespeare and Congreve are still "good theatre". So, in the period in question, were the plays of Ibsen and Chekhov. Why, then, was Henry James, with his immense knowledge, not only of the craft of writing, but of the stage itself, such a spectacular failure as a playwright?

Reviewing, in 1895, the second volume of *Theatricals*, the critic of the *Pall Mall Gazette* observed: ". . . we wish very much that Mr. James would write such farces to please himself, and not to please the stage." And on the same occasion William Archer expressed the opinion that "Mr. James has never taken up a natural and unconstrained attitude towards the stage . . . If he will only clear his mind of critical cant . . .

and write solely for the ideal audience within his own breast, he will certainly produce works of art, and not improbably successful plays". These are shrewd hits, but Henry James might have answered that the dramatist, if his aims are realistic, must write for the audience that actually exists in his time, must study the successes and be guided by the failures, and generally conform to the taste of the period. Oddly enough, James had one supreme object in writing plays—to make money. He had been writing novels for a quarter of a century, and had only met with a modest *succès d'éstime*. He had a comfortable private income from property in America that would make most writers envious, but he had also an expansive view of his social rights and obligations. Cash was a prime necessity, and the theatre was the most direct way of earning it. At first he had avoided that way because he realized, from his close observation of the theatre in Paris and London, that the world one enters, in knocking at a manager's door, is one of "deadly vulgarity and illiteracy". He describes very vividly, in the fourth chapter of *The Tragic Muse* (the novel in which he exposed all his theatrical aspirations), the limitations that beset the Victorian dramatist (the position has not changed). "What can you do," he asks pathetically, "with a character, with an idea, with a feeling, between dinner and the suburban trains?" In 1889 he confides to his journal that he had "practically given up my old, valued and long-cherished dream of doing something for the stage for fame's sake, and art's, and fortune's: overcome by the vulgarity, the brutality, the baseness of the condition of the English-speaking theatre today. But after an interval, a long one, the vision has revived, on a new and a very much humbler basis, and especially under the lash of necessity. Of art and fame *il est maintenant fort peu question*: I simply *must* try, and try seriously, to produce half a dozen—a dozen, five dozen—plays for the

183

sake of my pocket, my material future. Of how little money the novel makes for me I needn't discourse here". The new and humbler basis was to be a dramatization of his novel, *The American*, with Edward Compton as producer and leading actor. It ran for seventy performances—not by theatrical standards a success, but tantalizing enough to encourage both Compton and James to try again. *The Album* and *The Reprobate* followed almost immediately, but these were not produced; and then, in 1895, came the decisive event of James's dramatic career—the production of *Guy Domville* with George Alexander as manager and leading actor. The disastrous first night of this play, when James was hissed and booed as he came on the stage to take the author's call, has become legendary. It was more than the reaction of a disappointed audience: it was an audience divided against itself, one half applauding the subtlety and grace that had proved to be beyond the coarse sensibilities of the other half. It was the battle of the high-brow and the low-brow in all its raw violence, its inequality of weapons. It was a war for which Henry James had no strategic aptitude. He once more retired from the field.

He was to return, twelve years later, with a final group of plays. Meanwhile the battle for Ibsen had been fought and won on all fronts with the possible exception of the box-office. James had been an interested, indeed, a fascinated spectator. He might deplore in this Norwegian intruder "the absence of humour, the absence of free imagination, and the absence of style"—especially the absence of style, all the more mystifying in that "its place was not usurped, as it frequently is in such cases, by vulgarity". But humourless, flat and parochial as they might be, James had to recognize that plays like *Hedda Gabler* and *The Wild Duck*, had a vitality and a verisimilitude such as he had never achieved. This might be partly due to "the artistic exercise of a mind saturated with the vision of human infirmities; saturated, above all, with a sense of the infinitude, for all its mortal savour, of *character*. But it was also due to something for which James had always had the highest regard—a high sense of "the sacred mystery of structure". It is perhaps too facile to suggest that the influence of Ibsen is present in this last phase of James's dramatic career, but in one play at least, *The Other House*, the comparison is unescapable, and is made by Mr. Edel. "In *The Other House*'s provincial setting, the retrospective method employed in the prologue, the small cast, the use of Dr. Ramage as a family adviser (an Ibsen type recalling Judge Brack or Rector Kroll) and Mrs. Beever as the objective outsider, able to view the struggling characters with judicial calm, James has reproduced all the Ibsen externals." Mr. Edel goes on to compare the plot of this play with *Rosmersholm*, and the parallels are indeed very close. But for all that, he claims, *The Other House* stands on its own feet as a distinct Jamesian work. But he claims rather too much in claiming that it is also "British" in its motives and emotions.

It remains to ask what, if anything, was wrong with James's plays. One may express a hope that one day they will be tried out on a more sympathetic stage (actors and actresses of the Irving-Alexander age were, with rare exceptions like Elizabeth Robins, totally unsuited for such plays); one may express such a hope and yet at the same time ruefully admit that all is not well with these plays. Actors and critics complained of the artificiality of the dialogue, but this was no objection in the case of Congreve, or even in the contemporary case of Wilde. As Bernard Shaw said of *Guy Domville*: "Line after line comes with such a delicate turn and fall that I unhesitatingly challenge any of our popular dramatists to write a scene in verse with half the beauty of Mr. James's prose . . . I am speaking of the delicate inflexions conveyed by the cadences of the line." Nor can there be any criticism of the dramatic structure of the plays. Some of them are too long, but all are shapely, and move with perfect tempo to their appointed intervals. The real difficulty, in my opinion, lies elsewhere.

James was a master of the interior drama—of the subjective processes that are rarely, in real life, expressed in overt action. He writes, said George Moore, "like a man to whom all action is repugnant". "Why does he always avoid decisive action? In his stories a woman never leaves the house with her lover, nor does a man ever kill a man or himself. Why is nothing ever accomplished? In real life murder, adultery, and suicide are of common occurrence; but Mr. James's people live in a calm, sad, and very polite twilight of volition." This is very true of the novels, but it does not make them any the less great works of art. In this sphere James created a *genre* of which George Moore had no conception, and could have had no aptitude. But when it came to writing plays, James was at a loss, and resorted to some of the crudest melodrama ever intended for the stage. He tried to make up for it by elaborate stage directions—surely the most elaborate stage directions ever written by a dramatist. The concluding directions of *The Other House* are an extreme example of this, and far too long to quote: but apart from various visible actions, the actors are called on to "smother revulsions", to "take in" another character's fidelity to his vow, to choke impulses and to give a word "but the form of a look". The stage directions in his last play, *The Outcry*, are even more subtle in their intentions —and impossible of exteriorization ("On which, as having so unanswerably spoken, he turns off again in his high petulence and nervous, restless irritation and goes up and away—the thought of something still other, and not yet quite at the surface, seeming to work in him beneath and behind all this . . ."). This was the hand of the novelist annotating the play, increasingly as time went on. But the novelist would never have been responsible for the crude drinking scene in *Guy Domville*; nor for the astonishing figure of Rose Armiger in *The Other House*, who seems rather to have strayed from *East Lynne* or one of the more lurid romances of Hall Caine.

That interior drama can be bodied forth on the modern stage has been proved by the author of *The Family Reunion* and *The Cocktail Party*. One must conclude that in this matter James never had the courage of his convictions. He had been dazzled, as a youth, by the Parisian stage, about which he wrote so well and so enthusiastically in the articles now collected in *The Scenic Art*. The theatre of Dumas *fils* and Sardou must have had some point for its contemporaries, but it is now astonishingly dead—so dead that it would be an arduous task to discover to what extent its example was fatal to its fervent disciple. It is, at least, under suspicion.

Was all this dramatic effort of James's in vain? Theatrically, there can be no doubt. Some of James's plays will be revived when the theatre is less vulgar and commercial; they will be given by private societies to small but delighted audiences. But they will never command the stage as Ibsen does, or even Shaw. The defects are too inherent. But indirectly the experience was of incalculable value to James, for without the dramatic years it is not likely that his narrative art would have reached its wonderful perfection in such works as *The Wings of the Dove* and *The Golden Bowl*. That was Henry James's own conclusion. Looking back on the "whole tragic experience", "compensations and solutions" seemed to stand there with open arms for him. "Has a *part*," he asked himself, "of all this wasted passion and squandered time . . . been simply the precious lesson, taught me in that roundabout and devious, that cruelly expensive, way, of the singular value for a narrative plan too of the (I don't know *what* adequately to call it) divine principle of the scenario?" Certainly this was the divine principle which he applied with such success in his last great phase. In retrospect those days of struggle and disillusion in the theatre became a "strange sacred time", infinitely precious, for they had yielded up the secret of "the sacred mystery of structure."

I had intended, in this essay, to make some comparison of Henry James and Sean O'Casey. I thought that some lesson might be drawn from the success of O'Casey's plays when contrasted with the failure of Henry James's plays. But on consideration I find that their worlds do not meet at any point. Mr. O'Casey is good Theatre—in that respect he has the advantage of Henry James. But is he good drama? Good drama, in my opinion, should also be good reading. I enjoy reading a play like *Guy Domville* or *The Other House* even though I criticize many of its features; and this is because it has a literary texture, a verbal wit and dignity. "I think a poet's claim to greatness depends upon his power to put passion in the common people," says one of Mr. O'Casey's characters, and he is probably expressing Mr. O'Casey's own opinion, though another character answers: "The poet ever strives to save the people; the people ever strive to destroy the poet." The people certainly tried to destroy Henry James; his poetry was too refined for them. But they will not destroy Sean O'Casey; his rhetoric shakes the diaphragm and draws their tears, but the sound of it diminishes down the corridors of time.

23

Two Notes on a Trilogy

I

IN THE PREFACE which Henry James himself wrote for the "New York" edition of *The Wings of the Dove* he discussed in nearly exhaustive detail the aims or intentions he had had in writing this novel, and all that is left for a later and less qualified voice to add are a few things which modesty, or a fear of egoism, forbade the author himself to utter. *The Wings of the Dove* is the first member of the great trilogy which constitutes the final phase of James's work. In the past there has been a tendency—not now, I think, so widespread—to depreciate this final phase, to suggest that it is really a little too much of a good thing. That attitude shows a complete misunderstanding of the whole of our author's evolution, which was always, from the beginning, a reaching after the perfection which this novel, *The Ambassadors* and *The Golden Bowl* together represent—a perfection at once intellectually formal and deeply moving.

On the question of the form of the novel in general no modesty held back the author: on this theme he expatiates endlessly, not only in the Preface already mentioned, but also in his letters and essays, whether in connection with his own work or the work of other writers. No approach to Henry James is valid that does not recognize his intention to give the novel a shape, a structure in its way as rigid, as proof against sentimentality, weakness, irrelevance, inappropriateness, dullness, exaggeration and all the other sins of literary composition as, say, the classical drama of Aeschylus or Racine. Considering the previous history of the novel (or, for that matter, its subsequent history, which at no point has come within reach of Henry James in this respect), his ambition was already overweening: the public was not—is not yet—ready for such a discipline. Novel reading, even in intellectual circles, is regarded as a relaxation—as compared with the reading of philosophy, science or poetry. That, Henry James would have said, is precisely what is wrong with the novel, and with the reading public. Art has no outer courts: it is absolute—it either *is*, on the level of *Phèdre* or *King Lear* or *Samson Agonistes*, or it is *not*; it does not admit of adulteration. To give the novel the intensity of the great masterpieces—that, briefly, was James's ambition; and there can be no doubt, to some of us, that he succeeded, in *The Wings of the Dove* and equally in *The Ambassadors* and *The Golden Bowl*—succeeded beyond his own hopes, and certainly beyond the achievements of any other novelist who has ever conscientiously practised the art.

As for the form which fiction should take—should discover as it were, for itself—here again James left us in no doubt. The Preface to *The Wings of the Dove* is perhaps the supreme occasion for an exposition of what he called "the compositional key", though the other Prefaces are not less suggestive of it. There is, naturally, a centre round which the whole drama is to revolve—though one might equally well use a more static image and call it the keystone whose firm placing locks the whole structure into rigidity. This centre is then illuminated from various points of vantage, each of which is another subordinate arch or vault held in position by its own keystone (however baroque, even "mannerist", the *style* of Henry James, his structure must be thought of in terms of Gothic architecture). In the Preface to this novel he speaks of the

"fun" of "establishing one's successive centres—of fixing
them so exactly that the portions of the subject commanded
by them as by happy points of view, and accordingly treated
from them, would constitute, so to speak, sufficiently solid
blocks of wrought material, squared to the sharp edge, as to
have weight and mass and carrying power; to make for construction, that is, to conduce to effect and to provide for
beauty". He also speaks of the tension, even the conflict,
between drama and picture, between the action as such and
the prefigured elements within the dimensions of which the
action must take place, elements which are not mere stage
scenery, but mute presences which contribute *their* share to the
development of the action. One has to go no farther than the
first chapter—indeed, the first paragraph—to see the upholstery taking, as it were, the impress of the characters, the
mirrors reflecting their least movements. This kind of effect
is not achieved without the highest skill—the art of indirect
presentation, and with it what James called "the recording
consistency" of the author.

For these reasons, which are highly rewarding in the end,
it may nevertheless be some time before the reader gets the
"hang" of the story. The heroine does not appear before the
Third Book, and even thereafter the situation is developed in
such a leisurely fashion that the author was compelled, as he
confesses, to skimp the scenes as the plot drew to its loaded
conclusion. The motive was one which James had for a long
time nursed in his imagination. "The idea, reduced to its
essence, is that of a young person conscious of a great capacity
for life, but early stricken and doomed, condemned to die
under short respite, while also enamoured of the world; aware,
moreover, of the condemnation and passionately desiring to
'put in' before extinction as many of the finer vibrations as
possible, and so achieve, however briefly and brokenly, the

sense of having lived." The young person who is to embody this idea is Milly Theale, an American girl—"the fine flower of an 'old' New York stem"—who has wealth and charm, intelligence and independence—everything, as it turns out, except health. The author plunges her, eager and ingenuous, into a corner of English society which might be described as a little gamy—at least, it mingles its finer feelings with speculations that are calculating, even in the crude sense. Kate Croy, who threatens to dominate the novel by the forcefulness of her character, is more than a foil to Milly's wistful innocence: she represents the moral ambiguity of a diplomatic approach to life—which is the typical Jamesian theme, not less important for being so seemingly subtle. Her emissary, who is also her lover, is a weaker figure: indeed, we can never quite believe in Merton Densher, so deeply is his masculinity compromised in this petticoat government. The plot which these two concoct is staged in Venice, in an atmosphere of watery corruption which James knew as no one else how to convey. Kate instigates a particularly foul piece of deception—foul because, however extenuating the circumstances, it did involve the sanctity of the passions: the passion which was hers and Densher's by natural development, and poor Milly's only on the basis of their unconscionable pretence.

A moral tragedy cannot be epitomized: its excitement is in its subtleties of observation, its accuracy of discrimination, its accumulated perception of issues and dilemmas; and above all in the author's conscious control of the final issue. It might be objected that in this tragedy the heroine is not a victim claimed by exacting gods: she dies full of pity and forgiveness, and the retribution is left to work its poison in the consciences of the calculating lovers. We must admit that the pattern is not the classic one. But it would not have been like James to confine himself within such banal limits. Life itself does not conform

to a traditional pattern, and it was life, in all its immediacy
and contemporaneity, from which James drew his motives,
and in which he could not honestly find the classical formula.
But the effect is none the less cathartic; and when Milly dies
we feel, if we have given the story the attention it demands,
not perhaps that a great queen has gone to her doom, but
rather that once more a martyred spirit has proved the moral
grandeur of simple virtue.

II

The Golden Bowl, which Henry James began to write in
April, 1903, was to be the last completed full-length novel,
and it was written, as he himself said, "with the rarest perfection"—the perfection of all those arts, narrative and dramatic,
to which he had by then devoted the concentrated energies
of forty years. The "germ" of the story had been planted in
his mind some twelve years earlier—there is an entry of
November 28, 1892, in the *Notebooks*: "something lately
told one about a simultaneous marriage, in Paris (or only
'engagement' yet, I believe), of a father and a daughter—an
only daughter. The daughter—American, of course—is engaged to a young Englishman, and the father, a widower and
still youngish, has sought in marriage at exactly the same time
an American girl of very much the same age as his daughter."
James immediately began to elaborate the suggestion. "Say
he has done it to console himself in his abandonment—to
make up for the loss of the daughter, to whom he has been
devoted. I see a little tale, *n'est-ce pas?*—in the idea that they
all shall have married, as arranged, with this characteristic
consequence—that the daughter fails to hold the affections of
the young English husband, whose approximate mother-in-law
the pretty young second wife of the father will now have

become. The father *doesn't* lose the daughter nearly as much as he feared, or expected, for her marriage which has but half gratified her, leaves her *des loisirs*, and she devotes them to him and to making up, as much as possible, for having left him ... The reason for all this ... resides in the circumstance that the father-in-law's second wife has become much more attractive to the young husband of the girl than the girl herself has remained. *Mettons* that this second wife is nearly as young as her daughter-in-law—and prettier and cleverer— she knows more what she is about. *Mettons* even that the younger husband has known her before, has liked her, etc., been attracted by her, and would have married her if she had had any money." He explores the possibilities a little farther and then remarks: "The *subject* is really the pathetic simplicity and good faith of the father and daughter in their abandonment", and adds: "the other woman and the father and daughter all intensely American".

This idea for a "little tale" occurred to James in the midst of his infatuation with the theatre. *Guy Domville*, the fatal play on which his highest hopes were fixed, was written during the next summer. The disillusionment came with the disastrous failure of that play in January, 1895. The next month we find James returning, as if for consolation, to the theme of this very novel. He had also on his mind the theme which became *The Wings of the Dove*, but first there stood in his path, "brightly soliciting", "the idea of the father and daughter ... who marry—the father for consolation—at the same time, and yet are left more together than ever, through their respective *époux* taking such a fancy to each other". His fingers itched for it—"I seem to see it as something compact, *charpenté*, living, touching, amusing ... For God's sake let me try: I want to plunge into it: I *languish* so to get at an immediate creation." And then follows a rueful glance back over the dramatic years, and the daring thought that perhaps after all they had not been wasted—that he had "crept round through long apparent barrenness, through suffering and sadness intolerable, to that rare perception"—the rare perception being "the singular value for a narrative plan too of the . . . divine principle of the Scenario".

"The divine principle of the scenario" is the key to the subsequent development of James's narrative art, and there can be no doubt that on what he meant by this phrase depends the singular grandeur of his final phase as a novelist. The principle involves the carrying over into the novel of the formal demands that are implicit in drama. Of the three novels of the final phase, *The Golden Bowl* is perhaps the least rigid in form, —the geometry, at least, is less complicated. He said himself, in his Preface to the New York Edition, "the thing abides rigidly by its law of showing Maggie Verver at first through her suitor's and her husband's exhibitiory vision of her, and of then showing the Prince, with at least an equal intensity, through his wife's; the advantage thus being that these attributions of experience display the sentient subjects themselves at the same time and by the same stroke with the nearest possible approach to a desirable vividness". And again: "We see very few persons in *The Golden Bowl*, but the scheme of the book, to make up for that, is that we shall really see about as much of them as a coherent literary form permits. That was my problem, so to speak, and my *gageure*—to play the small handful of values really for all they were worth—and to work my system, my particular propriety of appeal, particular degree of pressure on the spring of interest, for all that this specific ingenuity itself might be." How beautifully the hand is played can only be appreciated in the reading, and the re-reading, of the book. It is done with a felicity worthy of the high theme.

To this theme I will return before I conclude, but it should be noted first that among the felicities of this novel is not only "the better form", but also what James in his Preface described as "the finer air", and which we all too prosaically would call the prose style. ("It all comes back to that, to my and your 'fun'—if we but allow the term its full extension; to the production of which no humblest question involved, even to that of the shade of a cadence or the position of a comma, is not richly pertinent.") We realize from his remarks on the subject in this Preface, and perhaps with surprise, that James would insist on the vocal test even for prose—for his own prose especially: "The highest test of any literary form conceived in the light of 'poetry'—to apply that term in its largest literary sense—hangs back unpardonably from its office when it fails to lend itself to *viva-voce* treatment." And he does not hesitate to define such finer airs. "We talk here, naturally, not of non-poetic forms, but of those whose highest bid is addressed to the imagination, to the spiritual and the aesthetic vision, the mind led captive by a charm and a spell, an inculculable art. The essential property of such a form as that is to give out its finest and most numerous secrets, and to give them out most gratefully, under the closest pressure—which is of course the pressure of the attention articulately *sounded*." James's prose, in this novel above all, answers to those conditions; it has everywhere "the touch that directly evokes and finely presents, the touch that operates for closeness and for charm, for conviction and illusion, for communication, in a word." Here, in fact, in this final trilogy, is to be found the greatest poetry of our time. Such a scene as that on the terrace at Fawns (Book Fifth, ch. II), gleams with whatever contemporary equivalent we possess for the Shakespearean magic.

As for the wisdom which this story embodies, it is one more

application of the subtlest ethical intelligence of our time. Moral values are not easy to define, except in action, and to describe Maggie Verver's quality as "simplicity" or "innocence" is to give no notion of its dynamic intensity. Nor do such words as "sophistication" and "decadence" at all adequately express the complexity of the values represented by Charlotte and Amerigo (the only character in the book who is not quite convincing—there was always a shade of sentimentality in James's transatlantic approach to European aristocrats). The truth is that James would have shrunk from any categorization, any codification, of moral values. The conduct of life is an art, and the work of living art is the creation of a fine aesthetic sensibility, and is to be appreciated only by a similar sensibility. In the scene I have referred to James describes Maggie at one point as being unable to give herself "to the vulgar heat of her wrong". To insist on moral rights, to cry out against moral wrongs—that is precisely the rough justice that leaves its victims bleeding. The whole of James's work is a protest against such obtuseness, and in *The Golden Bowl* he found finally that "large and confident action", that "splendid and supreme creation", which he had, over the years, so assiduously sought.

24

C. G. Jung

ONE DAY as we sat in his study overlooking the lake of Zürich, I asked Jung what had been the fundamental aim of all his life's work, and he answered simply: "I wanted to understand. . . . To understand is my only passion. But also I have a doctor's instinct. I want to help people when they are in pain. But to do that, I have to understand them."

Carl Gustav Jung is the son of a Protestant pastor, born in the village of Kesswill, in the canton of Thurgau, "in the year of the pig". That is Jung's own humorous comment, for in the Chinese calendar the year 1875 is given this symbol, a symbol of darkness. As a child Jung noticed that the world was dark and obscure: the reality did not tally with the superficial explanations given him by his elders. There was the darkness of the past—a night in which untold races of men had lived and left their undeciphered traces: he would study archaelogy. There was the darkness of language: different races speaking in different tongues, and many languages that men had once spoken had disappeared, leaving only traces in faded manuscripts and broken inscriptions—he would study philology. There was the darkness of life itself—the mystery of biological evolution of the human body, of the human mind. In this last region was the darkest mystery of all, and to this he would, in the end, devote all his inquisitive energy.

There is little wonder he had this bent in his nature. His ancestors for several generations on both sides of the family had been either theologians, seeking to solve the mystery of life by spiritual insight, or doctors, probing into the secrets of the body. His paternal grandfather, a German by birth, was a poet as well as a physician, who had had to leave his native country on account of his revolutionary sympathies, and had come to Basle with a recommendation from that great humanist Alexander von Humboldt. Here this ancestor became professor of anatomy and later founded the first asylum for the insane and the first institution for mentally-defective children. He married the daughter of an old patrician family, and so did his son. It was to Basle that Jung himself came, at the early age of four, and Basle is the city where, so to speak, he wove together the two strands of his inheritance.

In Basle he went to school and college, and completed his medical studies. He had already discovered his particular bent and had been drawn to the psychiatrical side of medicine. In 1900 he became an assistant to the famous mental specialist Bleuler, who was in charge of the cantonal asylum and psychiatrical clinic at Zürich. Two years later he had completed his doctor's thesis—on *The Psychology and Pathology of so-called Occult Phenomena*.

In this first publication of nearly half a century ago Jung already foreshadows, not only certain theoretical concepts which we will mention later, but also two characteristics of his method—his choice of a subject-matter (in this case "the occult") which is dangerous in so far as it suggests that the author has some personal predilection for it; and at the same time a refusal to accept the current and mystifying label attached to this subject-matter—the phenomena are *so-called* occult, but will prove in the author's opinion to be within the scope of a scientific method, and as such explicable, understandable.

This early essay sets out from a consideration of those forms of hysteria that take the form of somnambulism (sleep-walking), but the main evidence is drawn from the analysis of a spiritualistic medium made by Jung in the years 1899 and 1900. This case was replete with psychological problems—far more than Jung could deal with at the time; but its importance lay in its challenge to accepted notions of the workings of the mind. The idea that part of the mind is unknown to us, below the level of consciousness, was not new, of course. Presentiments of it are present in Greek philosophy, and we find it as an *idea* in Leibniz, Kant, Coleridge, Hartmann and Carus. Freud had made the idea a demonstrable fact, and though Jung did not meet Freud until 1906, he was from the first in friendly and fruitful relationship with the man and his work. The hypothesis of a dynamic unconscious is basic in this first essay of Jung's, but already Jung has taken a step beyond Freud's position. Having discussed all the essential features of the case significant for an understanding of the structure of the mind, Jung goes on to point out that "certain accompanying manifestations" must be mentioned and these, he fears, are sure to encounter "a not unjustifiable scepticism" in scientific circles. He calls this new material "unconscious additional creative work". By this phrase he meant to indicate the possibility that apart from the results of unconscious activity which can be explained in terms of ordinary associative processes, and by reference to the past history of the patient, there are other results (the "thought reading" of numbers, for example) which seem to depend on a state of receptivity in the unconscious greater than any known to conscious mental activity. In short, the unconscious has creative capacities beyond the range of the conscious. That was the suggestion forced on Jung by this case he observed as a young man of twenty-four, and his life-work to a considerable extent has consisted in a substantiation of this early intuition. His patient had been unable to explain how she had acquired the knowledge stored in her unconscious. Jung, however, could discover a number of parallels in occultist and gnostic sources scattered throughout all kinds of works of different periods quite inaccessible to the patient. That paradox sent him on a journey of exploration which is not yet at an end.

There is a current misconception which sees in Jung an early disciple of Freud who subsequently deserted his master. Nothing could be more misleading. From the very beginning there were differences of procedure and of outlook that were bound to lead to divergent results. Freud's work is based on a scientific method restricted to the principle of causality: that is to say, it is assumed that everything that happens has an explanation in prior causes, and is merely the result of those causes. The world is a mechanism that can be taken to pieces and we can only understand how it works if we know how to dismantle and reassemble its constituent parts. Jung does not deny this causal principle, but he says that it is inadequate to explain all the facts. In his view we live and work, day by day, according to the principle of directed aim or purpose, as well as by the principle of causality. We are drawn onwards and our actions are significant for a future we cannot foresee, and will only be explicable when the final effect of the impulse becomes evident. In other words, life has a *meaning* as well as an explanation; a meaning, moreover, that we can never finally discover, for it is being extended all the time by the process of evolution.

Is such an affirmation mystical? Not at all, Jung would say: it is merely the recognition of objective facts—awkward facts they may be for minds trained in the discipline of causal logic, but facts none the less. In this first carefully observed case of hysteria, it was already obvious that the unconscious, in the elaboration of systematic fantasies, followed certain patterns unknown to the waking consciousness, and that these patterns were not given by the facts of the case, but could nevertheless be related to patterns in other systems of thought and imagery. That is to say, the unconscious may be said to have an innate bias towards the formation of specific symbols, and these symbols have a significance which is more than personal— which is historical, racial, collective—at that time Jung could not say which.

But he affirmed the positive and super-personal value of the symbol, and already in that early act he chose another road than Freud, who can only see in the symbol a sign or representation of the individual's primitive sexual tendencies. All symbols, in Freud's view, could be, *must be*, reduced to products of biological (specifically sexual) instincts. That may be their scientific explanation, replied Jung, but "causality is only one principle, and psychology essentially cannot be exhausted by causal methods only, because the mind lives by aims as well". We know that man cannot live by bread alone: nor even, Jung would add, from the energy generated by suppressed infantile desires for pleasure or power. Man must also possess *hope*; and hope, or belief in the purposive value of life, is a vital necessity. Because it is a vital necessity, the unconscious has created (over many thousands of years) symbolic images or moulds of thought by which the hopes and aspirations of mankind can be shaped and expressed. The symbol thus has an evolutionary function. "The further development of man," Jung has written, "can only be brought about by means of symbols which represent something far in advance of himself, and whose intellectual meanings cannot yet be grasped entirely. The individual unconscious produces such symbols, and they are of the greatest possible value in the moral development of the personality."

This view, which threatened to reverse the scientific materialism of the nineteenth century, especially as it affected religious beliefs, has been bitterly opposed, not only by empiricist psychologists of the school of Freud, but by the whole of the positivistic and marxist trend in modern thought. Jung remains unperturbed, for he has no axe to grind, political or ecclesiastical. He remains objective. As for religion, he agrees with Cicero in deriving the word, not from "religare" (to bind fast, as the Church Fathers would have it) but from "relegere", which means to observe carefully, to look for hints and wait for hunches, and never seek to be dogmatic.

It is not necessary to be a theologian to get those intimations: they come to all sorts and conditions of men, and to men, like St. Paul, who least expect them, or want them. They come, of course, from the unconscious, and our only clue to their nature and operations is the scientific study of dreams.

We may perhaps get a better notion of the function ascribed to the dream in Jung's psychology by looking at the whole process in reverse. We must imagine, then, a single continuous psychic process, as pervasive and universal as the cosmic process or "nature", and equally removed from our human scale of time and space. As individual persons we are "carriers" of this force—we depend on it very much in the same way as our bodies depend on air. We have to keep it under pressure, contained within a sensitive envelope, and it is only this envelope of which we are normally conscious, and which we present to our fellow-men. But we are not allowed to forget our dependence on this psychic force—we are not allowed to assume that we are self-sufficient and exclusively personal. So in certain states of inattention (day-dreaming, sleep, hysteria, etc.) the unconscious force is revealed to us, not as an individual possession but as impersonal, racial, even primitively animal. We call this revelation a dream, and as such it cannot be explained with a psychology taken only from individual consciousness. Again, it is only a hunch we get, for the dream is back and behind, dominating our psychic life: "we do not dream—we are dreamed". We submit to the dream, we are in part the creation of our dreams, and the created cannot fully understand the purpose of the creator. "The dream is a mysterious message from our night-aspect"— from the darkness that we strive to understand. It is never, as the Freudians would argue, fully explicable in terms of our reason, or of our instinctive drives. Jung reiterates: it has a purpose which does not necessarily correspond with the purposes of the conscious mind and causality. It follows that there can be no *standard* symbols, good for all dreams, as there are in Freudian psychology, for the purpose of the dream will vary with every individual and every situation. There is always a complementary or compensatory relation between the conscious situation of the dreamer and the dream, and dream interpretation can proceed only if we have the requisite knowledge of the conscious situation. It is always helpful, says Jung, when we set out to interpret a dream, to ask: "what conscious attitude does it compensate?" There is a language of dreams and it has certain "roots" in the past, but it is a language that has become full of inflexions, complex and subtle. The task of interpretation is bound to be difficult but it is nevertheless an essential part of psychotherapy.

The dream is not an isolated event: it is part of a continuous unconscious mental process which by chance we interrupt, and succeed in bringing to consciousness. For that reason it is important to study dreams in series: they are connected by unconscious threads of meaning, and perhaps the analyst, by taking readings at various points, can guess the lines of communication. He may find that they cross at a certain point, which becomes the "centre of significance". Once such a centre is established, the task of interpretation becomes immensely simplified.

But not complete. At the centre of significance may be a symbol, and again Jung is too cautious to give such symbols a simple equivalence in our conscious life. "The dream speaks in images, and gives expression to instincts that are derived from the most primitive levels of nature." We may not be able to interpret such images in our conscious sophisticated language. But we can recognize them for what they are, messages from another psychic layer and we can assimilate them, make them our familiars. We shall find their parallels in our myths and fairy tales, even in popular fiction and pictorial art. Sometimes they signify positive forces, the forces of life, the power of healing and of fertility; sometimes negative forces, the forces of self-destruction and death. Contrary to Freud, who regards the unconscious as a depository of evil forces, Jung treats it as "that really very natural thing". "The unconscious," he says, "is not a demonic monster, but a thing of nature that is perfectly neutral as far as moral sense, aesthetic taste and intellectual judgment go. It is dangerous only when our conscious attitude towards it becomes hopelessly false. And this danger grows in the measure that we practise repressions."

Elsewhere he has given an example of this danger—the Nazi cult of collective forces, of tribal gods, of men of demonic power. Nobody saw the significance of the rise of Nazism as clearly as Jung; nobody gave such clear warnings. His voice was ignored and afterwards his clear understanding of the situation was misconstrued as a sympathetic attitude towards it! The physician must be the carrier of the disease he would cure; the prophet must be stoned for daring to prophesy war and pestilence!

But to return to the dream. Jung as a scientist has not found it possible to explain the unconscious by the rigid laws of causality. It had been Freud's tendency to regard the unconscious as an empty pit or "cauldron" which each individual gradually fills as he grows up and adapts himself to a hostile world. Envy and hatred of the father, sexually possessive feelings towards the mother, love of its own excrements— these and many other frustrated instincts are the material out of which the unconscious, according to Freud, is principally fashioned. His illusion, according to Jung, was to believe that what had in this manner been filled, could, by some technique of analysis, be emptied! It is true that towards the end of his career Freud began to speak of man's archaic heritage, of "inherited trends", which could not be got rid of, of "some primeval phylogenetic experience" which each child is destined to repeat. But that concession was not supported by any extensive evidence that Freud cared to publish, and it is doubtful if he would ever have come to regard the unconscious as possessing "possibilities of wisdom that are completely closed to consciousness", as having at its disposal "the wisdom of untold ages, deposited in the course of time and lying potential in the human brain". It was left to Jung to elaborate a theory of this kind, which he has called the theory of the archetype, and some explanation of this term is essential in any account of Jung's psychology.

We have already seen that in his first published case-history Jung was driven to the conclusion that the unconscious, in the elaboration of its fantasies, follows, as it were, certain well-worn tracks. There is some kind of pre-determined pattern which the individual unconscious falls into, like jelly into a mould. The fantasy, the process of fabulation, "sets" along defined lines. To this predetermined stress in the unconscious Jung gives the name *archetype*.

It is important to realize that the archetype is not a ready-made image. It is merely an inherited predisposition or tendency to fabricate definite types of imagery; certain lines of force along which the imagery in the unconscious will "automatically" arrange itself. It may be that the unconscious will "automatically" rely on certain symbols—the mother, the horse, the phallus, etc.; or that its dramatic constructions (our dreams) will follow the formulas we find embedded in ancient mythology. In any case, the evidence Jung derived from his own clinical experience, as well as from his reading in religious and mystical literature, anthropology, folklore, etc., convinced him of the existence of such patterns of symbolic expression, and a large part of his work consists of an elaboration and consideration of this hypothesis.

The division of the mental personality into two contrary forces—conscious and unconscious—corresponds with a polarity that runs throughout nature and history. The positive and negative fields of electro-magnetism, the male and female sexes, good and evil—everywhere we are confronted with pairs of opposites. The dialectic of the life process is based upon this fact, yet in our conscious practical life, we try to hide the fact. We think of ourselves as single in consciousness, of one sex, and generally as wholly good in intentions. But this illusion of unity does not correspond with the reality. Not only has psychotherapy proved that our mind is divided into levels or processes opposed to each other, but this opposition is expressed in recognizable ways. Such "ways of expression" are the archetypes, unknown and perhaps unknowable in their unconscious existence. Inasmuch as they determine the form taken by events in consciousness, they become perceptible. Among them we can distinguish two that are of universal significance. The first Jung has called the Shadow: it is the personification of all that we do not admit about ourselves, our "other aspects", our "dark brother", and since we do not like consciously to own this disreputable side of our nature, we think of it as outside ourselves, and we create images (archetypes) like Satan, or Caliban, or Mr. Hyde, or Adolf Hitler, to represent our other self. The process that Jung calls "individuation", a process of coming to terms with oneself and striking a balance among our conflicting impulses, is at first largely a question of becoming aware of our Shadow and of accepting this inevitable presence. We can make no progress towards mental health until we become fully conscious of this other self and accept it as part of the total reality of our being.

Another such archetype is the "soul-image", the reflection of the opposite sex which each of us, in varying degrees of intensity, carries in our unconscious. The male carries an "anima", or female image; the female an "animus" or male image. "Everyman carries his Eve in himself," says an old alchemical sentence. But in practice again we project the image—we seek its counterpart among our fellow human beings, and woe to the man or woman who makes a wrong choice! "Despite the fact that such a choice may seem to be as ideal as he feels it to be, it is perfectly possible in the long run that a man finds he has married his own worst weakness." "Every man carries within himself an eternal image of woman, not the image of this or that definite woman, but rather a definite feminine image. This image is fundamentally an unconscious, hereditary factor of primordial origin, and is engraven in the living system of man, a 'type' ('archetype') of all the experiences with feminine beings in the age-long ancestry of man . . . in short, an inherited psychical system of adaptation."

Jung took a further step beyond all contemporary psychology when he recognized in certain religious images of the past archetypes unconsciously designed to help the struggling soul towards fulfilment, or wholeness. These images, or *unifying symbols*, take different forms in different religions, but are all essentially the same. One of the most frequent images of this kind is the mandala, or "magic circle". In the East it is used as an aid to contemplation. Generally it consists of an intricate pattern in the form of a flower, a cross, or a wheel, with a tendency to four-fold arrangement. A Buddhist mandala, for example, will take the form of a highly stylized sacred building, with a figure of Shiva or some other divinity at the centre surrounded by an eight-leaved lotus. At the four cardinal points are the four gateways to knowledge and beyond this an enclosing circle, the horrors of the burial ground. In Christian iconography Christ is often represented within a circle or almond-shaped compartment, enclosed in a square whose spandrels are occupied by the symbols of the four Evangelists. The infinite variations of the Christian cross in Celtic, Caroligian and Gothic art are further illustrations of the expression of this archetypal symbol.

Another and more recent discovery of Jung's reveals the significance of ancient alchemy. The alchemists were apparently concerned with the transmutation of base metals into precious metals, for example, lead to gold; but in their secret writings and recipes, they used a symbolism which was derived from the unconscious and Jung has shown that this symbolism actually represents the transformation of the personality through the mixing and joining together of noble and base constituents, of elements drawn from the conscious and unconscious. The gold sought was not the substance which is "at the root of all evil", but rather philosophic gold, the elixir of life. In alchemical representations it becomes a symbol comparable with the Golden Flower of oriental mysticism, and alchemical experiments have their analogy in Yoga and other spiritual disciplines.

What all these researches lead to is an affirmation of religious symbolism, a proof of its necessity in the development of the psyche. At this point one should remember that Jung is first and foremost a scientist. His aim has never been to substantiate "religion"; it has been to make sick people well again, and in the clinical experience of "curing their souls", he has discovered that the symbol is not the arbitrary creation of mystics and poets, but a concrete psychological reality, as necessary to psychological health and wholeness as oxygen is to physical health and wholeness. The unconscious, in its general or collective aspect, is an organic system of such symbols, and we are only at the beginning of our understanding of its vast and complicated workings. It is permissible, for those who can make the leap into faith, to believe that these symbols are evidences of the living and transcendent God; but Jung himself has not, so far as we know, made that leap. He remains the scientist, the spectator *ab extra*, and though he may lead his patients to the threshold of the Church, the decision to cross or not to cross it must be their own. All that Jung shows to the patient (and in this sick world we are all potential patients) is that in one way or another we have to return to the Mother, to abandon our adolescent longing for independence, our protest against instinctual bonds, our intellectual pride. We have to learn that we are part of a process, a leaf on the Tree of Life, and that our freedom and happiness lies in the recognition of the bonds, visible and invisible, that bring to us the flowing sap. But the way back to integration, involving as it does a coming-to-terms with the collective psyche, is not easy, and is perhaps never wholly secure. It depends on a factor which Jung has not hesitated to call "moral"—on the recognition of a direction in life and on a certain faithfulness to oneself. "Being analysed" is no cure in itself—that way lies deception and self-delusion, and an opportunity for the clarlatan. Jung has always been severe with his patients. He does not promise to rid them of their neuroses, to banish their bad dreams, or even cure their complexes. On the contrary, these are the symptoms which the patient must learn to observe for himself: a psychic barometer to be read whenever he wants to know his mental climate. The art—and health is an art— lies in this reading, in this weather-wisdom.

Such a view of man's psyche has many repercussions in philosophy, and especially in political philosophy. It is true that Jung has repeatedly emphasized that re-integration is an individual process—it is up to each man to save his own soul.

But the diagnosis of our age that he has made leads to certain broad conclusions of a political nature, and Jung has not hesitated to express them. "We are living in times of great disruption," he has declared; "political passions are aflame, internal upheavals have brought nations to the brink of chaos, and the very foundations of our *Weltanschauung* are shattered. This critical state of things has such a tremendous influence on the psychic life of the individual that the doctor is bound to follow its effect on the individual psyche with more than usual attention. The storm of actual events does not only sweep down upon him from the great world outside; he feels the violence of its impact even in the quiet of his consulting-room and in the privacy of the medical consultation. As he has a responsibility towards his patients, he cannot afford to withdraw to the peaceful island of undisturbed scientific work, but must constantly descend into the arena of world events, in order to join in the battle of conflicting passions and opinions. Were he to remain aloof from the tumult, the calamity of his time would only reach him vaguely from afar, and his patients' suffering would find neither ear nor understanding."

Jung has realized, with every considerable psychologist of our time, that the crowd or the mass develops a psychological force of its own. In the crowd the individual loses his identity, not only physically, but also spiritually, and what merges, and emerges as crowd psychology, is the irrational side of the collective unconscious. We freely admit such a possibility when confronted with the barbarian horde, or the riotous mob. What we do not so readily recognize is that the individual, in those mass-organizations which we call the State, has dwindled away to mere nothingness. He has surrendered his power of decision, his social responsibility, and finds himself a rivet (not even a cog!) in a machine whose movements and direction he has no power to control. That might not matter if he could be assured that some exceptionally wise and gifted individuals were in control, but in effect every man is similarly riveted, similarly powerless, and what motivates the machine is a demonic force issuing directly from the collective unconscious. No other hypothesis can explain the release against mankind itself of the terrifying weapons of destruction now in the possession of world States.

Freud, as is well known, was wholly pessimistic about the future of mankind. The death instinct drives us on, and the only end is the universal destruction of life. But Jung does not agree with him. The unconscious, he says, does not believe in death. There is a *libido*, a general urge to life, and it is true that this urge can be split, so that it works against itself. But fundamentally it seeks to flow onwards, to gather force and intensity. That fundamental characteristic of the *libido* allows us to hope that mankind will become aware of the threat to its existence before it is too late. We must *dare* to hope, and it is the daring rather than the hope that will carry us through. But the means, for Jung, is still the integration of the individual personality. The group, the party, the nation, the union of nations, have no freedom of choice. Within such collectives, psychic powers work themselves out as if by an unconscious law of life. "There is set going a causally connected process that comes to rest only in catastrophe." The epoch, Jung thinks, calls for the liberating personality, "for the one who distinguishes himself from the inescapable power of collectivity . . . who lights a hopeful watchfire announcing to others that at least *one* man has succeeded in escaping from the fateful identity with the group soul".

This distinction between the leader who (like Hitler) is the expression of unconscious forces that are evil and demonic, and the leader who has stood apart and avoided the general panic, is perhaps easier to draw in theory than in practice. Jung admits the difficulty. "There are times in the history of the world (our own may be one of them) when something that is good must make way; what is destined to be better thus appears at first to be evil. This last sentence shows how dangerous it is even to touch on these problems, for how easy it would be, according to this, for evil to smuggle itself in by simply explaining that it is the potentially better!" But t he risk must be run, and Jung reminds us how, in myth and legend, the life of the infant hero is always threatened—the serpents and Hera threatened to destroy Hercules, and only by a miracle did Jesus escape from the slaying of the first-born in Bethlehem. Life would become meaningless if it were deprived of its tragic element, for it is danger and desperation that generate the intense awareness, the finer consciousness, that carry life to ever higher manifestations. The "way" to this new dimension of existence must be discovered. Each of the great religions has been a journey of exploration, and each has its symbol of the pilgrim's progress along this way. The Chinese call it *Tao*, and Jung often speaks with admiration of the wisdom of this ancient philosophy.

As we sat, on that day already mentioned, looking across the still lake, under the cloudless sky, Jung related the story of the Rain-maker, as told to him by Professor Richard Wilhelm, the famous Chinese scholar. There had been a terrible drought in Kiou Chou and a man from Shantung was sent for, of whom it was said that he could make rain. When he arrived he asked for a little hut to be built for him outside the town. When it was ready he retired into it and asked not to be disturbed. He stayed in his hut for three days and three nights and on the morning of the fourth day a snow-storm broke out such as had never been seen at this time of the year.

When Wilhelm heard this he went out to the man and asked him how he had set about to make that snow. The man answered that he had not made it. It was simply that he came from Shantung where everything was right. Here in Kiou Chou heaven and earth were separated, everything was wrong and it took him three days to become right again himself. But as soon as he was right rain or snow would naturally fall.

Tao, Jung explained, is meaningful coincidence in time—when heaven and earth are working together properly, then things are all right, everything has its due place and function.

Like most Chinese stories, at first it seems too simple and pointless, but the meaning grows as we meditate upon it. The inactivity it seems to advocate is merely external. The invisible spheres revolve, and at a certain point in time, they coincide, and at that moment we find ourselves in harmony with nature. At such times things happen as we wish them to happen: we are instruments of the divine power, vessels filled with grace. That is the full meaning of *integration* in Jung's psychology, and he believes that the world will be saved, if it is saved at all, by integrated personalities.

Jung is serene in his retirement. I mentioned the attacks that had been made on him in America and Great Britain, but he dismissed them with a smile. It is always the fate of a pioneer, he said, to be misunderstood, to be reviled. And there is still work to be done, mysteries to be solved, darkness to be dispelled. There is no trace of anger or of scorn in his reaction. We have moved into the garden in the course of our long talk, and he now sits in the cool shade of a tree, more than ever like a Chinese sage. We listen to the plash of oars on the water, to distant voices, and we fall silent, feeling that here too is a meaningful coincidence. It seems as if earth, sky and water had been listeners, too, and the unity of the impression is the unity of perfect sympathy, of the Sympatheia that, according to the old Stoics, draws all elements together, in peace and harmony.

24
'The Prelude'

ONE WINTRY EVENING, a hundred and forty years ago, a party of friends, deeply attached to each other, was gathered round the fire at a farmhouse near Coleorton, in Leicestershire. There were present William Wordsworth and his family, his sister Dorothy, his wife's sister, Sarah Hutchinson, Coleridge, and Coleridge's son, Hartley. To this group Wordsworth read, for the first time, his great poem on "the growth of an individual mind", as he then described it. Everyone present was deeply moved . . . Coleridge so much so that he retired to his room and in the middle of the night composed those lines beginning:

> O Friend! O Teacher! God's great gift to me!
> Into my heart have I received that Lay
> More than historic, that prophetic Lay
> Wherein (high theme by thee first sung aright)
> Of the foundations and the building up
> Of a Human Spirit thou hast dared to tell
> What may be told, to the understanding mind
> Revealable . . .

They had listened to

> An Orphic song indeed,
> A song divine of high and passionate thoughts
> To their own music chaunted!

and when it was finished—when, said Coleridge addressing Wordsworth in this poem, when

> Thy long sustained Song finally closed,
> And thy deep voice had ceased—yet thou thyself
> Wert still before my eyes, and round us both
> That happy vision of beloved faces—
> Scarce conscious, and yet conscious of its close
> I state, my being blended in one thought
> (Thought was it? or aspiration? or resolve?)
> Absorbed, yet hanging still upon the sound—
> And when I rose, I found myself in prayer.

The poem which Wordsworth read to his friends in January, 1807, was not to be published until the year of the poet's death, 1850, and it was then given the title *The Prelude or Growth of a Poet's Mind; an Autobiographical Poem*. It is said that Mrs. Wordsworth invented the title *The Prelude*, and as a title it is appropriate enough, considering the poem's origin, and the place it occupies in Wordsworth's work. Nine years before that first recitation of *The Prelude*, Wordsworth and Coleridge had discussed the possibility of Wordsworth composing a great philosophical poem, to be called *The Recluse, or Views on Man, Nature, and Society*. Coleridge suggested that Wordsworth "should assume the station of a man in mental repose, one whose principles were made up, and so prepared to deliver upon authority a system of philosophy. He was to treat man as man—a subject of eye, ear, touch, and taste, in contact with external nature, and informing the senses from the mind, and not compounding a mind out of the senses; then he was to describe the pastoral and other states of society, assuming something of the Juvenalian spirit as he approached the high civilization of cities and towns, and opening a melancholy picture of the present state of degeneracy and vice; thence he was to infer and reveal the proof of, and necessity for, the whole state of man and society being subject to, and illustrative of, a redemptive process in operation, showing how this idea reconciled all the anomalies, and promised future glory and restoration".

That grandiose conception was never to be realized. We have, as part of it, *The Prelude*, a poem of twelve Books and 7,883 lines, *The Excursion*, nine Books and 8,850 lines, and a noble fragment of 107 lines of *The Recluse* itself, which Wordsworth printed in his Preface to the first edition of *The Excursion*, "as a kind of Prospectus of the design and scope of the whole poem". In that same Preface he refers to the unpublished *Prelude* in these terms:

Several years ago, when the Author retired to his native mountains, with the hope of being able to construct a literary Work that might live, it was a reasonable thing that he should take a review of his own mind, and examine how far Nature and Education had qualified him for such employment. As subsidiary to this preparation, he undertook to record in verse, the origin and progress of his own powers, as far as he was acquainted with them. That Work, addressed to a dear Friend, most distinguished for his knowledge and genius, and to whom the Author's Intellect is deeply indebted, has been long finished; and the result of the investigation which gave rise to it was a determination to compose a philosophical poem, containing views of Man, Nature, and Society; and to be entitled, *The Recluse,* as having for its principal subject the sensations and opinions of a poet living in retirement. The preparatory poem is biographical, and conducts the history of the Author's mind to the point when he was emboldened to hope that his faculties were sufficiently matured for entering upon the arduous labour which he had proposed to himself; and the two Works have the same kind of relation to each other, if he may so express himself, as the ante-chapel has to the body of a gothic church.

Admittedly, all this sounds a little pompous, even portentous. But we shall never understand Wordsworth, much less sympathize with him, unless we realize that he regarded himself as "a dedicated Spirit". At the conclusion of one of the most mangificent passages in *The Prelude*, in which he had recalled "one particular hour" of his youth, a moment of unreflective ecstasy, he breaks off to address Coleridge in these words:

> Ah! need I say, dear Friend, that to the brim
> My heart was full; I made no vows, but vows
> Were then made for me; bond unknown to me
> Was given, that I should be, else sinning greatly,
> A dedicated Spirit. On I walk'd
> In blessedness, which even yet remains.

No great poet has ever taken himself so seriously as Wordsworth. His whole life reveals an obstinate, at times a selfish determination to fulfil his poetic destiny. It was perhaps this very determination, involving as it did seclusion and a limitation of experience, which explains Wordsworth's failure to achieve his great plan. Poetry depends, to an extent not always appreciated by poets themselves, on the maintenance of normal contacts, on the daily stimulus of unanticipated events. *The Recluse* was not the happiest title for a poem on man, nature and society, nor was "retirement" of the prolonged kind which actually occurred the right condition. We must realize that when he set out on his great self-imposed task, Wordsworth hoped to complete the whole of the great philosophical poem he envisaged in less than two years. In the Advertisement which precedes the 1850 edition of *The Prelude* it is stated that this part of the plan "was commenced in the beginning of the year 1799, and completed in the summer of 1805". That statement is not quite accurate. Professor Garrod has proved that the Preamble to the poem was written in September, 1795. The first draft of *The Prelude* as a whole was complete by 1806; *The Excursion* was not published until 1814;

and as late as 1824 Dorothy writes as though *The Recluse* were
still to be regarded as "work in progress", though she says
that her brother "seems to feel the task so weighty that he
shrinks from beginning with it". But Professor de Selincourt
was probably right in suspecting that by this time Wordsworth himself knew that he would never go on with *The
Recluse*. What had been conceived as a two-years' task had
petered out after nearly thirty years of slow, frustrated effort.

It was "*comparatively* with the *former* poem", that is to say,
with *The Prelude*, that *The Excursion* disappointed Coleridge's
expectations, and in his letter to Wordsworth about *The Excursion* (written reluctantly nine months after that poem had
been published) Coleridge conjectured that its inferiority
"might have been occasioned by the influence of self-estab-
lished convictions having given to certain thoughts and expressions a depth and force which they had not for readers in
general". Later critics did not seek any such subtle explanations: a few passages excepted, which were of earlier composition, they found the poem desperately dull. But it is only
against the achievement of *The Prelude* that this judgment
becomes of critical interest. I do not wish to engage in a
defence of *The Excursion*, which stands in relation to *The
Prelude* very much as *Paradise Regained* stands to *Paradise Lost*.
The failure is one of organic continuity. The later poem was,
as Coleridge said, "to have sprung up as the tree" from "the
ground plot and roots" which had been prepared in *The
Prelude*, and as far as there was the same sap in both, they
should have formed one complete whole, each revealing, for
its distinct purpose, "the vital spirit of a perfect form". Well,
let us admit that *The Excursion* has no organic power of this
kind: let us return to the groundwork of *The Prelude*, to that
"Orphic song" which Coleridge could praise without reservations, and which remains, a hundred and fifty years after its

conception, a poem unique in kind and unsurpassed in its particular brand of eloquence.

The poem is unique, not in its form, but in its subject-matter. In form it is an epic, like *Paradise Lost*, but the subject is the poet's own mind—not the poet himself, as eponymous hero, but the poet as dedicated spirit—as a spirit dedicated to a task for which, without scrupulous self-examination and self-assessment, he might not deem himself sufficiently disciplined, sufficiently worthy. Wordsworth admitted that "it was a thing unprecedented in literary history, that a man should talk so much about himself", but he added, in perfect sincerity, that it was not self-conceit that induced him to do this, but real humility. He began the work, he said, because he was unprepared to treat any more arduous subject, and diffident of his own powers. At the same time he confesses, in the first Book of *The Prelude*, that when in this way he makes "rigorous inquisition" of himself, "the report is often cheering": for, he continues,

> I neither seem
> To lack that first great gift, the vital soul,
> Nor general Truths, which are themselves a sort
> Of Elements and Agents, Under-powers,
> Subordinate helpers of the living mind.
> Nor am I naked in external things,
> Forms, images, nor numerous other aids
> Of less regard, though won perhaps with toil,
> And needful to build up a Poet's praise.

This is self-confident enough, but a little later he confesses that when it comes to his "last and favourite aspiration",

> some philosophic song
> Of truth that cherishes our daily life

that then

> from this awful burthern I full soon
> Take refuge and beguile myself with trust
> That mellower years will bring a riper mind
> And clearer insight.

Already, in 1805, he had made a very shrewd analysis of his powers and capacities, of the psychological inhibitions that would defeat his greater purpose:

> Thus from day to day
> I live, a mockery of the brotherhood
> Of vice and virtue, with no skill to part
> Vague longing that is bred by want of power,
> From paramount impulse not to be withstood,
> A timorous capacity from prudence;
> From circumspection, infinite delay.
> Humility and modest awe themselves
> Betray me, serving often for a cloak
> To a more subtle selfishness, that now
> Doth lock my functions up in blank reserve,
> Now dupes me by an over-anxious eye
> That with intrusive restlessness beats off
> Simplicity and self-presented truth.

Wordsworth must undoubtedly be described as an egoist—romantic artists commonly are. But do not let us make the mistake of assuming that he was naïve. He is as subtle as Shakespeare in his psychological penetration, and like Shakespeare he was, as Coleridge pointed out, always the *spectator ab extra*—the merciless, objective analyst. From this point of view, the poetic work that comes nearest to *The Prelude* is *Hamlet*.

I should now perhaps say something about the structure of *The Prelude*. It is in narrative form, divided into books which represent various stages in the growth of the poet's mind. But the narrative is interspersed with reflective passages which sometimes, as in the case of Book VIII (entitled *Retrospect*) and Book XIV (*The Conclusion*), extend over the greater part of that section. The epic character of the poem is undoubtedly diluted by such philosophic musings. Various versions of the poem survive. These were collected and collated by the late Ernest de Selincourt, the greatest Wordsworthian scholar of our time, and his edition of *The Prelude* makes a comparison of the texts very easy. The conclusion that Professor de Selincourt came to after a careful study of the two main texts was that from a poetic or technical point of view, the final version, all things considered, is undoubtedly the better one. "Weak phrases are strengthened and its whole texture is more closely knit," he says, and he adds: "The 1805 text . . . leaves often the impression of a man writing rapidly, thinking aloud or talking to his friend without waiting to shape his thought into the most concise and telling form, satisfied for the moment if he can put it into metre by inverting the prose order of the words."

If our schools and universities were to take an interest in the writing of poetry (they generally confine themselves to its history and classification) then a study of the evolution of the text of *The Prelude* would be of incomparable value. There is no document in the whole of our literature which has so much to teach the practising poet. Take, for example, the use of the verb "to be" as an auxiliary. The auxiliary is always to be avoided in poetry because it produces a softening or dimming of the statement made. 'The gentleness of heaven *is on* the sea' was the original reading of a line in one of Wordsworth's best-known sonnets ("It is a beauteous evening, calm and free"). Wordsworth later altered this line to read: "The gentleness of heaven *broods o'er* the sea", and there is an obvious gain in vividness. In the same way, in *The Prelude*, to make use of an example given by de Selincourt, the descrip-

tion of the morning of Wordsworth's poetic dedication
originally ran:

> Magnificent
> The morning was, in memorable pomp,
> More glorious than I ever had beheld.
> The Sea was laughing at a distance; all
> The solid Mountains were as bright as clouds.

"Many a poet," observes de Selincourt, "would have rested
satisfied with those lines as they stood, but no one can miss the
gain in strength and vividness effected by the simple changes:

> Magnificent
> The morning rose, in memorable pomp,
> Glorious as e'er I had beheld—in front
> The sea lay laughing at a distance; near,
> The solid mountains shone, bright as the clouds.

The difference is simple—the substitution, for "was" and
"were", of the active verbs "rose", "lay" and "shone".

In this way, and in the revision of many other details of
composition, the whole text of *The Prelude* was cleaned up
between 1805 and 1850, and we cannot but agree with de
Selincourt that "the cumulative effect of such changes, each
one perhaps trifling in itself, cannot easily be over-estimated".
Not all the changes, even of diction, are for the better—there
is a tendency to substitute abstract and grandiloquent phrases
for simple words—thus "thought and quietness" becomes
"meditative peace" and even a "woman" is dignified as a
"female". Other changes are due to a shift in intention—the
original version was addressed directly to Coleridge and had
some of the intimacy of a confession made to a friend; the

final version, though it does not abandon this device, is much more circumspect and discreet. On balance, we have to conclude with Professor de Selincourt that the ideal text of *The Prelude* would follow no single manuscript, and we must each construct, from the material supplied by de Selincourt, our ideal text.

The Prelude is written in blank verse, the unrhymed metre that Shakespeare habitually used, and Milton in his great epics. It is usual to compare Wordsworth's diction with Milton's, and there are a few passages of striking similarity. But in general Wordsworth's diction bears little resemblance either to the rich imaginative texture of Shakespeare's verse, or to the baroque pomp of Milton's. We must remember that Wordsworth's declared intention was to use in his poetry "a selection of the real language of men in a state of vivid sensation". Coleridge, with his usual perspicacity, found a parallel in "well-languaged Daniel".

Samuel Daniel is still, as he was in Coleridge's day, a "causelessly neglected poet", but we know that Wordsworth admired him greatly. His contemporaries thought him prosaic, and most succeeding critics have agreed with them. Coleridge thought his style and language "just such as any very pure and manly writer of the present-day—Wordsworth, for example—would use; it seems quite modern in comparison with the style of Shakespeare". He further characterized this style as "the neutral ground of prose and verse . . . common to both", but such a neutral style is not negligible. On the contrary, Daniel's diction, wrote Coleridge in *Biographia Literaria,* "bears no mark of time, no distinction of age, which has been, and as long as our language shall last, will be so far the language of the today and for ever, as that it is more intelligible to us, than the transitory fashions of our own

particular age". As an example of this neutral style in Wordsworth, Coleridge gave the famous description of skating from
the first book of *The Prelude*:

> So through the darkness and the cold we flew,
> And not a voice was idle; with the din
> Smitten, the precipices rang aloud;
> The leafless trees and every icy crag
> Tinkled like iron; while far distant hills
> Into the tumult sent an alien sound
> Of melancholy not unnoticed, while the stars
> Eastward were sparkling clear, and in the west
> The orange sky of evening died away.

That is the neutral style—no "multitudinous seas incar-
nadine": no Hallelujahs from the Empyrean rung, but simple
words in natural order, creating, we do not know why, a
curiosa felicitas, a subtle beauty beyond analysis.

Coleridge distinguished several other virtues in Wordsworth's poetic diction: I will only mention one further one—
what he called "meditative pathos—a union of deep and
subtle thought with sensibility; a sympathy with man as man;
the sympathy indeed of a contemplator, rather than a fellow-
sufferer or co-mate . . . but a contemplator, from whose view
no difference of rank conceals the sameness of the nature;
no injuries of wind or weather, or toil, or even of ignorance,
wholly disguise the human face divine". "In this mild and
philosophic pathos", Coleridge continues, "Wordsworth
appears to me without a compeer. Such he *is*: so he *writes*."
This meditative pathos pervades the whole poem, but a
specific instance of it will be found in the story of Vaudracour
and Julia.

The philosophy which emerges from this great exercise in
self-examination is a philosophy—or rather, a philosophic
faith—that has some relevance to our present quandary and

incessant heart-searchings. Coleridge once—it was in their
early days—characterized Wordsworth as a "semi-atheist",
and in spiritual matters he did indeed question some of the
complacent assumptions of his contemporaries. But the more
we ponder that faith of his, and contrast it with nihilism on
the one hand and intolerant dogma on the other, the more
appealing and satisfying it becomes. Wordsworth has also
been called a pantheist; that, too, is a misleading label. He was
essentially a humanist—not a sceptical humanist like Montaigne, but a pious humanist, like Spinoza or Erasmus. The
poet, he said,

> hath stood
> By Nature's side among the men of old
> And so shall stand for ever.

And Nature was valued by the poet because it has the power
to "consecrate", "to breathe Grandeur upon the very
humblest face of human life".

This faith is so clearly expressed in the two concluding
books of *The Prelude* that it is difficult to understand how so
many misconceptions of Wordsworth's philosophical position
could have arisen. It is true that the poem is not all plain
sailing—no poet has written 8,000 lines without lapses into
flatness or obscurity. I doubt if Wordsworth is ever hopelessly
obscure, but he could be dull. When he attempts the description of scenes for which he has no innate sympathy—as in
the account of his residence in London—he can be painfully
stilted, and at times grotesque. But the style is the man himself, a man, like most of us, of imperfect sympathies. I do not
think we can say with Coleridge that Wordsworth does to
all thoughts and *all* objects

> add that gleam,
> The light that never was, on sea or land,
> The consecration, and the poet's dream.

But he added that light to the widest, the most entrancing landscape in English literature. He did not people that landscape with the vivid figures of a Shakespeare, nor shake its shores with Milton's "trumpet-tones of harmony". Wordsworth is by no means devoid of imaginative sympathy, and he had a perfect comprehension of the simple folk of his native fells. But the characteristic figure in his landscape is a Solitary, a Wanderer, a man for whom every common sight has significance, who from a fund of natural wisdom can communicate perfect understanding. The best description of such a figure is his own, in *The Excursion*:

> Early had he learned
> To reverence the volume that displays
> The mystery, the life which cannot die;
> But in the mountains did he *feel* his faith.
> All things, responsive to the writing, there
> Breathed immortality, revolving life,
> And greatness still revolving; infinite:
> There littleness was not; the least of things
> Seemed infinite; and there his spirit shaped
> Her prospects, nor did he believe—he *saw*.

A spirit that *sees*, a faith that is *felt*—Wordsworth's uniqueness as a poet lies in his affirmation of this correspondency between subject and object, between existence and transcendence, between the many and the one, between Man and God. It is a faith that inspired him to write some of the greatest poetry in our language, poetry that has lost none of its significance with the passing of a hundred years.

26

Barbara Hepworth

IN APPROACHING the work of any contemporary artist one has always to dispose of the tiresome question of influences—tiresome because, being a contemporary question, it is bound to involve those not very creditable emotions we generally hide under the French phrase *amour propre*. To the objective student of art these emotions seem unreasonable, for the whole history of art is a close texture of such influences, and those who are most free from them are certainly not the greatest artists. One might even risk the generalization that the great artist emerges precisely at the point where the greatest number of strands meet, to create, not a confusion, but a pattern of universal significance. Michelangelo is such a *nodus*, and in our own time, Picasso.

Barbara Hepworth has mentioned the main influences in her own development, and I shall comment on them presently. But she might have mentioned more, for by quite consciously situating herself in the historical tradition of sculpture, she allowed her roots to strike deep into the past, as well as to spread widely in the present. One might as well begin with the Aphrodite of Knidos, for a *Torso* carved by Barbara Hepworth at the age of twenty-five is conceivably a derivative of the lost masterpiece of Praxiteles. One must mention African tribal sculpture, Mexican sculpture, Egyptian sculpture and certainly the sculpture of the Italian Renaissance, for the secrets of all these styles were absorbed in an apprenticeship that was as profound as it was passionate. But an artist must finally submit to the strongest influence of all, which is the influence of one's age—that insistent and all-pervasive demand

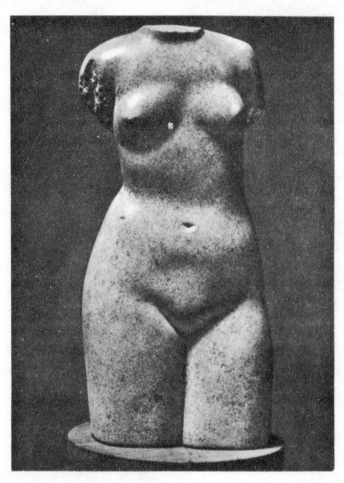

BARBARA HEPWORTH: *Torso* 1928

for an idiom that will express the dumb consciousness of a generation resolved to find its own answer to the enigmas of existence. In this situation the artists of a period are the language-makers, inventing visual symbols for the hitherto unexpressed intuitions of an evolving humanity—but expressing them in a *common* language, a language with a logical syntax and a flexible articulation.

Barbara Hepworth has been a contemporary, a compatriot and fellow student of Henry Moore. Five years older than her, he was five years nearer to these influences which were to be their common source of inspiration. Until about 1935 they are tacking against the same wind, and their courses though separate are often parallel. Then the wind drops and they move out into the open sea, each to pursue a different direction. The metaphor is commonplace, but capable of elaboration (I am thinking of the common dangers they encountered, of the signals they exchanged). But there was, from the beginning, an innate difference of temperament. This is well illustrated by the statements which they both contributed to *Unit One*, the manifesto of a group of English architects, sculptors and painters published in 1934. Barbara Hepworth evokes a landscape, speaks of "the relationship and the mystery that makes such loveliness", of "projecting her feeling about it into sculpture"; of "building up a new mythology" and of "an impersonal vision *individualized* in the particular medium". It is a "sense of mystery" that gives her the power to project "some universal or abstract vision of beauty" into her plastic medium. If we turn to Henry Moore's statement we find a similar concern for nature, but no mention of mystery or loveliness, but an explicit disclaimer of beauty ("Beauty, in the later Greek or Renaissance sense, is not the aim of my sculpture.") He goes to nature for a vocabulary of form—"form-knowledge experience", he calls it;

and gives as the aim of his art, vitality. "Between beauty of expression and power of expression there is a difference of function. The first aims at pleasing the senses, the second has a spiritual vitality which for me is more moving and goes deeper than the senses."

The two ideals, distinct in their essence and expression, are denoted by the words "beauty" and "power", and these two words express the divergence that was to take place in the development of the two sculptors. It is possible to argue that these qualities, in a work of art, can never be wholly separated; there is power in beauty ("the terrible crystal"), and there is beauty in power (Blake's "tyger burning bright"). But if these qualities are sufficiently differentiated as ideals, it must not then be supposed that the one is sentimental or feminine, the other realistic and masculine. What one might venture to suggest is that they represent those two components of the psyche which Jung has differentiated as the *anima* and the *animus*. According to this hypothesis, we all carry in us an image of the other sex, "the precipitate of all human experience pertaining to the opposite sex", and as we tend to project everything that is latent and undifferentiated in the psyche, man projects his "Eve" and woman her "Adam". But the projection of images from the unconscious is never direct (except in dream or trance); the woman has to disguise her animus in feminine attributes (loveliness), the man his anima in masculine attributes (vitality, virility). In each case the secret power of the projected image comes from this state of tension, this sexual ambiguity or dialectic.

The dialectic which Barbara Hepworth was to develop from 1934–5 onwards was between the antitheses of Geometry and Grace (one is tempted to use Simone Weil's terms Gravity and Grace, especially as she always conceived gravity as a geometrical or mechanical phenomenon). It may be objected that geometry is not necessarily graceless, but this is to confuse grace, which is lively, rhythmical, *mouvmenté*, and essentially labile and organic, with proportion, which is measured, mathematical or algebraic, and essentially non-vital. To infuse the formal perfection of geometry with the vital grace of nature—that might be taken as a description of the ideal which Barbara Hepworth now began to desire and achieve. The basic studies generally taking the form of drawings, are geometric. But when we compare the finished sculptures with such preparatory drawings, we see immediately that a subtle but substantial change has taken place. There is a deviation towards organic form. The form, though still geometric, seems to have a vital function, as though a perfect geometrical spiral has been transformed into an organic shell, a *nautilus pompilius*. As Dr. Johnson observed (it is a quotation used by D'Arcy Thompson at the beginning of *Growth and Form*): "The mathematicians are well acquainted with the difference between pure science, which has to do only with ideas, and the application of its laws to the use of life, in which they are constrained to submit to the imperfections of matter and the influence of accident." (*Rambler*, May 5, 1750.) The sculptor is not constrained to submit to the imperfections of matter, but rather to its limitations—to its tensile strength, its texture or toughness; and what Johnson calls "the influence of accident" becomes, in the artistic process, the influence of the artist's own organism—the sense of vitality, of change, of growth. One might say that space is transformed by time, but that is too abstract a formula; we should say rather that idea, in becoming material mass, is transformed by the human pulse, by vibrations that spring from the heart and are controlled by the nerves of a living and creative being.

In the formulation and development of this dialectic Barbara Hepworth was aided by two artists who worked in close touch with her for a number of years—Ben Nicholson and Naum Gabo. The closer influence—that of Ben Nicholson—was no doubt the deeper influence. He himself had been influenced—not so much directly, as idealistically—by Piet Mondrian, and the ideal which all these artists share is one which has become known under the confusing name of "abstraction". Abstraction was logical enough as a term for those compositions which were derived, or abstracted, from the natural object—the various stages of cubism were stages in abstraction. The term became ambiguous once the artist began with a non-figurative or geometrical intuition of form, and either clothed this with features reminiscent of the natural object (Juan Gris), or pursued the intuition until all naturalistic reference had been excluded. But after a certain stage in his development Mondrian, and Gabo from the beginning of his Constructivist period, began with a purely formal concept, and what they then create, as an objective work of art, has no reference whatsoever to naturalistic forms—it is a "new reality".

The daring originality of this attempt—daring from both an artistic and a philosophical point of view—has not yet been sufficiently appreciated by the critics of modern art. It is not only assumed by these artists that they can produce, by a subjective mental process, images which have no reference to the natural world but which nevertheless are logically coherent (in the sense that they can be communicated to other people), but even that these images express an essential reality which is beyond, or in some sense superior to, the reality of appearances. It is as if the artist were a demi-god, capable of creating a new satellite, a world dependent on this world but not of it; a new world. It is not a question of creating a pleasing pattern (for which reason all objections to this type of art based on its merely decorative function are beside the point):

232

BARBARA HEPWORTH: *Pelagos* 1946

it is a question of origination, of what Heidegger calls *Stiftung* (establishment). To quote Gabo: "I am constantly demanding from myself and keep on calling to my friends, not to be satisfied with that gratifying arrangement of elemental shapes, colours and lines for the mere gratification of arrangement; I demand that they shall remain only means of conveying a well-organized and clearly defined image—not just some image, any image, but a new and constructive image by which I mean that which by its very existence as a plastic vision should provoke in us the forces and the desires to enhance life, assert it and assist its further development."[1]

Abstract art, like realistic art, is always in danger of degenerating into academicism. It fails to renew its forces at the source of all forms, which is not so much nature as the vital impulses which determine the evolution of life itself. For that reason alone it may be suggested that an alternation between abstraction and realism is desirable in any artist. This does not mean that abstract art should be treated merely as a preparatory exercise for realistic art. Abstract art exists in its own rights. But the change-over from one style to another, from realism to abstraction and from abstraction to realism, need not be accompanied by any deep psychological process. It is merely a change of direction, of destination. What is constant is the desire to create a reality, a coherent world of vital images. At one extreme that "will to form" is expressed in the creation of what might be called *free* images, so long as we do not assume that freedom implies any lack of aesthetic discipline; and at the other extreme the will to form is expressed in a selective affirmation of some aspect of the organic world—notably as a heightened awareness of the vitality or

[1]"On Constructive Realism", *Three Lectures on Modern Art*, by Katherine S. Dreier, James Johnson Sweeney and Naum Gabo. New York, 1949, p. 83.

grace of the human figure. Some words of Barbara Hepworth's express this antithesis perfectly: "Working realistically replenishes one's *love* for life, humanity and the earth, Working abstractedly seems to release one's personality and sharpen the perceptions, so that in the observation of life it is the wholeness or inner intention which moves one so profoundly: the components fall into place, the detail is significant of unity."

A new and constructive image which provokes in us a desire to enhance life, assert it, and assist its further development—there we have the definition of the kind of work of art which a sculptor like Barbara Hepworth tries to create. Whether the emotions before such a work of art are *sui generis* and distinct from the emotions evoked by a classical work of art—say the Aphrodite of Knidos—must still be discussed. We need not refer to a Roman copy of Praxiteles' work—let us make the adequate comparison of the *Torso* already mentioned and a constructive image such as that presented in *Pelagos* (see Plate 6). There is no doubt that both images—the one realistic, the other abstract—convey life-enhancing values. *Pelagos* conveys them directly: the wood is carved into a tense form which suggests the unfolding point of life itself (as in a fern frond, or a spiral shell; or the tense coil of a snake). By duplicating the point of growth in a screw-like torsion an infinitely prolonged rhythm is created, but held in momentary stability by the strings connecting the two terminations. The experience of the spectator is purely emphatic —that is to say, our senses are projected into the form, fill it and partake of its organization. If we live with such a work of art it becomes a *mandala*, an object which in contemplation confers on the troubled spirit a timeless serenity. To object that such a state of passive serenity is not "life-enhancing" is to miss the whole significance of art, which is not a stimulus to biological vitality so much as to that apprehending consciousness or cosmic awareness upon which life itself finally depends.

The directness of such an aesthetic experience may now be compared with the indirectness of the experience conveyed by the *Torso*. One should perhaps first dismiss, as irrelevant, the sexual appeal of this particular work (or of others like it). It is not that its sexual appeal is to be despised; but one does not begin to appreciate a work of art with the aesthetic sensibilities until one has set it apart from actuality. This is what Susanne Langer has called "the primary illusion" in art—the form must be closed and must exist in itself and for itself. "The work of art has to be uncoupled from all realistic connections and its appearance made self-sufficient in such a way that one's interest does not tend to go beyond it."[1] It may be that what one might call the *duplicity* of representational art has been a necessary stage in the social evolution of art; and it may be that socially speaking many of us are not ready to dispense with "realistic connections" in a work of art; but at least let us all realize that these values are secondary and unrelated to the perceptual experience of form. This is not to separate art from life, or the artistic experience from the sexual experience of any other kind of sensuous experience; on the contrary, it is merely to distinguish, for unalloyed enjoyment, "the pattern of vitality, sentience, feeling, and emotion". The analogy of music may help the reader at this point.

Having, I hope, made this distinction clear we may return to a consideration of the new plastic image, its origins and functions. We have seen that according to Gabo the image is of intuitive origin. It is a projection from the visualizing con-

[1] "Abstraction in Science and Abstraction in Art", by Susanne K. Langer. *Essays in Honor of Henry M. Sheffer.* New York (Liberal Arts Press), 1951, p. 180.

sciousness, from the *imagination* (the image-making faculty), and though one must suppose that this function is only possible to a mind that has had normal visual or tactile experience (experience of natural objects), the image, in Gabo's case, is always "mentally constructed".

The process is not so clearly defined in the case of Barbara Hepworth. Obviously she sometimes begins with geometrical constructions (generally in the form of preliminary drawings) and modifies these vitalistically in the process of transforming them to a sculptural mass. But equally obviously she sometimes begins from a life-study, and many of her forms suggest, however indirectly, naturalistic prototypes. In a few instances she gives a naturalistic emphasis to an otherwise abstract form by the addition of a naturalistic detail. This, in my opinion, is an unhappy compromise. I can perfectly well understand a decision not to follow Gabo into a world of mental construction unrelated to immediate visual experiences; but having chosen to remain in the world of organic symbolism, it was surely unnecessary to label the symbol with a representational motive. I admit that I myself in the past have spoken of a "counterpoint" of realistic and abstract motives—the kind of counterpoint which Klee practised so successfully, where there is a continuous interpenetration of organic feature and abstract form; but the naturalistic motives that occasionally get caught up in Klee's free fantasies are incidental, and not direct pointers to a perceptual image. It is partly, perhaps, a question of scale. The more monumental sculpture becomes, the less appropriate is such a "playful" emphasis on the perceptual image. We may admire the tact with which this counterpoint is always stated, but still retain a suspicion that it is a concession to a non-plastic sentiment of some kind.

Barbara Hepworth's greatest achievement, up to the pre-

sent, undoubtedly lies in those monumental carvings destined
for a civic setting—the *Contrapuntal Forms* commissioned for
the Festival of Britain and later erected in the new town
of Harlow, and the *Vertical Forms* commissioned for Hatfield
Technical College. The significance of such sculpture is more
than aesthetic—it is a social challenge. Modern sculpture (and
we might say the same of modern painting) has yet to assume
the functions and achieve the status of a public art, and unfortunately that will not depend on any specific efforts of the
sculptor. One must first reckon with a disunity of the arts,
and however willing the architect and town-planner may be
to co-operate with the sculptor, the fact remains that as artists
they have different origins, different ideals, and different social
functions. A unified plastic vision, embracing all the arts, is
a thing of the past. But even more detrimental to any social
acceptance of modern sculpture on a monumental scale is the
almost complete atrophy of plastic sensibility in the public
at large. The bored or busy eyes that contemplate these sculp-
tured monuments will only very rarely penetrate to their
secrets, to discover a pattern of vitality. Harwell may be a
"new town" but it is not ready for the impact of a "new
reality". All the more credit, it should be said, to those in
authority who have had the courage to mount those mono-
liths as advance guards to a new civilization.

I have known Barbara Hepworth throughout most of her
active career, and what has been astonishing and of some
general significance is the fact that she has remained a completely human person, not sacrificing either her social or her
domestic instincts, her feminine graces or sympathies, to some
hard notion of a career. This deserves emphasis because it is
often suggested (and the suggestion is often accepted) that an
artist must lead a monachal existence, denying himself if not

all human contacts, at least all human entanglements—what Cézanne called *les grappins*. Any consideration of the lives of typical "great" artists should have shown the absurdity of this idea. Art is a reflection, however indirect, of the basic human experiences, and all these daily tensions and conflicts, these surrenders and obsessions which seem at the time to distract the artist from his work are secretly replenishing the sources of his inspiration. The solitariness of the artist, so necessary for the intermittent flux of this inspiration, he must carry within himself; the artist is a man capable of being solitary in a crowd. The serenity of the artist is not achieved by isolation, but by the cultivation of those powers of attention which make him the spectator *ab extra* of the human scene.

The other factor in Barbara Hepworth's career which seems to me to be of particular significance is her devotion to the technique of carving. Somewhere I have called this a moral, and not an aesthetic prejudice, and I would still maintain that art must be judged by its results, and not by the means used to obtain those results. But the moral factor is not irrelevant in any total estimate of an artist's achievement. The act of carving is not only technically, but one might almost say "mystically" distinct from any other method of creating solid forms in space. Chinese mysticism makes much use of the symbol of the Uncarved Block; it represents the possibilities latent in the universe, to be released by contemplation, by mental "attention". The plastic images latent in that same block can only be released by similar disciplines—there is in art a law of compensation by which the greatest impression of ease is the effect of the highest degree of skill. It is not necessary to deny skill to the crafts of modelling clay or forging iron; but one does deny these materials the capacity for fully satisfying the full range of aesthetic sensibility. The heirarchy of materials is natural, related to profound aspects of human experience, to that nostalgia which ever seeks, in the flux of life, perenniality in its monuments.

27

Susanne Langer

GREAT BOOKS do not always take the world by storm; especially in philosophy they may lie neglected for many years before their significance becomes apparent. This may be due to their *novelty*, for we are always suspicious of new ideas that may upset our complacency; or to their *difficulty*, for most of us instinctively shy away from a book that obviously demands time and mental effort for its assimilation. And then, of course, there is the element of mere chance: an important work is neglected because it is in a difficult language, or is published in a small country. For these reasons Kierkegaard was neglected for nearly a century. In the case of Susanne Langer's *Philosophy in a New Key*, none of these reasons holds good. It was first published by the Harvard University Press in 1942, and was even issued, some time later, but only in the United States, in a cheap popular edition. What success such a recondite book had in that form I do not know; but similar books, such as Whitehead's *Adventures in Ideas*, have had a wide circulation in the same format. But Whitehead was already a famous name, and thousands of people with no specific interest in philosophy may be willing to spend a shilling or two to satisfy their curiosity about anything famous—"to see", as they might put it, "if they can see anything in it". But

Susanne Langer was an unknown name, and what fame has come to her in the past fifteen years has been due to the slow recognition of the unusual interest of her book.

I acquired *Philosophy in a New Key* as soon as it was published—by accident, for it came to me for review. I have to confess that I neither reviewed it nor returned it to the art magazine that had sent it to me with the query: Worth a review? The sub-title I must have read: "A Study in the Symbolism of Reason, Rite and Art"; the dedication to "Alfred North Whitehead, my great Teacher and Friend", should have aroused my interest; and then I probably glanced down the long analytical list of contents, and seeing chapter headings such as "The Logic of Signs and Symbols", and sectional headings such as "The Influence of Semantic Problems on Genetic Psychology", "The Logical Characteristics of Language", etc., I jumped to the conclusion that here was another of those teasing books on "the meaning of meaning" that would have little interest for the readers of an art magazine. The book found its way unread on to a shelf, and there it remained for about five years. I don't know what eventually impelled me to take up Susanne Langer's book again. Unread books on my shelves have a way of looking at me with an accusing eye. Perhaps unconsciously, in first glancing through its pages, I had absorbed a phrase or two, and these phrases had lingered as an irritant in my brain. Or perhaps, in my general reading, I had come across Susanne Langer's name more than once and had been prompted to attach some more definite significance to it. In any case, I began to read this neglected book, and gradually realized that it was something I had been waiting for for many years—one of those synoptic works which, by bringing together separate areas of knowledge, suddenly reveal the pattern of reality, and give a new meaning to all one's piecemeal explorations.

My first suspicion, that this was another essay in the meaning of meaning, was confirmed. Mrs. Langer's work branches off from the science of semantics, as it is called, to establish a new meaning of meaning. She begins by pointing out the steady divergence of philosophy and science during the past three or four hundred years. "The only philosophy," she writes, "that rose directly out of a contemplation of science is positivism, and it is probably the least interesting of all doctrines, an appeal to common sense against the difficulties of establishing metaphysical or logical 'first principles'." Some people profess to be satisfied with a system of sense-knowledge or fact-finding that leaves out of account, as stages already discarded in the advance of humanity, all non-physical spheres of interest, all those forms of art and ritual, of myth and religion, which for other people seem alone to make life worth living.

But meanwhile science itself, without the help of philosophy, has come to the surprising conclusion that our sense-data are primarily symbols, and it is this development that has provoked the new issue. "In all quietness," writes Mrs. Langer, "along purely rational lines, mathematics has developed just as brilliantly and vitally as any experimental technique, and, step by step, has kept abreast of discovery and observation and all at once, the edifice of human knowledge stands before us, not as a vast collection of sense reports, but as a structure of *facts that are symbols* and *laws that have their meanings*. A new philosophical theme has been set forth to a coming age: an epistemological theme, the comprehension of science. The power of symbolism is its cue, as the finality of sense-data was the cue of a former epoch."

A pre-occupation with symbolism is the new key in philosophy, and it is therefore very important to know what is meant by symbolism. As a matter of fact, as Mrs. Langer points out, there are two distinct conceptions of symbolism. She writes, "One leads to logic, and meets the new problems in theory of knowledge; and so it inspires an evaluation of science and a quest for certainty. The other takes us in the opposite direction—to psychiatry, the study of emotions, religion, fantasy, and everything but knowledge. Yet in both we have a central theme: the *human response*, as a constructive, not a passive thing. Epistemologists and psychologists agree that symbolization is the key to that constructive process, though they may be ready to kill each other over the issue of what a symbol is, and how it functions."

Before arriving at her own definition of symbolism, Mrs. Langer makes a thorough survey of previous definitions, but I must confine myself to what is original in her presentation. In the first place, however, it should perhaps be made clear that there is nothing non-scientific, irrational or mystical in Mrs. Langer's approach to the subject. It is true that she differs radically from the semanticists, according to whom thought begins and ends with language, including, of course, mathematical and scientific symbols. What is not a language with a scientific grammar, according to this point of view, is merely unanalysed feeling. Mrs. Langer, in common with certain philosophers such as Cassirer and Whitehead, maintains that the field of semantics (the science of meaning) is wider than language: that there are systems of symbolism, subject to their own logic, that constitute another mode of thought. In other words, there is both *discursive* thought (thought that begins and ends with language) and also *non-discursive* thought (thought that is expressed in non-linguistic forms). Visual forms, for example—lines, colours, proportions, etc.—"are just as capable of *articulation*, i.e. of complex combination, as words. But the laws that govern this sort of articulation are altogether different from the laws of syntax that govern language". They are non-discursive, and do not present their constituents successively, but simultaneously. And generally we may say that poetry, myth, ritual, the plastic arts and music, provide forms which in a purely sensory way constitute a *non-discursive symbolism*, "peculiarly suited to the expression of ideas that defy linguistic 'projection'". But this non-discursive symbolism remains within the realm of rationality; for though, as Mrs. Langer says, "the recognition of presentational symbolism as a normal and prevalent vehicle of meaning widens our conception of rationality far beyond the traditional boundaries, yet (it) never breaks faith with logic in the strictest sense".

We can put it this way: Feelings have definite forms—there is a pattern of sentience—and these forms or patterns become progressively articulate and clear in the course of individual and racial evolution. The Gestalt psychologists, on whom Mrs. Langer relies for some of her most pertinent evidence, have already shown that there is in our receptor apparatus an inherent tendency to organize the sensory field into "groups and patterns of sense-data, to perceive forms rather than a flux of light impressions . . . This unconscious appreciation of forms is the primitive root of all abstraction, which in turn is the keynote of rationality; so that it appears that the conditions of rationality lie deep in our pure animal experience—in our power of perceiving, in the elementary functions of our eyes and ears and fingers. Mental life begins with our mere physiological constitution". Or, as Mrs. Langer, who has a gift for the summary phrase, says: "A mind that works primarily with meanings must have organs that supply it primarily with forms." "Rationality is embodied in every mental act . . . it permeates the peripheral activities of the human nervous system, just as truly as the cortical functions." "Rationality is the essence of mind, and symbolic transformation its elementary process. It is a fundamental error, therefore, to recognize it only in the phenomenon of systematic, explicit reasoning. That is a mature and precarious product."

Mrs. Langer makes a good deal of use of the phrase "symbolic transformation". She needs it, not only for the processes of symbolic logic, but also to introduce the idea of the progressive evolution of systems of symbolism, such as language itself, such as ritual, myth, music, and art in general. She has a brilliant chapter on the origins and evolution of language, in which she adopts and develops the hypothesis put forward sixty years ago by J. Donovan in two articles contributed to the journal *Mind*. These articles were called "The Festal Origin of Human Speech", and they set out to demonstrate that ritual antedates language, and that song antedates speech. Once vocal sounds had acquired an expressive value and become representative, they still constituted a very primitive mode of communication until there arose a new principle of language which we now call *metaphor*. "One might say," says Mrs. Langer, in another of her aphoristic phrases, "that if ritual is the cradle of language, metaphor is the law of its life." "It is the power whereby language, even with a small vocabulary, manages to embrace a multimillion things; whereby new words are born and merely analogical meanings become stereotyped into literal definitions." And again, "Every new experience, or new idea about things, evokes first of all some metaphorical expression. As the idea becomes familiar, this expression 'fades' to a new literal use of the once metaphorical predicate, a more general use than it had before." Language as we use it in discursive reasoning, the practical, prosaic language of everyday logic and science, is metaphorical language devitalized, refined and split into easily combined elements. But at the root of it is the basic human act of symbolic presentation.

Mrs. Langer follows her chapter on language with an easier illustration of her thesis in ritual and myth. Here I think the essential point to emphasize is that "the birth of symbolic gesture from emotional and practical movement probably begot the whole order of ritual, as well as the discursive mode of pantomime. The recognition of vague, vital meanings in physical forms—perhaps the first dawn of symbolism—gave us our idols, emblems, and totems; the primitive function of dream permits our first envisagement of events. The momentous discovery of nature-symbolism, of the pattern of life reflected in natural phenomena, produced the first universal insights. Every mode of thought is bestowed on us, like a gift, with some new principle of symbolic expression . . . The origin of myth is dynamic, but its purpose is philosophical. It is the primitive phase of metaphysical thought, the first embodiment of *general ideas*." But beyond myth is a further transformation: "The highest development of which myth is capable is the exhibition of human life and cosmic order that epic poetry reveals . . . The epic is the first flower—or one of the first, let us say—of a new symbolic mode, the mode of *art*."

Philosophy in a New Key ends with a discussion of symbolic transformation in the art of music, and this discussion is the connecting link with Mrs. Langer's second book, *Feeling and Form* (1953), in which she extends her general theory to account for all forms of art and all art-forms. It is again a brilliant book, a little diffuse in structure, perhaps, but full of original observations expressed in a clear and expressive style. The range of reference is immense, and in at least two of the arts—music and drama—Mrs. Langer gives an impression of direct acquaintance with the creative process. Her handling of the plastic arts is not so convincing.

Mrs. Langer remains in this work primarily a philosopher, and she is therefore much concerned with definition—with the definition of art itself, and with the meanings we should attach to such words as expression, creation, symbol, import, intuition, vitality, and organic form. Most of her definitions can be related to a theory of symbolism which she has inherited from her master, Ernst Cassirer, and we need not be surprised, therefore, to discover that all the manifestations of art are to be comprehended by this theory. Art, that is to say, is a symbolic activity, and is to be distinguished from other symbolic activities by the nature of the material it symbolizes. Mrs. Langer has no doubt about the proper sphere of art's symbolizing activity—it is charged with "the creation of forms symbolic of human feeling".

Almost every term in this definition might be challenged. The notion of "creation", for example, is a cause for much perplexity. Mrs. Langer pays little attention to the possibility of unconscious motivation—though artists have often disclaimed the notion of originality and have spoken rather as if angels dictated to them. Even the word "human", which looks so innocent in the definition, is a little suspect—if the Pyramids are works of art, what *human* feeling do they symbolize? Mrs. Langer has a plate illustrating Stonehenge, but impressive as this monument is, especially at sunrise or sunset, the feeling it symbolizes is again not human. And is the word "feeling" itself adequate? Here one is somewhat baffled by the absence of any reference to a basic psychology—one does not know whether Mrs. Langer is using "feeling" in the sense, for example, in which it would have been used by William James, or in the quite different sense in which a psychologist like Jung would use the word. What range of somatic and psychic phenomena does it cover? If, as would seem to be the case, Mrs. Langer uses the word in its customary sense to indicate a subjective state of sensation, desire or emotion, then it is very doubtful if the definition would cover whole categories of works of art where what is symbolized by the work of art might more accurately be called an intuition. An intuition of what? In the case of architecture and of certain modern abstract paintings, it is an intuition of harmony, of a "good" *Gestalt*. The work of art symbolizes nothing but an intuitive apprehension of formal relationships. We may say the result is "pleasing", but Mrs. Langer spends a lot of time arguing that the intention of the artist is to present feelings not to enjoyment, but to conception. She does not share what Otto Baensch has described as "the erroneous opinion . . . that the percipient's delight and assent are the criteria of art". The significance of a work of art, be it a painting, a poem, a statue or a sonata, lies in its formal organization. Such form is not representational, nor is it merely sensational in its appeal. It is symbolic, and if we ask: Symbolic of what? the answer is: symbolic of the feeling it is designed to present. The work of art is not a stimulus to evoke feelings, nor a signal to announce them: it is a logical structure corresponding to the pattern of sentience, a form which the feeling fits. The form has the power to present the feeling, and by virtue of the form we apprehend or conceive the nature of the feeling.

Such finely articulated symbols cannot be translated into any other mode of expression. Art is "formally and essentially untranslatable", and the pretence to interpret art is vain. Mrs. Langer says she strongly suspects, though she is not ready to assert it dogmatically, "that the import of artistic expression is broadly the same in all arts as it is in music—*the verbally ineffable, yet not inexpressible law of vital experience, the pattern of affective and sentient being. This is the 'content' of what we* perceive as 'beautiful form'; and this formal element is the artist's 'idea' which is conveyed by every great work of art". It is a definition that covers, not only the traditional forms of classical and romantic art, but music in its purest form, and the visual arts in their most "abstract" form.

It follows that artistic truth is the truth of a symbol to the form of a feeling—"nameless forms, but recognizable when they appear in sensuous replica". But art is a witness to truth that can easily be denied, or disregarded. "The worst enemy of artistic judgment," says Mrs. Langer, "is literal judgment, which is so much more obvious, practical, and prompt that it is apt to pass its verdict before the curious eye has even taken in the entire form that meets it. Not blindness to 'significant form', but *blindedness*, due to the glaring evidence of familiar things, makes us miss artistic, mythical, or sacred import." It is very easy to "do without" music, or poetry, or ritual; but "doing without" these things means doing without so many means of communication, so many insights into the nature or reality. We become "partial minds", as Yeats called us; and I would agree with Mrs. Langer that much of the misery and distress of the modern world is due to this "blindedness", this incapacity to communicate the pattern of our feelings. We have language, but "the limits of language are not the last limits of experience, and things inaccessible to language may have their own forms of conception, that is to say, their own symbolic devices". To suppress such symbolic devices is to block the free functioning of the mind. And Mrs. Langer ends *Philosophy in a New Key* with this warning: "A life that does not incorporate some degree of ritual, of gesture and attitude, has no mental anchorage. It is prosaic to the point of total indifference, purely casual, devoid of that structure of intellect and feeling which we call 'personality'."

It would be possible to argue that the main object of art is to do away with symbols. Mrs. Langer defines a symbol as "any device whereby we are enabled to make an abstraction". But one tendency of art is to strive to avoid abstraction—to come to terms with what the artist apprehends directly as the reality of the object. This may be a delusive aim on the artist's part, but when Cézanne painted the Montagne Sainte-Victoire, he thought he was presenting us with a piece of nature. "The *littérateur*," he said, "expresses himself by means of abstractions, the true painter by means of design and colour, his sensations and perceptions." That is to say, a painting by Cézanne is not so much a symbol, but, in Charles Morris's sense of the word which Mrs. Langer adopts, a signal. When we come to consider more recent types of non-representational and constructive art, the lack of any symbolic reference is all the more obvious. The "feeling" in such works is not in any sense referential: it is contained within the work of art, it is self-subsistent. Mrs. Langer admits the "virtual" character of works of art, their "disengagement from belief", but she then states, rather arbitrarily, that "abstract form as such is not an artistic ideal. To carry abstraction as far as possible, and achieve pure form in only the barest conceptual medium, is a logician's business, not a painter's or a poet's. In art, forms are abstracted only to be made clearly apparent, and are freed from their common uses only to be put to new uses to act as symbols, to become expressive of human feeling".

There is the crux of my disagreement with Mrs. Langer. Abstraction is not necessarily a process of achieving pure form "in only the barest conceptual medium". Chardin achieves pure form in the exact representation of a wine-bottle, a tumbler, a loaf of bread and a carving knife. It would be a misuse of the term "expression" to say that these objects, as arranged and painted by Chardin, "express" a state of feeling about bread and wine, or any feeling for these objects in their everyday uses. Juan Gris or Braque might have used the same objects and have carried abstraction "as far as possible"—that is to say, to a point where the objects were no longer recognizable. But the painting would not on that account be necessarily less of a work of art. All such works of art are essentially structures representing what Mondrian called "pure reality", and as devoid of feeling as a mathematical equation.

In her earlier book Mrs. Langer made frequent use of a phrase, "the pattern of sentience", which seemed to me a perfect description of the work of art. But I see now that it is an ambiguous phrase, for everything depends on where we discover the pattern. If we find the pattern within ourselves, and faithfully depict it, then we can say that the work of art is symbolic of human feeling. This is an exact definition of expressionistic art, so characteristic of the Germanic tradition. But more often the artist is possessed by intuitions, promptings from the unconscious, which have no basis in sentience, *but which he reduces to concreteness and precision in the act of creating a work of art*. Art is a process of crystallization; but the form is not imposed from without, nor dictated from within. It is a dialectical development, and the final synthesis is a unique event, a new reality.

28

Henry Miller

THE SIMPLEST THINGS to say about Henry Miller is that he can write, but the temptation is then to add, if only below one's breath, some word like "beautifully", and that at once gets away from the truth. At the beginning of his first book, *Tropic of Cancer*, Miller wrote: "A year ago, six months ago, I thought I was an artist. I no longer think about it. *I am.* Everything that was literature has fallen from me. There are no more books to be written, thank God." That was in 1934, but in whichever is his latest volume, he will list more than twenty volumes, about half of them already published, half "in preparation". But not one of them, Miller would explain, is a book in the ordinary sense of the word. His whole work is "a prolonged insult, a gob of spit in the face of Art, a kick in the pants to God, Man, Destiny, Time, Love, Beauty . . ." Miller has written consistently in that spirit, and the result, as it mounts up, is one of the most significant contributions to the literature of our time.

Literature. That again is the wrong word. Anais Nin, the subject of one of Miller's essays in *Sunday After the War* and one of the few writers who can possibly be associated with him, wrote a Preface to *Tropic of Cancer* in which she said: "The poetic is discovered by stripping away the vestiture of art; by descending to what might be styled 'a pre-artistic level', the durable skeleton of form which is hidden in the phenomena of disintegration reappears to be transfigured again in the ever-changing flesh of emotion. The scars are burned away—the scars left by the obstetricians of culture. Here is an artist who re-establishes the potency of illusion by gaping at the open wounds, by courting the stern, psychological reality which man seeks to avoid through recourse to the oblique symbolism of art."

There are clues in *Sunday After the War* to Miller's underlying purpose. He confesses that he has "the itch" to write, but that he already regards as a confession of failure. "The truly great writer does not want to write: he wants the world to be a place in which he can live the life of the imagination. The first quivering word he puts to paper is the word of the wounded angel: pain." And on another page he says that no man would set a word down on paper if he had the courage to live out what he believed in. But later on Miller seems to wriggle out of his nihilistic dilemma, and he does so by making a distinction between art and "an egotistical performance on the part of the intellect". What he is protesting against all through is not art, in any vital sense of the word, but culture, symbolism, clichés and conventions of every sort. He recognizes that it is only through art that one finally establishes contact with reality—"that is the great discovery". As for "establishing contact with reality", that, as Plato held long ago, and as Miller holds now, is a matter of putting ourselves in unison with the world order—"to know what is the world order in contradistinction to the wishful-thinking orders which we seek to impose on one another . . . We have first to acquire vision, then discipline and forbearance. Until we have the humility to acknowledge the existence of a vision beyond our own, until we have faith and trust in superior powers, the blind must lead the blind . . . The great joy of the artist is to become aware of a higher order of things, to recognize by the compulsive and spontaneous manipulations of his own impulses the resemblance between human creations and what is called 'divine' creations. In works of fantasy the existence of law manifesting itself through order is even more apparent than in other works of art. Nothing is less mad, less chaotic, than a work of fantasy. Such a creation, which is nothing less than pure invention, pervades all levels, creating, like water, its own level".

Genius is the norm—that is another axiom of such a theory of art. Miller uses a word which Cézanne was fond of—*realization*. "Seeing, knowing, discovering, enjoying—these faculties or powers are pale and lifeless without realization. The artist's game is to move over into reality." It sounds so simple, but as an individual psychological process it is supremely difficult; it is also tragic, because it involves a complete break with what at any given moment is implied by one's *civilization*. Realization and civilization are contradictions, as a psychologist like Trigant Burrow has long maintained: as D. H. Lawrence, who was influenced by Dr. Burrow, also maintained: and as Miller, in many respects a successor to Lawrence and his fervent admirer, also maintains. "*Civilized*, we say. What a horrible word! What bedeviled idiocy skulks behind that arrogant mark! Oh, I am not thinking of this war, nor of the last one, nor of any or all the wars men waged in the name of *Civilization*. I am thinking of the periods in between, the rotten stagnant eras of peace, the lapses and relapses, the lizard-like sloth, the creepy mole-like burrowing-in, the fungus growths, the barnacles, the stink-weeds; I am thinking of the constant fanatical dervish dance that goes on in the name of all that is unreal, unholy and unattainable, thinking of the sadistic-masochist tug of war, now one getting the upper hand, now the other. In the name of humanity when will we cry *Enough*?"

Many people will sympathize with the vivid indignation of that outcry, but will not be prepared for all that might be involved in the opposite process of realization. Consider, for example, what the law would call Henry Miller's obscenity. Ignoring the underground circulation of pornography, Miller is probably, in this technical sense, the most obscene writer in the history of literature. At least, he exceeds the considerable efforts of writers like Catullus, Petronius, Boccaccio and Rabelais. But he is never obscene for obscenity's sake—there is no "effort" about his obscenity—it is all part of the process of realization, a natural consequence of his devastating honesty, and also of his vitality. The nearest parallel I can think of is the obscenity of the unexpurgated *Thousand Nights and One Night*—those tales are essentially innocent, apparently not designed to shock the unsuspecting reader. But such a comparison is false if it suggests that Miller is in any sense a manufacturer of *pastiches*. As Anais Nin says so well in the Preface already referred to, "it is no false primitivism which gives rise to this savage lyricism. It is not a retrogressive tendency, but a swing forward into unbeaten areas. To regard a naked book such as this with the same critical eye that is turned upon even such diverse types as Lawrence, Breton, Joyce and Céline is a mistake. Rather let us try to look at it with the eyes of a Patagonian for whom all that is sacred and taboo in our world is meaningless".

The war, which found Miller in Greece, forcibly translated him to his native States. He reacted violently, and the pages he has since written about his mother country, published under the title *The Air-Conditioned Nightmare*, constitute the most shattering attack ever launched against the American "way of life". *Sunday After the War*, which is a collection of extracts from various works in progress, contains fragments from this book, and others from an autobiographical narrative called *The Rosy Crucifixion*. Another narrative piece, "Reunion in Brooklyn", is also autobiographical and describes the return of the prodigal son to his poor and depressing home: it is a masterpiece of realism, as was the episode from the same background which appeared in an earlier volume, *Black Spring*, under the title "The Tailor Shop".

What makes Miller distinctive among modern writers is his ability to combine, without confusion, the aesthetic and prophetic functions. Realization, one might imagine, is such a disinterested process that the result would be the purely objective naturalism of a *Madame Bovary*. But Flaubert's limitations have become somewhat obvious, and though his method is perfect for as far as it goes, Miller is aware that it must be carried much further, into the realm of ideas, and that the writer must not be afraid to declare his ideals. Miller's ideals I find very acceptable—they are the ideals of what I call anarchism, and have never been expressed better than in these words which come from an essay on "Art and the Future" in *Sunday After the War*.

The cultural era is past. The new civilization, which may take centuries or a few thousand years to usher in, will not be *another* civilization—it will be the open stretch of realization which all the past civilizations have pointed to. The city, which was the birthplace of civilization, such as we know it to be, will exist no more. There will be nuclei of course, but they will be mobile and fluid. The people of the earth will no longer be shut off from one another within states but will flow freely over the surface of the earth and intermingle. There will be no fixed constellations of human aggregates. Governments will give way to management, using the word in a broad sense. The politician will become as superannuated as the dodo bird. The machine will never be dominated, as some imagine; it will be scrapped, eventually, but not before men have understood the nature of the mystery which binds them to their creation. The worship, investigation and subjugation of the machine will give way to the lure of all that is truly occult. This problem is bound up with the larger one of power—and of possession. Man will be forced to realize that power must be kept open, fluid and free. His aim will be not to possess power but to radiate it.

A power that is open, fluid and free—Miller is thinking of the relation of man to his environment, but the words describe the essential quality of his own writings.

29

'De Stijl'

THE SIGNIFICANCE of the movement associated in its beginnings with the Dutch review *De Stijl* undoubtedly lies in the fact that it carried to a logical conclusion certain implications of Cubism. When Mondrian went to Paris in 1910 Juan Gris had already established the priority of the abstract composition (against the priority of the object to be analysed). But Mondrian was quick to realize that neither Gris, nor Picasso, nor Léger, had followed to its end the path they had chosen. It had led them to the banks of a dyke which they then refused to cross. Beyond the dyke was an undiscovered country—a realm of "pure reality", and Mondrian was determined to reach it. But "pure reality" was only to be attained by means of "pure plastics", that is to say, by means of forms unconditioned by subjective feeling and conception. The artist was compelled to eliminate all the variable and transient elements of perceptual experience—"to reduce natural forms to the *constant* elements of form, and natural colour to *primary* colour". Pure reality could only be apprehended by intellectual or intuitive processes; subjective states of feeling, such as are evoked by the particularities of form and the colours of nature, obscure pure reality.

Such was the basis theory and practice of Mondrian, to which Van Doesburg gave a more verbal and intellectual formulation in the pages of *De Stijl*. It is one of the most coherent doctrines in contemporary art, and must be subjected to a fundamentally philosophical criticism.

Such criticism should, I think, in the first place be directed to the process of "depersonalization". But we should make a distinction between the "depersonalization" and the "de-humanization" of art. What is created by man, particularly by a man of Mondrian's great intelligence and sensibility, is not and cannot be in any real sense "inhuman". What Mondrian and his colleagues were doing was to separate and distinguish among faculties, all of which are human, but some of which are not (in their opinion) so valuable as others. We might say that they were making a distinction between two classes of symbols—(1) symbols which refer back to the phenomenal world with all its emotional associations and are therefore liable to create confusion; and (2) symbols which are original and unique and can be related only to an immediate intuition of "reality".

What, then, is "reality"? Not, evidently, the subjective vision of circumstance and environment which is the conventional notion of reality. The Neo-plasticist is committed to one of two possible alternative views of reality. Either he must assert that by a process of intuition he is able to see through the realm of appearances to a realm of *essence*; or he must claim the ability to create an entirely new and valid reality. It seems to me that Mondrian was committed to the first alternative. He was a Platonic artist, whose purpose was, in his own words, "to discover fixed laws which govern and point to the use of the constructive elements of the composition, and of the inherent interrelationships between them. These laws may be regarded as subsidiary laws to the *fundamental* law of equivalence which creates dynamic equilibrium and reveals *the true content of reality*". This is the dividing line between Neo-plasticism and Constructivism, for a constructivist like Gabo rejects such idealism and claims to create *a new reality*, a concrete reality, not to discover reality in some metaphysical region.

Nevertheless, Mondrian's ideal reality is expressed in concrete plastic symbols, and there is evidence to prove that these symbols are not irrelevant to our daily life, to the evolving consciousness of society. To give but one example: the Royal Festival Hall in London is the creation of two architects, one of whom, Leslie Martin, has for many years been a devotee of Mondrian and has admittedly been profoundly influenced by Mondrian's art.

Neo-plasticism did not emerge from a social vacuum. It is intimately related, not only as M. Jaffé has claimed, to the life and landscape of Holland, but to wider economic and social pressures. It is obvious that the modern style in architecture, in so far as it can be called a style, has evoked in response to specific discoveries in the scientific and technological sphere, and also in response to economic and social factors. The consequent style in architecture is severely rectangular, materially parsimonious, and whatever aesthetic satisfaction it can give must come from the inherent relationships of its constructive elements and from what Mondrian called "dynamic equilibrium". A congruity has been established between modern abstract art (especially Neo-plasticism and Constructivism) and modern architecture, not on the superficial level of imitation, but at the profound level of emergent social symbolization. The art and the architecture are equally the expression of our time.

But now to express one reservation. If we compare paintings by Mondrian, Van Doesburg and Malevich with certain architectural drawings or plans, we observe that they are nearly identical—the architect's ground-plan looks like a neo-plasticist painting, the neo-plasticist painting looks like an architectural ground plan—what conclusion must we draw from this identification? That art and architecture are one in principle? That all art is architectoric and universally geometric? That would seem to be the argument of the *De*

Stijl group. It might be argued, however, that in such cases painting has lost its identity—or, to be more exact, it has lost its freedom. For architecture is not a free art: it is, as we have boasted in our time, a functional art. But the plastic arts of painting and sculpture are not *functional* arts. They are imaginative arts. It only remains to assert that nevertheless an imaginative art may be abstract.

There remains a problem that cannot be fully discussed within the limits of a short essay: the denial of the human craving for representational symbols. Though it is possible that a civilization can altogether dispense with the figurative symbol (we have the Mohammedan civilization to prove it), nevertheless it is doubtful whether our own humanistic civilization can do so without profound changes in its spiritual condition. I think the chances are that the arts will evolve a compensatory balance—that certain arts, such as architecture, sculpture and music, will tend to become more and more abstract, and that other arts, such as the film and drama, will adequately satisfy the craving for representational symbols. We must not attempt to force a totalitarian unity on the arts. "The complexity of art," said Mondrian, "is due to the fact that different degrees of its evolution are present at one and the same time. The present carries with it the past and the future. But we need not try to foresee the future; we need only take our place in the development of human culture, a development which has made non-figurative art supreme."

That, of course, is a claim that no objective critic can admit —that the present development of human culture has made non-figurative art *supreme*. The most we can claim is that non-figurative art has become a necessity, a necessity for a limited number of people. The masses remain indifferent to it, and one might even say that critics in general remain hostile to it. But the same people may be indifferent to existentialist philosophy, or any other significant movement of our time. We must not be intimidated because we are in a minority. The indifference of the majority is a species of inarticulateness: a failure to make any connection between a way of life which they accept and the art which is its prefiguration.

30

Ezra Pound

I WILL BEGIN this tribute with some personal reminiscences for they will show more clearly than my subsequent arguments why I approach the case of Ezra Pound in a sympathetic mood. Between 1912 and 1914 I was a student in a provincial university. I had just begun to write poetry and had been infected by that spirit of adventure or experiment that was about in those days. The fashionable poets were the Georgians—their annual anthology began to appear in the year 1913, and when the war broke out one of their number —Rupert Brooke—suddenly became a national poet, representative of much that was good in the spirit of the times. But, also representative of something that I had begun to recognize as sentimental and weak. My enlightenment was not due to native perspicacity, so much as to the tutoring I had received from journals like *The New Age* and Wyndham Lewis's *Blast*, which journals carried on a rowdy opposition to all that the Georgians represented in literature and art. By far the most active part in this opposition was played by a young

American who had come to London in 1908, and had quickly made contact with the few figures in contemporary art and letters whom he could respect—W. B. Yeats, Wyndham Lewis, then just emerging as a self-styled Vorticist, and the belligerent philosopher T. E. Hulme. The intimate history of those pre-war years has still to be written, but a group, quite distinct from the Georgians, began to form. Pound was joined by a young poet, Richard Aldington, along with his American wife, who signed her poems with the initials H. D., by another American, John Gould Fletcher, and by a London poet, F. S. Flint. In the spring or early summer of 1912, Pound, H. D., and Aldington decided that they were agreed upon certain principles of poetry, which they proceeded to formulate. In January that year Hulme had collected in *The New Age* (25 January, 1912) five poems with the heading "The Complete Poetical Works of T. E. Hulme"—poems which were afterwards reprinted as an appendix to one of Pound's volumes (*Ripostes*, 1915), and it is certain that Hulme had a good deal to do with the clarification of the group's ideas. The group itself launched an anthology called *Des Imagistes*, which was edited by Pound and published in March, 1914. By the next year the group had split and a new anthology, *Some Imagist Poets*, was published, containing work by Aldington, H. D., Fletcher, Flint, D. H. Lawrence and Amy Lowell, but nothing by Pound.

Meanwhile the European War had broken out, and all these groups were forcibly dispersed. But the same event had dispersed the group of students to which I belonged, and for the first time—it was early in 1915—I went to London. There were, of course, many people whom I would have liked to meet at that time, but the poet with whom I most eagerly sought contact was Ezra Pound. I forget exactly when I first met Pound, but I had written to him and he immediately invited me to tea. He then lived in a triangular room in the Holland Park district of London. The person I met was probably as shy and embarrassed as I was, and I took away the impression of an agile lynx, beautiful in features, aggressively dressed, who sprang from conversational point to point very much in the manner that the animal he reminded me of might spring from branch to branch. We met occasionally in the ensuing years, but never became intimate; and then, shortly after the end of the war (I think it was in 1920) Pound left England in disgust and went to live at Rapallo, and from that time I saw less of him than ever. I met him for the last time the year before the Second World War, during a visit of his to London. I took away from that final meeting an impression of a man who had become agitated and elated to a dangerous degree.

There are, as everyone knows, degrees of mental disturbance, many of which do not merit incarceration. No unprejudiced observer will fail to observe in Pound's letters[1] a progressive egocentricity, and even the cause of it is not far to seek. A man who sets out (1908) with the idea that "no art ever yet grew by looking into the eyes of the public" is bound to find himself increasingly isolated from the social matrix that ensures "sanity" (which admittedly may be no more than an accepted code of conduct). Pound started kicking against the pricks from the moment he landed in Europe, and the inertia of the brute that bore the pricks produced in him the frenzy of shrill vituperation, scatological abuse, and mere spluttering invective which give his letters their wearisome unity. Of course one sympathizes, and sometimes the invective rises to a withering temperature. But then one remembers the inconsistency of it all. Pound professes a great admiration for Confucius; he has translated the *Ta Hio* and

[1] *The Letters of Ezra Pound.* Edited by D. D. Paige. London, 1950.

other Confucian classics. But nothing could be further from the Confucian demeanour than Pound's roaring crusade. The Master said, "He who speaks without modesty will find it difficult to make his words good." That is only one of a hundred maxims from the *Analects* that might be brought to the attention of his self-styled disciple. The one virtue Confucius insisted on was "inperturbedness"; it is the one virtue that Pound has never possessed or professed. The fault lies in his displacement, his lack of "rootedness", his contempt for human failings. He lacks all humility—not so much personal humility, for he has never sought high rewards; but humility towards his art and towards his destiny. The disintegration which increasingly invades his poetry, and his correspondence, is simply a reflection of his failure to achieve any degree of social, and therefore personal, integration. "Galdós, Flaubert, Tourgenev, see them all in a death struggle with provincial stupidity . . . All countries are equally damned, and all great art is born of the metropolis (or *in* the metropolis). The metropolis is that which accepts all gifts and all heights of excellence, usually the excellence that is *tabu* in its own village. The metropolis is always accused by the peasant of 'being mad after foreign nations'." There, in 1913 (and in spite of an admiration, expressed elsewhere, for such "peasant" poets as Homer and Hardy), is the Alexandrian heresy, of which Pound, in our time, has been the most gifted exponent.

What had drawn me to Pound, and made of me a devoted disciple, was his poetry and his poetics. But we both belonged to another and wider circle—that which centred round A. R. Orage, the editor of *The New Age*, one of the most influential personalities in the cultural life of that time. From Orage we had both acquired similar ideas about politics and economics, and though these were to lead us to very different conclusions, we always agreed on two points—the evil wrought in post-medieval society by the Church's admission of the principle of usury, and the dependence of any social revolution on its ability to deal with the monetary problem. There was another if a less urgent bond of interest—an enthusiasm for Chinese art and philosophy, but Pound was to develop this interest to a much deeper extent than I have done. On these three subjects—poetics, economics and sinology—Pound and I have always agreed, and this has perhaps enabled me to penetrate with more sympathy than would otherwise have been possible into the difficult problems raised by his work and conduct.

I shall concentrate mainly on Pound's poetry and poetic principles, but his poetry is so involved with his ideas that some appreciation of these is also essential. Pound would maintain, and I think I would agree with him, that there is an intimate connection between the general decline of sensibility which has led to the most vulgar civilization in the history of mankind and the economic fallacies which begin with the religious and legal recognition of usury at the end of the Middle Ages. In other words, poetics and economics cannot be separated. But for the moment let us turn our attention to the poetics.

So far as the English-speaking world is concerned, Pound is the animator if not founder of the modern movement in poetry. His experiments—with the exception of the five or six poems which T. E. Hulme wrote in 1908[1]—predate any similar experiments by other English or American poets. By this I do not mean that there was no free verse before 1912. Pound did not invent free verse—he re-formed free verse, gave it a musical structure, and to that extent we may say

[1] I have given the evidence for Hulme's priority in *The True Voice of Feeling*. London, 1953. Ch. VI.

paradoxically that it was no longer free. But let us try to trace the historical process in Pound's own work. As a youth in the Middle West he must have modelled himself on romantic poets like Chatterton and Poe, on Rossetti and Swinburne. Then he discovered Italian poetry, possibly via Rossetti, and then the Troubadours and Browning. The result was an eclectic style to which, as time went on, were added accents from Lionel Johnson and Dowson, W. B. Yeats and Fiona Macleod. These *pastiches* are not to be despised—a poem like "The Goodly Frere" has found its way into many anthologies, and it is indeed a good fake of a medieval ballad. Most of the verse included in the first three volumes Pound published in England between 1909 and 1911 is of this nature —romantic poetry in the true historical meaning of that ambiguous word. Several of these poems are accompanied by learned footnotes—Mr. Eliot was not the first poet to indulge in this practice. A footnote to "La Fraisne", for example, refers the reader to Janus of Basel, the "Daemonalitas" of Father Sinistrari of Ameno (1600 *circ*.), the Book of the Dead, and the Provençal sources of the legend on which the poem is based.

Such was the stage of development Pound had reached by 1911 or 1912, when he began his discussions with Hulme, Aldington and Flint. What then emerged was "The School of Images", or Imagism as it was to be called. Like the sonneteering of the sixteenth century, it was of foreign inspiration, mainly French, though we must not forget Walt Whitman, who at any rate served as a terrible warning. Later Pound was to make "A Pact" with him:

> I make a pact with you, Walt Whitman—
> I have detested you long enough.
> I come to you as a grown child
> Who has had a pig-headed father;

I am old enough now to make friends.
It was you that broke the new wood,
Now it is a time for carving.
We have one sap and one root—
Let there be commerce between us.

But for the moment it was "a time for carving", and it was the French poets, Gautier and the later Symbolists, Verlaine, Francis Jammes, Paul Fort, Tristian Corbière, Max Elskamp, Mallarmé, Maeterlinck and Verhaeren, and, of course, Rimbaud, who were the master-carvers. But in France itself a new group of *vers libristes* had come into existence, and with this group, Jules Romains, André Spire, Vildrac and Duhamel, the English group soon established a sympathetic exchange of ideas. The guiding critic was Remy de Gourmont, whose *Livre des Masques* had given definition to the whole movement, and whose *Problème du Style* is a source-book for many of the ideas that inspired the literary developments in both France and England at this time. I am afraid it has been forgotten how much we all owed to this brilliant critic. Pound was in direct communication with him until his death.

When, as a result of all this cross-fertilization of ideas, the group in England began to formulate their principles, they took the following shape: I give them in Pound's own words:

In the spring or early summer of 1912, "H. D.", Richard Aldington and myself decided that we were agreed upon the three principles following:

1. Direct treatment of the "thing" whether subjective or objective.

2. To use absolutely no word that does not contribute to the presentation.

3. As regarding rhythm: to compose in the sequence of the musical phrase, not in sequence of a metronome.

And here are some further injunctions which Pound wrote in a poetry magazine in 1913:

Use no superfluous word, no adjective, which does not reveal something.

Don't use such an expression as "dim lands of peace". It dulls the image. It mixes an abstraction with the concrete. It comes from the writer's not realizing that the natural object is always the *adequate* symbol.

Go in fear of abstractions (Remy de Gourmont had said: "*En littérature, comme en tout, il faut que cesse le règne des mots abstraits*" —this was on the 27th February, 1898—Preface to *Le deuxième livre des masques*).

Do not re-tell in mediocre verse what has already been done in good prose.

Don't imagine that the art of poetry is any simpler than the art of music, or that you can please the expert before you have spent at least as much effort on the art of verse as the average piano teacher spends on the art of music.

Use either no ornament or good ornament.

And so on, to advice of a more technical nature.

The Imagist Anthology of 1915 (in which Pound did not appear) had a more elaborate statement of principles, but they are mostly covered by Pound's statement. There is one of the paragraphs in this manifesto which gives a clear definition of the word Imagist and may therefore be usefully quoted:

To present an image. We are not a school of painters, but we believe that poetry should render particulars exactly and not deal in vague generalities, however magnificent and sonorous. It is for this reason that we oppose the cosmic poet, who seems to us to shirk the real difficulties of his art.

We might explain Pound's later development by saying that he began with free verse of a vaguely rhetorical kind, and arrived at a specific kind of free verse to which he gave the name "imagism". Imagism differs from Whitmanesque and other varieties of free verse in insisting on a concreteness of imagery, and on a tight musical or rhythmical structure. Nothing is in a certain sense less free than good free verse, for it achieves an exact correspondence between the verbal and rhythmical structure of the verse and the mood or emotion to be expressed. The result is a quality which Mr. Eliot has recently called "transparent"—"that is to say, you listen not to poetry as poetry, but to the meaning of poetry". In Pound's words, you get rid of the ornament. And when you are rid of the ornament you are left with the image, the direct percept. The trouble in our kind of language is that we have to express ourselves in words which do not visually convey the image. It is different in the Chinese language where the ideogram is developed from a visual representation of the image, and where, however remotely, a suggestion of the concrete object is present in the verbal sign.

I must now deal briefly with Pound's theory of poetry, as it developed beyond imagism. This is based almost entirely on one short treatise, *The Chinese Written Character as a Medium for Poetry*, by Ernest Fenollosa. Fenollosa was an American orientalist who died in 1908. I have never known whether Pound had direct contact with this distinguished scholar, but it was Pound who first published this particular essay in 1918. It is undoubtedly one of the basic documents of the aesthetics of modern art, and provides the bridge between the oriental and occidental cultures.

Fenollosa begins with an analysis of the Chinese sentence, and more particularly of that sentence when it constitutes a poem. I cannot enter into the details of Fenollosa's argument, but he brings out the essential concreteness of the language, a concreteness that extends to verbs, conjunctions and pronouns as well as to ordinary nouns. More significantly still, he shows how the Chinese have built up their intellectual fabric, their logical categories, in the same concrete way. They have done this by the use of metaphor, that is to say, the use of material images to suggest immaterial relations. The rest of the argument can be given in Fenollosa's own words:

The whole delicate substance of speech is built upon substrata of metaphor. Abstract terms, pressed by etymology, reveal their ancient roots still embedded in direct action. But the primitive metaphors do not spring from arbitrary *subjective* processes. They are possible because they follow objective lines of relations in nature herself.

Metaphor, the revealer of nature, is the very substance of poetry. The known interprets the obscure, the universe is alive with myth. The beauty and freedom of the observed world furnish a model, and life is pregnant with art. It is a mistake to suppose, with some philosophers of aesthetics, that art and poetry aim to deal with the general and the abstract. This conception has been foisted upon us by medieval logic. Art and poetry deal with the concrete in nature . . . Poetry is finer than prose because it gives us more concrete truth in the same compass of words.

Our ancestors built the accumulations of metaphor into structures of language and into systems of thought. Languages today are thin and cold because we think less and less into them.

In diction and in grammatical form science is utterly opposed to logic. Primitive men who created language agreed with science and not with logic. Logic has abused the language which they left to her mercy.

Poetry agrees with science and not with logic.

The moment we use the copula, the moment we express subjective inclusions, poetry evaporates. . . . We need in poetry thousands of active words, each doing its utmost to show forth the motive and vital forces. . . .

We should beware of English grammar, its hard parts of speech, and its lazy satisfaction with nouns and adjectives. We should seek and at least bear in mind the verbal undertone of each noun. We should avoid "is" and bring in a wealth of neglected English verbs.

. . . the great strength of our language lies in its splendid array of transitive verbs. . . . These give us the most individual characterizations of force. Their power lies in their recognition of nature as a vast storehouse of forces. . . . Will is the foundation of our speech. . . . I had to discover myself why Shakespeare's English was immeasurably so superior to all others. I found that it was his persistent, natural, and magnificent use of hundreds of transitive verbs. . . . A study of Shakespeare's verbs should underlie all exercises in style.

In this last passage we have indicated the clue to the technique of Pound's later verse—the verse of the Cantos. It achieves its poetic effect by the *juxtaposition* of words whose *overtones* blend into a delicate and lucid harmony. A shorter definition still: Poetry is the placing of words to produce metaphorical overtones. "The overtones vibrate against the eye." Shorter still, a definition suggested to Pound by a Japanese student: "Poetry consists of gists and piths."

Pound's literary criticism is developed in several volumes, beginning with *The Spirit of Romance* (1910), *Instigations* (1920), *Indiscretions* (1923), *How to Read* (1931), *The ABC of Reading* (1934), *Polite Essays* (1937), *Guide to Kulchur* (1938), but the cream of it all is contained in the volume of collected essays called *Make It New*, published in 1934. Here are Pound's articles on the Troubadours, on the Elizabethan Classicists, the Translators of Greek, on French poets, on Henry James and Remy de Gourmont, and on Cavalcanti, the late thirteenth-century Italian poet to whom Pound has devoted so much attention.

Criticism, according to Pound, has two functions. First, it is a rationale of composition—it tries "to fore-run composition, to serve as gun-sight". Secondly, it is a process of "excernment". "The general ordering and weeding out of what has actually been performed. The elimination of repetitions. The work analogous to that which a good hanging committee or a curator would perform in a National Gallery or in a biological museum." Even this second function is for the benefit of the actual composer, for it is further defined as "the ordering of knowledge so that the next man (or generation) can most readily find the live part of it, and waste the least possible time among obsolete issues". It will be seen at once that this very drastically limits the scope of criticism. That scope, as defined by representative critics, such as Coleridge, Matthew Arnold and T. S. Eliot, has included not merely the composer but also the audience. Admittedly much criticism suffers from not clearly separating these two points of view, and most of our critics make for confusion by continually jumping without warning from one point of view to the other. Pound avoids that danger. His intention is always clear, his judgment unequivocal. Not the shade of an ethical prejudice discolours his purely literary opinions. We may say that he has one general principle of criticism, and one only: "Civilization is individual." That principle is often re-iterated throughout his work, and underlies his poetics, his ethics and even his economics. As to what Mr. Pound believes—his answer to Mr. Eliot's worried question was: "I believe in the *Ta Hio*." That is not a witticism: Pound has studied Confucius and devoted a great deal of time to the translation and elucidation of the Confucian texts. There is one famous saying of the Chinese sage which perfectly expresses the general character of Pound's criticism: "What the superior man seeks is in himself: what the small man seeks is in others." Pound, as we have seen, is in some sense a traditionalist: he has studied the past; but in the end he relies on his individual sensibility. Literature, he would say, depends for its cultivation and continuance on the peculiar sensibility of a few artists within each generation. Criticism is a professional activity—a process of refinement, above all, a refinement of language—to make it new, to make it precise, to make it clear.

There is plenty of evidence to show that he has applied his critical faculties to his own work, and there is no modern poet whose work shows such a decisive development from birth to maturity. I shall not try to illustrate this development —it would require too much quotation. Any educated reader who knows an early romantic poem such as "La Fraisne", a perfect free verse cadence such as "Doria", one of the "translations" from the Chinese such as "The River-Merchant's Wife", and the "Hugh Selwyn Mauberley" sequence (the most "carved" satirical verse in the language), will be incited, if liable to the poetic contagion, to fill in the evolutionary gaps.

By 1920, when "Mauberly" was published, Pound was already engaged on the immense work which was to occupy him for the rest of his life, and which is still unfinished. It has never been given a definite title, but is known as "The Cantos", and more than ninety of these have been published.[1] They are of varying length, but they already amount to more than 500 pages of verse, and constitute the longest, and without hesitation I would say the greatest, poetic achievement of our time.

Technically the poem is the perfection of Pound's taut free verse, and there are passages of the purest lyricism which in themselves, if extracted, would constitute a body of poetry for which there is no contemporary parallel. In the complex

[1] Section: Rock-Drill 85–95 de los Cantares was published in 1956, New York: New Directions.

structure of the Cantos these passages are relatively rare, and what we have to explain is a mosaic of images, ideas, phrases, —politics, ethics, economics—anecdotes, insults, denunciations—English, Greek, Latin, Italian, Provençal, Chinese—without division, without transition, without cohesion—apparently without structure and without pattern. But all the same there *is* pattern, there *is* structure, and there is a controlling force. Pound himself has used the image of the magnet and the iron filings: "The *forma*, the immortal *concetto*, the concept, the dynamic form which is like the rose-pattern driven into the dead iron filings by the magnet, not by material contact with the magnet itself, but separate from the magnet itself. Cut off by a layer of glass, the dust and filings rise and spring into order. Thus the *forma*, the concept rises from death."

The dust and filings—these are the detritus of a civilization in decay, in dissolution. The Cantos must be conceived as a massive attack on this civilization, an exposure of its rottenness and active corruption. It is an analysis of history—of European and American history since the Middle Ages, and of the grandiose epochs of Chinese history. Corruption is traced to its source in usury, and those who have opposed usury and tried to eradicate it—Malatesta and Jefferson, for example—are treated as heroes in this epic. Against this corruption is set the harmony and ethical rectitude of Confucius.

I am not going to deny that for the most part the Cantos present insuperable difficulties to the impatient reader, but as Pound says somewhere, "you can't get through hell in a hurry". I am not going to defend the poem in detail—there are stretches which I find boring, but that too is no doubt a characteristic of hell. But I am convinced of the greatness of the poem as a whole, and the more I read it the more I get out of it. It will need in the future an immense work of exegesis, and in America that work has already begun. In the end the poem cannot fail to have its effect. In his criticism Pound frequently uses the phrase "ideas in action", and that is the general characteristic of the texture of this immense poem. Ideas do not exist as abstract counters in a process of logical reasoning: rather, they are dropped into the mind of the reader as separate concrete entities which then set up mental reactions. Conceptual reasoning is not the poet's business: it is his business to see, to present, to condense, to combine—all active processes. Pound's favourite Chinese ideograph represents man and word side by side: a man standing by his word, a man of his word, truth.

If I do not discuss these ideas on the present occasion, it is not because I consider them nonsense. On the contrary, I think that Pound is one of the few men who have talked sense in our time. The mistake he has made, in my opinion, is to believe that his ideas could be realized by a modern state. He did not see that the modern totalitarian state is an incarnation of the principle of usury, an instrument of war and oppression. Because Mussolini was fighting the international bankers, Pound thought that he had turned his back on the monetary game, had seen through "the great illusionistic monetary monopoly". But he was wrong—tragically blind and wrong, and he is now paying the penalty. Pound has always hated war—he did not think that youth and beauty should be sacrificed

> For an old bitch gone in the teeth,
> For a botched civilization.

His broadcasts from Italy during the last war were legal acts of treason against the United States. But Pound would never admit that the United States, in any human sense, were committed to the war: the United States were involved in a disaster precipitated by Wall Street. Usury is a cancer, Finance a disease, and War the dying agony of a civilization strangled by debt and taxation. These were the ideas that Pound attempted to put into action during the war. The war is suspended, Pound is confined to a mental hospital, but his ideas are still in action.

31

The Architect as Universal Man

IN DUSSELDORF a naked figure of a man realistically modelled by Georg Kolbe stands incongruously in front of an office building designed by Helmut Henrich and Hans Heuser. The building is not particularly severe—its façade is masked by balconies that are decorative in effect though no doubt functionally justifiable.

There are many other examples in other countries of architecture's last concession to figurative art—the Henry Moore groups outside the Hertfordshire schools is the typical example from our own country. Sometimes a figure will be clamped to a blank wall, like Lipchitz's bronze on the side of the Ministry of Education and Health in Rio di Janeiro, but such an arbitrary juxtaposition of sculpture and architecture serves only to emphasize the totally distinct plastic conceptions that the two arts now represent. Even the Moore screen on the Time-Life building in London, though it represents a solution reached by architect and sculptor in association, and though the sculptures have been "denaturalized" to conform better with a functional building, nevertheless has the air of a concession: the architecture *admits* the sculpture, swallows it up without digesting it. The character of the building would not change if the sculpture were to be replaced by a blank wall.

Architecture was the parent of sculpture—indeed, the earliest architecture *is* sculpture, and even the primitive African hut of our own time is still a work-of-art-to-live-in. Architecture was perhaps the parent of all the plastic arts; certainly the patron. The palaeolithic cave was a painted crypt, and even the art of writing may have been first conceived as an inscription on a monument. We must think of the archaic temple as a vast Christmas tree, which is then gradually stripped of the votive works of art that hang on it. But we must also think of the architect as a Father Christmas, capable of distributing those gifts.

The specialization of the arts, like the division of labour, is a process which, as we look back on the history of civilization, seems inevitable. An art like painting would never have become so various and so expressive if it had remained an adjunct of architecture. Nevertheless, it is useful to remind ourselves how comparatively recently that independence was established. There was no "free" painting before the fifteenth century, and no "free" sculpture before Donatello. Indeed, a unitary conception of art was normal until the beginning of the Industrial Age, and as industrial processes have developed in the direction of mass production, so artistic processes have developed in the direction of isolation and individualism. The *artist* once signified *a man of total plastic sensibility*, just as the artisan was a man of total practical capability. Music and poetry were not arts in this sense, but rather accomplishments, modes of communication. Plato distinguished the arts that are based on manual ability from the arts of rhetoric that are mental.

That this condition of separation is fatal to the arts is shown in various ways. There is, in the first place, no "monumental" achievement in the contemporary arts; and many of our individualistic painters, perhaps in some measure aware of their failure to function in this total sense, have, after a period of restless experimentation, expressed their frustration in forms of art that are essentially private. In this way the plastic arts seem to aspire to the condition of music and poetry—that is, become voices, modes of subjective communication between individual and individual, or between individual and coterie. The monument, on the other hand, is always an autonomous object—a transfusion of personality into a timeless and impersonal construction. An Egyptian pyramid, or the Temple of Somnathpur, or the Parthenon, or a Gothic cathedral, does not "express a personality", or even "convey a message". We can, it is true, read "serenity" into Greek architecture, or "transcendentalism" into Gothic architecture, but such exercises have nothing to do with the objective reality of the building as such: and in any case, serenity and transcendentalism are universal concepts rather than sensuous reactions.

The quality that concerns me for the moment, however, is the complexity of such monuments—their *esemplastic* power as Coleridge used to call it—the reduction of a multiplicity of purposes to a unity of effect. This quality may sometimes be due to some kind of collective intuition—the working of several minds to a common conception; the spontaneous overflow of a group consciousness. It is difficult to explain the Gothic cathedrals on any other supposition. But more usually the unity of effect is due to a single controlling mind, that of the master-builder, a man who was capable of conceiving the monument, not as a shell to be adorned (or as a Christmas tree to be "decorated") but as an organism, every particular cell of which is morphologically and functionally related to the whole.

The last metaphor is misleading if it suggests that every function is utilitarian (in biology or architecture). Nineteenth-century materialism left us with a very narrow conception of utility—the useful was anything that promoted the health, wealth or comfort of mankind—in short, happiness. Those nations that have already secured such blessings (such as the Americans and the Swiss) have discovered that there is something missing—an intangible ethos, wonder, "worship", glory, or simply beauty. We begin to suspect that this intangible something is just as necessary for life—for life in the strict biological sense—as comfort or wealth; that it is one of the conditions of complete health. Slowly we have become aware of the presence of a psychosomatic equilibrium in life itself, as well as in the human body. Beauty after all is not an elegant addition to the good life: it is the tone or temper of all that actually makes life "good". It is the style of life when life is positive, expansive, affirmative.

Architecture, which is so intimately concerned with the basic activities of human life (as providing the necessary shelter —the biological shell for a sensitive organism) is thus required to be always affirmative in this sense—stylistically *vital*. But the solution of a practical problem is not stylistically vital in this sense. What moves us, inspires us, incites us is not satisfaction, but curiosity, wonder, endless search for an ideal perfection. Such ideal perfection cannot be limited by necessity or contingency (by functional needs); it must of necessity ignore and transcend the practical.

Fiedler, and probably Semper and Hegel before him, pointed out that Greek architecture (which they assumed to be the highest point of architectonic genius) had never been concerned with practical needs or technical solutions. "The

Greeks invented nothing in their architecture, but developed only that which they received, and with such a clear awareness that they necessarily arrived at a result in which everything directly reminiscent of the demands of needs and wants, of the nature of the material used and of the conditions of construction, had disappeared except for faint echoes."[1] The Greek temple is a pure expression of form, a monument dedicated to ideal beauty and to nothing else. In this sense Fiedler thought it superior to the Gothic cathedral, which was inspired by practical needs—"the pointed arch was only a technical development; artistically it was an evasion. In a struggle with practical needs man was not attempting to find a higher expression of form and did not hesitate to mutilate the form in order to devise a solution to a practical problem, and thereby renounce any artistic progress from the beginning". One may protest that nevertheless a higher expression of form did emerge on the basis of this technical development: that at Amiens and Lincoln the intellect has elaborated a practical device into a free form. But Fiedler has made his point—and it is a good one: architecture is a formal and not a technical development; it is a development of the relatively chaotic and the pragmatic towards ideal form, ideal order: a development which takes place in the aesthetic consciousness of man and not as the solution of a practical problem.

I have already hinted at a distinction between an aesthetic consciousness determined by time-sense (music and poetry) and an aesthetic consciousness determined by space-sense (the plastic arts). There may be intercommunications, but I am more concerned with the unity of plastic aesthetics. I mean that, *a priori*, the sensibility of the plastic artist should be expressible in any and all the plastic arts: the segregation of architect,

[1] Conrad Fiedler: *On the Nature and History of Architecture.* 1878. Trans. Carolyn Reading. Privately printed by Victor Hammer at the Transylvania University, Lexington, Kentucky, 1954.

sculptor, painter and craftsmen (woodworker, silversmith, weaver, etc.) is merely a *division of consciousness* and has had altogether deplorable effects on the development of the arts, above all, of architecture.

We know that the great monuments of Greece and of the Renaissance were, at their best, conceived in their entirety by a single clear intellect and we marvel at the capacity of an individual like Pheidas or Brunelleschi, or Bramante, or Michelangelo or Wren. But what should cause us more surprise is the complexity of an architectural enterprise that leaves the structure to engineers or builders who work by calculation and not by visual intuition; that then expects sculptors and painters to adapt their personal vision (or fragments thereof) to a technical formula; and expects from this conjunction of compromised talents a work of art!

To look at modern architecture from this point of view results in a new valuation. It does not necessarily mean a general condemnation of all functional architecture. On the contrary, we may find among the strictly functional monuments of our time a few that carry technical means to a new clarity of form—that repeat the Greek achievements by intellectualizing all the material elements—the materials are, as it were, dematerialized and what remains is a form as pure as the Pyramids. Certain buildings and projects by Mies van der Rohe approach this condition. It is true that this architect has always been in the past associated with an antiformal conception of architecture. "We refuse to recognize problems of form, but only problems of building . . . Form, by itself, does not exist—Form as an aim is formalism, and that we reject" (1923). But there are later statements which are not so positive —e.g.: "My attack is not against form, but against form as an *end in itself* . . . Only what has intensity of life can have intensity of form . . . We should judge not so much by the

results as by the creative process . . . Life is what is decisive
for us. In all its plenitude and in its spiritual and material
relations." (Letter to Dr. Riezler, 1927.) "Let us not give
undue importance to mechanization and standardization . . .
For what is right and significant for any era—including the
new era—is this: to give the spirit the opportunity for existence" (1930). It is true that Mies van der Rohe continues to
oppose "the idealistic principle of order" to "the organic
principle of order" (inaugural Address of 1938), but the distinction is almost verbal, for the organic principle is defined
as "a means of achieving the successful relationship of the
parts to each other and to the whole", which was the Greek
ideal of form. He can repeat "the profound words of St.
Augustine: Beauty is the splendour of Truth".

I do not assemble these quotations to give a particular
emphasis to statements that might seem to imply a mystical
outlook in Mies van der Rohe: his buildings are a sufficient
refutation of any suggestion that architecture should be used
as a language expressive of states of mind or emotion. Architecture is always regarded as "the crystallization of its inner
structure, the slow unfolding of its form". But it is distinct
from technology, though dependent on it. "Our real hope is
that they (architecture and technology) grow together, that
some day the one be the expression of the other." That is
what happened in Greek architecture: the technology was
taken over, nothing was invented, but gradually porportions
were refined, forms were defined, until the fusion was complete: the ideal form was a purification, a simplification of
the organic structure.

I believe such a fusion has taken place in Mies van der
Rohe's work in Chicago—the Minerals and Metals Research
Building of 1942-3, the Alumni Memorial Hall of 1945-6,
the Apartment Houses of 860 Lake Shore Drive (1951), and

the project for the Architecture and Design Building (1952). To these we may now add the project for the National Theatre, Mannheim (1953). But what we must immediately note about such buildings is that they are "undecorated"— no sculptural groups on the façade or in the front—no Kolbe figure declaring its naked humanity on the porch— no "works" by individualistic artist of any kind. The details that may be called decorative on all these buildings are determined by the architect himself, and are usually a decorative use of normal structural materials—"structural elements are revealed with decorative effect", as Philip Johnson neatly expresses it. The Lake Shore Drive buildings have walls of glass, which might have been left with a smooth surface, as they are in the Lever building in New York; but Mies van der Rohe has welded vertical steel sections which may serve as windbraces or mullions, but whose real function is to project as decorative elements. The decorative use of material is more obvious in the Mannheim Theatre project, for the building is shown resting on a plinth of highly dramatic marble.

Mies van der Rohe, so far as I know, practises no art other than architecture, though he is an amateur of painting and has a fine collection of the works of his friend Paul Klee. Le Corbusier, to pass to another significant architect of our time, is a painter of considerable achievement, a sculptor in wood and concrete, a designer of tapestry and furniture, and a mosaicist. He is a universal artist of the Renaissance type, like Leonardo or Alberti. He does not hesitate to combine his various talents in a single architectural conception, but in general he has kept his versatility in the background, perhaps realizing that there is a contradiction between the personalist tendency of the painting and sculpture, for example, and the impersonal values of the architecture. A painting or a mosaic in a Corbusier building is by another artist—Charles Edoaurd Jeanneret-Gris, in fact. Nevertheless, if we look at Le Corbusier's achievement in its wider context—as town-planning, *la Ville Radieuse*, a way of life—we see that the décor is marginal or additive. It can be swallowed up as a play activity—something taking place *within* the architecture—but it does not fuse with the architecture, and is not a formal purification of the underlying technology. The architecture is a separate conception and a complete unity without the décor. The architecture expresses an intolerance of the detached work of art which extends to the architect's own personalist creations. It is only in the church at Ronchamp that Le Corbusier as universal artist has created a monument that exhibits all aspects of his genius in integral unity.

These two examples will serve to present the problem. To take further examples—Frank Lloyd Wright, or Gropius, Oscar Niemeyer or Pier Luigi Nervi, Aalto or Breuer—would not resolve the problem, which is basically a revolt against personalist art and an attempt to find in architecture a new universal art: an art represented proto-typically by Greek architecture and later by Byzantine architecture. The Parthenon and Hagia Sophia are the paradigmatic type, the unification of the arts in the monument, and this unification is not achieved by chance, or even by conscious co-ordination: it is the all-inclusive concept of a master mind, a master-builder. We do not know what kind of future lies beyond the threat of nuclear weapons—none at all if the threat becomes a reality and radiation falls like a fatal rain on all mankind. But if there is to be a constructive future, we may be sure that the transition from our present state of cultural fragmentation can only be effected through a new conception of the architect: the architect as a comprehensive man of intelligence, a single source of unity and universality. From that new concentration of formal values the arts might once more derive a common style and an organic vitality.

32

Gandhi

IT HAS been said that future ages will regard Gandhi as the most remarkable man of our time. In his own country he was a legendary hero long before his death; there is material enough, in his acts and sacrifices, to merge the hero into saint. "Mahatma" is already more than a reverent title, and his "autobiography"[1] is a didactic gospel. But it is also more—and less. It is as detailed and banal as a provincial newspaper; it is colourless and often tedious; it is disconcertingly honest and unaffectedly modest. It has neither fire nor force, and its monotony is never redeemed by the remotest breath of poetry. And yet the reading of it is a moving, an unforgettable experience. We have a Golden Legend from the Middle Ages; this is the first book of a Leaden Legend.

Let us begin with the essential dogmas:

What I want to achieve—what I have been striving and pining to achieve these thirty years—is self-realization, to see God face to face, to attain *Moksha* (freedom from life and death). The essence of religion is morality.

I have gone through deep self-introspection, searched myself through and through, and examined and analysed every psychological situation. Yet I am far from claiming any finality or infalibility about my conclusions. One claim I do indeed make, and it is

[1] *The Story of My Experiments with Truth*, by M. K. Gandhi, London, 1949.

this. For me they appear to be absolutely correct, and seem for the time being to be final!

For me, truth is the sovereign principle. This truth is not only truthfulness in word, but truthfulness in thought also, and not only the relative truth of our conception, but the Absolute Truth, the Eternal Principle, that is God. . . . I worship God as Truth only. I have not yet found Him, but I am seeking after Him. I am prepared to sacrifice the things dearest to me in pursuit of this quest.

As a background to these dogmas, let us place certain concrete events in Gandhi's life.

He was the youngest son of his father's fourth marriage. His mother was "saintly". He was married at the age of thirteen and "devoted to the passions that flesh is heir to". He was cowardly—haunted by the fear of thieves, ghosts, and serpents. "I did not dare to sit out of doors at night. I could not bear to sleep without a light in the room." He was guilty of petty thefts, and indulged in secret meat eating. He deserted his father's death-bed to make love to his girl-wife, and was forever remorseful. "The poor mite that was born scarcely breathed more than three or four days. Nothing else could be expected. Let all those who are married be warned by my example." Then came various colour-bar experiences in England and South Africa. His natural shyness ("Shyness my shield") was aggravated by his gaucherie in society.

Gandhi's importance, like Tolstoy's, lies in his fearless preaching of the doctrine of non-violence, in his belief that permanent good can never be the outcome of force. In this he claimed to be (and proved himself to be) more than a visionary. "I am not a visionary. I claim to be a practical idealist. The religion of non-violence is not meant merely for the *rishis* and saints. It is meant for the common people as well. Non-violence is the law of our species as violence is the law of the brute. The spirit lies dormant in the brute, and he knows no law but that of physical might. The dignity of man requires obedience to a higher law—to the strength of the spirit." Gandhi devoted the greater part of his teaching to the elucidation of this universal truth. Other aspects of his teaching must seem, at any rate for most western minds, less compelling: his indifference to beauty, his morbid denial of the sexual instinct ("If the observance of Brahmacharya—chastity —should mean the end of the world, that is none of our business"), his worship of the cow ("a poem of pity"). But Gandhi was well aware of his own inconsistencies, and with inborn humility did not insist on an intellectual acceptance of any of his doctrines. "Patient example is the only possible method to effect a reform."

In Christian terms, Gandhi might qualify as a martyr, not as a saint. He was granted no special revelation; whatever "grace" he possessed was human, not divine. He was, by any standards, a great humanitarian—his love of his fellow-men was disinterested, spontaneous. Yet it had in it an element of compensation for his feeling of inferiority. He became a typical "agitator"—he was not content to do good within his own competency—he sought to create instruments of power to redress wrongs. He knew that power corrupts, and he tried to avoid that corruption by blunting the edge of the sword—by the strategy of non-violence. He was repeatedly involved in compromise (and confesses: "All my life through, the very insistence on truth has taught me to appreciate the beauty of compromise"). His organized campaigns, by the very fact of organization, became factors in power politics. He ended by playing the Congress game, the game of war and revolution.

Contrast the humanitarianism of his contemporary, Albert Schweitzer—more limited in its immediate effects, but by its very purity producing throughout the world a sympathetic response of unmeasurable resonance. But Schweitzer's God has been Love, whose sphere is human and immediate. Gandhi's was Truth, indefinable, unattainable, insatiable. His sacrifices to this God were, to say the least, very inconvenient for the people nearest and dearest to him. He treated his wife with ruthless tyranny. He calls himself a "cruelly blind husband", and was himself the judge of what was good for the poor woman. He forcibly took away her jewels, for example. "I regarded myself as her teacher, and so harassed her out of my blind love for her." In similar ways, as he uneasily confesses, he deprived his children of education—and gave them instead "an object-lesson in liberty and self-respect".

His attitude to sex was as egotistical as the rest of his behaviour. He makes no distinction between passionate love and brutish lust. He decides, for his own good, that he must extinguish sexual passion in himself. If he had had any conception of the true nature of passionate love, he would have realized that it is a reciprocal bond, as precious to the wife as to the husband. A unilateral "extinction" of such passion is not admissible. But Gandhi's attitude to sex was not rational, and certainly not humane. It was a revulsion unconsciously motivated by his early association of love and death. In fact, the death-wish, as an underlying motive, is probably the key to all Gandhi's actions. His fanatical vegetarianism (which did not stop at risking the death of other people), his fasting, his will to chastity—all can be interpreted as unconscious opposition to life.

Perhaps it is vain to try to comprehend this mind and personality with the inherited prejudices of the humanist tradition. Breaking in on that tradition is the element of Christian asceticism, no doubt of oriental origin; but that too is in conflict with Christian charity, as well as with the older Greek conception of measure. According to this conception, we accept the human body for what it is—God's gift, but an untuned instrument, an indisciplined daughter of desires. The art of life is to introduce harmony and proportion into this impulsive complex. It was the belief of the Greek philosophers, as of the Chinese sages before them, that such harmony is possible of attainment, and that even sexual passion can be transformed into erotic beauty. It is significant that nowhere in the pages of Gandhi's autobiography is there once a mention of beauty. That is why it must be called a Leaden Legend—sullen and ugly. To say "base" would be to succumb to the temptation of the metaphor. However much we may be repelled by the insensitive fanaticism of this votary of Truth, we must recognize the heroism. It does not transmute the lead into gold, or make the martyr a saint; but it stirs the very life it strove to deny.

33

The Enjoyment of Art

"TELL ME WHAT IT MEANS?" How often that question is addressed to me as I stand with some friend or chance acquaintance before a modern painting. And just as often I evade the question, or give some flippant answer, not because I am unwilling to help the puzzled spectator, but because I realize that the question reveals an attitude towards art so hopelessly wrong that no simple words of mine can make any difference.

If I were honest on such occasions, I should say: "I am no miracle-maker. I cannot make the blind *see*!" And then my companion would feel insulted, and would certainly be in no better position to appreciate the work of art in front of us. Perhaps the less direct approach, which I am making in this essay, will have no such sad consequences.

The arts we are to discuss—painting, sculpture, drawing, etc.—are sometimes called the *visual* arts, and this indicates the simple fact that we are made aware of them through a particular organ of sensation: *the eye*. When we think of other arts which involve other organs of sensation—the ear in music, or the palate in cooking—it seems faintly obvious that there is a direct relationship between the art and the sensation. When we hear a melody we don't ask what it means, nor do we attempt to analyse the bouquet of a good wine. But art, it will be said, is more than sensuous pleasure—there is no comparison between Botticelli and a tender beefsteak! But there is. The connection may be remote, but we must accept as the foundation of our aesthetics the fact that all art is fundamentally sensuous. It can be many other things besides, but unless we begin with a sensational reaction to the work of art in front of us, we are lost.

For many reasons, some of which I will presently explain, most people no longer react sensuously to works of visual art. One sometimes has the impression that they no longer *see* the work of art—to such people the thing seen is like a letter in some language they do not understand, a symbol in some unfamiliar science. What is registered is a certain arrangement of lines and colours which has got into the wrong brain cell—it has been plugged into the wrong exchange. This was brought home to me vividly one day when J. L. Baird, the inventor of television, came to see me. It was during the last war, and he was feeling depressed. He looked at the pictures on the walls and at my books, and then confessed that it was a mystery to him how anyone could derive either pleasure or interest from painting or poetry. He did not speak with arrogance—he was genuinely puzzled, and as a scientist he wanted to satisfy himself that there was some explanation. But though we discussed the problem for a long time, we could only arrive at the conclusion that education and environment had made us two different creatures, and that nothing short of a long process of rehabilitation would enable him to appreciate Picasso, or my mind to move in a world of nuclear physics. I might have pointed out, but did not, that a great scientist like Einstein had retained his aesthetic sensibility, and had even claimed that some connection existed between scientific and artistic imagination.

The point I wish to bring out by this anecdote is that it is perfectly possible to deaden our aesthetic sensibility, and I would go further and assert that this is what normally happens nowadays. A local anaesthetic has been injected into our visual nerves, and most of us are artistically blind. How that has come about is another question, and a very complicated one, but in my own opinion what we call "education" is mainly responsible. People in general were not always like this—indeed, we know that until about 1820 what we now call "good taste" was endemic: everybody possessed it. We cannot explain an epoch of art like the Georgian Period, when everything from public buildings and cottages to silverware and furniture bears the impress of instinctive harmony, on any other supposition. The craftsman of such an age were not "educated"—they were apprenticed to a master and learned their craft in contact with tools and materials. In the same way we cannot help being struck by the unfailing aesthetic instincts of primitive peoples, tribes in Africa, for example, not yet contaminated by our export drive. Art, we must conclude, has nothing in common with literacy, with the spread of scientific knowledge, with "culture".

The education that deadens the sensibility is not confined to the schools—it is something we drink in all the time from our environment. We may, of course, react against our environment, and there is perhaps more genuine appreciation of art in the coalfields of Durham than in the villas of Surrey. We are not so easily seduced by positive ugliness as by all the counterfeits of art—the conventional objects which we accumulate in the course of a lifetime, largely because we have no alternative. Nowadays only the rich can discriminate, and they are a shrinking quantity. Most of us have to accept what we find in the stores, and what we find there are the insensitive products of the machine—objects made without love, without personal responsibility, for profit and utility. We can, if we are desperate enough, modify such an inheritance; but we can make very little impression on the scene as a whole. We resign; we accept; we live with ugliness and when beauty surprises us, we no longer recognize her features.

But, someone will protest, we do love art, we do love beauty; it is your beastly modern art we don't like and can't understand. Explain that if you can!

Again, I cannot explain the art, but only the situation in which the artist finds himself. It is true that there are many sensitive people who enjoy the art of the past—painting up to Cézanne, for example, music up to Debussy, the architecture of Lutyens, etc. To such people the paintings of Picasso or Klee, the music of Stravinsky or Alban Berg, seems a deliberate insult. Here again, I think, education is the explanation. The blinkers may not be so wide, but they are effective in a certain direction. Modern art does admittedly need more discrimination—it has not been sifted for us by the experience of generations. There are charlatans among us, skilful imitators and venal impressarios. But our best protection against such deceptions is a virgin sensibility. If we bring only convention and prejudice to the appreciation of modern art, we cannot discriminate between originality and eccentricity, between the unknown and the unknowable.

I may have given the impression that there is some relation between the appreciation of art and a state of naïvety, even of stupidity, but this is far from the truth. We are miseducated into a condition of aesthetic insensibility, but assuming we could start with a virgin sensibility, then the full appreciation of art would depend on another kind of education, for great art may be infinitely complex. There is such a thing as the education of the senses, and skill itself, which all great art demands, is an education of the senses. It is true that we do not need to be a skilful player to appreciate great music or (to mention another form of art) a great game of tennis. But we must possess and develop an intuitive understanding of skill, which is perhaps based on an imaginative participation in these skills—we anticipate, and mentally imitate, every minute and subtle action of the artist. But this is not intellectual understanding—it is not knowledge in the scholastic sense. It is an instinctive activity.

Marcel Proust, who had a profound understanding of all the arts, once wrote: "From the moment that works of art are judged by reasoning, nothing is stable or certain, one can prove anything one likes. Whereas the reality of genius is a benefaction, an acquisition for the world at large, the presence of which must first be identified beneath the more obvious modes of thought and style, criticism stops at this point and assesses writers by the form instead of the matter . . . This constant aberration of criticism has reached a point where a writer would almost prefer to be judged by the general public (were it not that it is incapable of understanding the researches an artist has been attempting in a sphere unknown to it). For there is more analogy between the instinctive life of the public and the genius of a great writer which is itself but instinct, realized and perfected, to be listened to in a religious silence imposed upon all others, than there is in the superficial verbiage and changing criteria of self-constituted judges." Proust was thinking of the artist as writer, but what he says is equally true of the artist as painter or sculptor. The instinctive approach of the unlettered public, of craftsmen and artisans, is surer than the sophisticated shying at art indulged in by the typical highbrow. But we must not ignore the qualification which Proust puts in brackets in the passage I have quoted. Art is an elaborate discipline, a relentless struggle with intractable materials, and unless the public appreciates this creative process, its instinctive approach to art will not penetrate to the inner court, where enjoyment is most intense.

34

D'Arcy Thompson

THERE ARE certain scientific classics, and *Growth and Form* is one, which have such a wide significance that they must become, as it were, layman's property and be given general currency. Sir D'Arcy Thompson described his volume as "an easy introduction to the study of organic Form", and though there are chapters which involve more mathematical knowledge than the layman can claim, it is nevertheless a book that must be brought to the notice of the general reader.

Sir D'Arcy Thompson was not a narrow specialist; he was in the best sense of the word a humanist, familiar with the speculations of philosophers and the visions of poets no less than with the multitudinous facts of natural science. He was of the same "blood and marrow" as Plato and Pythagoras, and he had something of the geniality of a Goethe or a Henri Fabre. Its theme apart, his book has an endless fascination merely as a collection of *faits divers*, of curiosities of nature; and all this knowledge is presented with such urbanity and charm, that I can imagine it being read for pleasure, like Buffon's *Histoire Naturelle*, long after its findings have become the unacknowledged commonplaces of science.

Its subject is what Goethe was the first to call Morphology: the study of the inter-relations of growth and form, and the part which physical forces play in this complex inter-action. It is "but a portion of that wider Science of Form which deals with the forms assumed by matter under all aspects and conditions, and, in a still wider sense, with forms which are theoretically imaginable"; but with the ancient Greek physicists, Sir D'Arcy Thompson would maintain that the same laws are operative throughout the known universe—"for the harmony of the world is made manifest in Form and Number, and the heart and soul and all the poetry of Natural Philosophy are embodied in the concept of mathematical beauty". *Growth and Form* is concerned with that harmony only as manifest in organic forms—in flowers and shells, in fir-cones and guillemots' eggs, in dolphins' teeth and the narwhal's horn, in deer's antlers and spiders' webs, in concretions, spicules, agglutinated skeletons and the branching of blood vessels. In all these divers and sometimes complicated forms, from the amoeba to man, physical forces are seen determining the specific forms assumed in the process of growth.

That Nature keeps some of her secrets longer than others is fully admitted by Sir D'Arcy, and there are forms which still elude mathematical or physical analysis: but in this work he has demonstrated clearly, and for all time, that "throughout

the whole range of organic morphology there are innumerable phenomena of form which are not peculiar to living
things, but which are more or less simple manifestations of
ordinary physical law". This revelation has disturbing consequences for two popular myths: the myth that form is
determined, as by some supernatural foresight, by the end or
function of the thing (Entelechy); and the doctrine that forms
are produced by natural selection in a process of continuous
historical evolution. We may still be a long way from a
mechanical theory of organic growth, but the facts which are
co-ordinated in this book suggest two conclusions, which to
some extent contradict the accepted theories. They may best
be given in the author's own words:

(1) When, after attempting to comprehend the exquisite adaptation of the swallow or the albatross to the navigation of the air, we
try to pass beyond the empirical study and contemplation of such
perfection of mechanical fitness, and to ask how such fitness came to
be, then indeed we may be excused if we stand wrapt in wonderment,
and if our minds be occupied and even satisfied with the conception
of a final cause. And yet all the while, with no loss of wonderment
nor lack of reverence, do we find ourselves constrained to believe
that somehow or other, in dynamical principles and natural law, there
lie hidden the steps and stages of physical causation by which the
material structure was so shapen to its ends.

(2) In so far as forms can be shown to depend on the play of
physical forces, and the variations of form to be directly due to
simple quantitative variations in these, just so far are we thrown back
on our guard before the biological conception of consanguinity, and
compelled to revise the vague canons which connect classification with
phylogeny. . . . In the order of physical and mathematical complexity
there is no question of the sequence of historic time. The forces that
bring about the sphere, the cylinder or the ellipsoid are the same
yesterday and tomorrow. A snow-crystal is the same today as when
the first snows fell. . . . That things not only alter but improve is an

article of faith, and the boldest of evolutionary conceptions. How far
it is true were very hard to say; but I for one imagine that a ptero-
dactyl flew no less well than does an albatross, and that Old Red
Sandstone fishes swam as well and easily as the fishes of our own seas.

I merely record, for I am not competent to discuss, this
fundamental difference between the Darwinian conception of
the causation and determination of form, and that which is
based by Sir D'Arcy Thompson on the laws of physical
science. It is a difference which must inevitably have wide
repercussions in philosophy. Meanwhile I feel more confidence in pointing out the significance which this science of
form has for the theory of art. There is no word which slips
more frequently from Sir D'Arcy's pen than the epithet
"beautiful". When he has revealed the physical laws which
determine a form, he again and again introduces what is in
effect an element of *value* to characterize that form. In this, of
course, he is but following the example of Plato, but never
before has such a range of specific natural forms been shown
to possess the harmony and proportion we usually ascribe only
to works of art.

In effect, efficient form in the organic world, in the inor-
ganic world, and in the world of art, is shown to be determined by identical laws. That, of course, is not the whole
story, either in biology or in art. We must not confuse form
with energy. To illustrate by an example from this book: if
a drop of water, tinged with fuchsin, is gently released at the
bottom of a glass of water, its momentum enables it to rise
through a few centimetres of the surrounding water, and in
doing so it communicates motion to the water around. In
front, the rising drop *thrusts* its way through, almost like a
solid body; behind it tends to *drag* the surrounding water after
it, by fluid friction; and these two motions together give rise
to "beautiful" vorticoid configurations. The "form" of these

JACKSON POLLOCK: *Convergence* 1952

liquid jets, like the form of a work of art, is beautiful; but it would not have existed without the initial pressure which released the drop of water. In the same way, the form of a work of art does not come into existence without an initial act of imagination, an inspiration. And it is as true in art as in physics, that the matter which is released in inspiration has no prevision of the form which, under natural laws, it will assume. At least, such is the distinction between an art that is vital and organic and one that is academic and dead.

35

A Seismographic Art

ABSTRACTION IS still the generic term for the tendency most characteristic of modern art, but the term must be redefined if we are to apply it to the only distinct movement that has arisen since the end of the Second World War. The new generation rejects the purism, the absolutism, that we associate with names like Mondrian, Ben Nicholson, or Victor Pasmore. Instead they present us with various forms of the formless—paintings that look like a scraped palette, arbitrary scribbles in colours that have the dramatic flourish of a signature, and do indeed signify a personality, and perhaps nothing but a personality. This type of art, which has not yet earned a generic name (unless we adopt *tachisme* from the French), is the only face that the atomic age presents to the world—a face of blank despair, of shame and confusion. But yet the features can be identified, are recognizable again once they have been seen.

Abstractionism or non-figurative art developed from cubism—as a process of universalization. It gradually shed the accidental details of natural phenomena, until an art of geometrical and harmonic relations, as detached as music from realism, became possible. The new art is not entirely original —the early Kandinsky paintings of 1909–12 are unacknowledged precursors—but it differs from cubism and its successors in that it deforms rather than refines the natural object. The identity of this object may be recorded in the title of the paintings—sometimes fancifully: "Altar on the Blue Diamond", "Yellow Heartbeat" (Alan Davie); sometimes directly: "Ant-hill", "Beast", "Head", "Cane Boxes" (Dova); "Winter", "Night Fantasy" (Hultberg). If the plastic mass of paint is not actually inspired by an object, it is manipulated until it can be associated with an object, either by virtue of its silhouette, or by some suggestive detail (an eye or a limb). But the recognition of the object is not essential: if the painting has any phenomenal significance, it is only like a signpost, which tells us where the inspiration came from, or where it might possibly be expected to lead us. Meanwhile it lies in our way, an object as stubborn as a rock or a tree-stump. We are invited to inspect its pattern of lichen, its veins of quartz or obsidian; and perhaps we may experience a dynamic force, a mana, a magic, that has somehow been communicated to the shaped form as it passed through the alembicating mind of the painter.

The odd thing is that an art so personal in its origins should be so universal in its distribution. It is sometimes said that it all began with the American painter, Jackson Pollock, who dribbled paint from pierced cans over a canvas laid like a carpet on the floor, and only stopped when the arbitrary result acquired some significant pattern. But Leonardo already recognized the fascination of such formless forms, and in

France painters of this kind like Fautrier, Dubuffet and Michaux have an independent origin. It is just possible that the widespread use of the Rohrschach test in experimental psychology may have had something to do with the origins of the movement, for that test showed how much (and what various) significance could be read into an apparently meaningless shape—if only we tried. It seems quite clear that the average reaction to a painting by Fautrier or Dubuffet is exactly the same kind as the average reaction to a Rohrschach blot. But is it necessarily an aesthetic reaction? Can a blot be elaborated into a work of art?

The mental reactions provoked by the Rohrschach blots prove that the creation of a blot-like painting (with infinite possibilities of informal variation. and with all the additional power given to it by colour and texture) is not necessarily non-sensical. A blot can be beautiful, and a painting by Fautrier or Dova is also beautiful. But when we make such a statement, are we stretching an already ambiguous term beyond all reasonable limits? We have only to consider works of art so diverse as a painting by Titian or a fountain by Bernini, a Greek vase or a Mexican mask, to see how different the meaning of beauty can be. It is our sensibility that is fickle, and some external magnetism sends it wavering round the compass of creative possibility. The particular magnetism that has exerted its power in these past ten post-war years is negative: a vacuous nihilism that renounces the visible world, and even the inner world of the imagination, and scribbles a graph of its uncertainty on the surface of a blank consciousness.

But can we seriously compare a blotch of colours, however powerful its sensuous and even psychic evocations, to Titian's "Sacred and Profane Love" or Bernini's "Apollo and Daphne"? Contemporary aesthetics is very accommodating, but we must make a fundamental distinction between objects that are imaginative, and objects that merely evoke images. In the one case there has been no exercise of the shaping power of a mind: an unshaped object enters the consciousness and as we contemplate it we (the spectators) make our associations, let our fancy play round it—each spectator becomes an artist, and each is creating his own work of the imagination. But the object that sets this process going is not in itself necessarily a work of art.

It would seem, therefore, that an arbitrary act of expression (as when we deliberately make a blot on a sheet of paper) is not sufficient to constitute a work of art: there must be an element of control, of shaping, though this may be undeliberate, as when an already shapely poem or visual image arises spontaneously in the mind. But the point to insist on is that spontaneity is not in itself a guarantee of beauty or vitality—a formal element must be present in what is spontaneously revealed.

This still leaves open the whole problem of what constitutes aesthetic form. The blotchers might maintain, quite correctly, that aesthetic form is not necessarily measured or metrical form—that there exist irregular forms that are of undoubted aesthetic appeal. Chinese art—oriental art generally—provides many examples, whilst in Europe the Rococo movement was an assertion of the aesthetic validity of such irregular forms. The word "rococo" is said to be derived from the French *rocaille*, and rockeries and grottoes were fashionable extensions of a deeper love of the formally irregular. Rococo ornament is sometimes as wildly arbitrary as a painting by Hartung or Mathieu, but the Rococo artist never claimed for it a more than decorative function. Rococo painting sometimes breaks out of its frame, as in Baciccia's fresco "The Triumph of the Name of Christ," in the Gesu church in Rome—though Baciccia (1639–1709) is too early to be more than a precursor of the Rococo style. In a Fragonard or a Watteau, rococo signifies no more than an open form, a composition that is imaginatively extendable beyond the rectangle of the picture's frame. By contrast, some of the blotch-paintings of which we are speaking are self-contained, monolithic, and have no reference to the rectangle of the canvas, which is merely a place where the painting "happens".

There is little purpose in longing for a type of art that has no sympathetic relationship to the prevailing "spirit of the age". Consciously or unconsciously the artists will refuse to supply it. Those who demand a return to realism, or to classicism, should first demand a return to sanity in economics and politics, a return to idealism in philosophy and to moderation in everything. Not that art is a direct expression of such conscious states of mind. Art springs from a deeper source and is prophetic. It expresses a sense of dissatisfaction with normal concepts of reasoning, with the conventional reality presented by newspapers, novelists and historians. Always in each epoch, the artist has been seeking a new orientation in a world grown indefinite and muddled—refocusing his sensibility on images that have grown dim and indistinct.

The new images presented by the younger artists are not indistinct for lack of focus: they are authentic symbols of chaos itself, of mind at the end of its tether, gazing into the pit on the other side of consciousness. This is not the Nothingness of the existentialists, but the Unconscious of the psychoanalysts. To attempt to reach this forbidden region is not unknown in the past; and in the recent past the surrealists came back with authentic discoveries. But surrealist painting was like the effort of remembering a dream: the images were the product of unconscious activities that had an arbitrary origin (in the psychosis of the individual artist, for example): they were seized on the confines of consciousness, and however much an André Breton might preach the doctrine of pure automatism they were not automatic because they were the product of the dream (or the day-dream), and that, as Freud has shown, is a purely deterministic mental activity. The successors to the surrealists, these artists without a generic name, without an identity, are much more genuinely automatic. They deliver themselves, not to the unconscious forces of the imagination, but to something as irresponsible as an angry gesture. In fact, their painting is instinctive, a reflex activity, completely devoid of mental effort, of intellection. As such, it may possess vitality, but never beauty. Beauty is not rational, but it always bears the marks of intellection— that is to say, of harmonies and proportions that can be analysed and intellectually appreciated. The artist must not deliberately create these values (that leads to academicism and death): he has a natural feeling for them, a disposition (perhaps innate, perhaps acquired by discipline) to make automatic use of them.

The automatism of the instinctive painter has no such natural limits: it is an emotional earthquake and the seismograph it leaves behind tells us only what happened to an individual sensibility at a certain moment. We do not even re-experience the earthquake—we merely observe the record of its force and duration.

Once in possession of this instinctively created graph, the artist can begin to elaborate it consciously. A Mathieu or a Soulages leaves his seismograph untouched: a Fautrier or a Sallés plays about with it—adds a vivid touch of colour here and there: scribbles in a suggestive line or two, even a recognizable feature, an eye or a breast. A "monster" may emerge —an idol or a "presence". Hence the claim, which Michael Tapié makes, for the *magic* quality of such paintings. We are fascinated, even terrorized, by the mysterious power that

FAUTRIER: *Otage* 1945

emanates from the object created by "the artist". But that, it may be said, depends on the spectator's sensibility (a sensibility that is in no sense aesthetic). Some people see ghosts, or receive telepathic messages: others do not. Some people, in the same way, respond to a vaguely suggestive mass of paint. We may envy them, but at the same time suspect that the experience has nothing to do with art.

But also at the same time we must remember that beauty has never been an all-inclusive principle of art. Combined with it, at times completely replacing it, is the alternative principle of vitality. Beauty takes us out of life, to contemplate eternal values; vitality puts us at the centre of life, to experience its essential quality, its source and power. There is such an essential dynaminism in some of the paintings of this new type, and before we react with scorn or fury, we should consider whether a willing submission to such forms of expression might not leave us with a heightened sense of reality. At least, such art is not tired, feeble, as was the art at the end of the nineteenth century; nor is it merely negative, like dadaism or a good deal of surrealism. It has much in common with the futurism of the period immediately preceding the First World War; but futurism was more conscious of its environment, machine-conscious, politics-conscious. The new art is conscious of nothing but the artist's own personality, and with an urgent sense of desperation seeks the principle of vitality in introspection, in subjectivity. Previous epochs of vital art, such as the paleolithic, or the Viking, or the Scythian, sought vitality in external life, usually in animals. The self, one feels, may not be a very constant source of vitality: it is subject to self-distrust and despair. But such is really the challenge of the new movement in art: to feel the pulse of vitality within one's own consciousness and then to convey its plastic rhythms in graphic form.

36

Tribal Art and Modern Man

THE RELATIONS between tribal art and modern art are as old as the Eiffel Tower—exactly, for the Eiffel Tower was built to commemorate the Universal Exhibition of 1889, and at that exhibition there were numerous anthropological objects which attracted the attention of the artists of Paris, above all, of Gauguin. "It is great," said Gauguin. "In the Java village there are Hindoo dances. All the art of India can be seen there, and it is exactly like the photos I have. I go there again on Thursday as I have an appointment with a mulatto girl." Van Gogh wrote to Emile Bernard:

There is something I am very sorry to have missed at the Exposition, that is the collection of dwellings of all the races. . . . So could you, since you have seen it, give me an impression of it, and especially a sketch with the colours of the primitive Egyptian dwelling. . . . In one of the illustrated papers I saw a sketch of ancient Mexican dwellings, they too seem to have been primitive and very beautiful. Oh, if only one knew about those times and could paint the people of those days who lived in such dwellings—that would be just as beautiful as Millet: I don't say as far as colour is concerned, but in character, as something significant, as something in which one has a solid faith.

This is eighteen years before Picasso painted *Les demoiselles d'Avignon*, and note what Van Gogh is saying (and what Gauguin and Emile Bernard were thinking at this time)—namely, that primitive art is beautiful, and that it is beautiful because it is primitive—that because it is primitive it has something which is significant, something in which one can have a solid faith.[1]

[1] In fact, it is often part of a very complex culture, and for this reason anthropologists prefer to call it "tribal" rather than "primitive".

Until that time, and indeed till long after that time, anthropologists and ethnologists had been completely blind to the aesthetic appeal of the objects which they piled up in rich confusion in their museums. Their favourite epithet for the description of such objects, throughout the nineteenth century, is "crude", and "crude" I suspect they remain for most anthropologists, who are not accustomed to give any scientific status at all to aesthetic values. Frobenius, towards the end of the nineteenth century, was probably the first anthropologist to use the word "art" in connection with tribal organizations, and he did not lay much stress on it.

Robert Lowie, as late as 1925, is probably the first anthropologist to recognize, in his own words, that "the aesthetic impulse is one of the irreducible components of the human mind . . . a potent agency from the very beginnings of human existence"; though he quotes Jochelson, whose work is unknown to me, as having previously admitted this truth. But what I wish to emphasize is the fact that the whole of this revaluation of tribal art—its very recognition as art—was due to artists, and not to scholars and scientists, who, in spite of their more intimate knowledge of the material in question, remained obstinately purblind to its aesthetic qualities.

All this is matter of fact, and perhaps not very important. What is more interesting and debatable is the motive underlying the recognition of the aesthetic value of primitive art, sixty years ago. Why did the artists of 1889 find tribal art not merely beautiful, but also significant—"something in which one has a solid faith"? That, I take it, is the real problem.

I think there is little doubt that the answer to this question lies in the artist's revolt, conscious or unconscious, against the industrial civilization which, by the third quarter of the nineteenth century, had become such a hideous reality. In the case of Van Gogh and Gauguin, European civilization was a "dismal swamp", corrupt beyond redemption. Gauguin deliberately turned his back on it, and went to Tahiti to seek the primitive reality. To a certain extent he found it, and this is how he describes it:

> A delight distilled from some indescribable sacred horror which I glimpse of far-off things. The odour of an antique joy which I am breathing in the present. Animal shapes of a statuesque rigidity: indescribably antique, august, and religious in the rhythm of their gesture, in their singular immobility. In the dreaming eyes is the overcast surface of an unfathomable enigma.

In the case of Van Gogh the reaction was less conscious, more introverted, and the end was madness. From the asylum in St. Rémy he wrote of his *horror of life*, but he also wrote that he considered the artist's duty was to think, not to dream, and he said of Bernard's and Gauguin's paintings: "the thing about them is that they are a sort of dream or nightmare—that they are erudite enough—you can see that it is someone who is mad on the primitives . . ." and that gave him "a painful feeling of collapse instead of progress". But his own concentration on the visual was an escape from the civilization around him—as he said himself: "It is really at bottom fairly true that a painter as man is too much absorbed by what his eyes see, and is not sufficiently master of the rest of his life."

Van Gogh died in this year 1889 which I have given as the one in which the relations between tribal and modern art began, so he does not really come into question. But Van Gogh is the father of that movement known as Expressionism, and the Expressionists were to become, twenty years later, the most consistent representatives of a primitive style in modern art. By a primitive *style* I mean a mode of expression more or less directly influenced by primitive prototypes. Emil

Nolde, like Gauguin before him, actually visited the South Seas, and there was the direct impact on other Expressionists, such as Schmidt-Rottluff, Pechstein and Kirchner, of Frobenius's publications, and of Carl Einstein's *Negerplastik*, published in Leipzig in 1915.

To return to France: I would like to suggest that there was no break in development between the discovery of primitive art in 1889 and its direct translation into cubism from 1907 onwards. Gauguin went on painting until 1903, and his works, of course, gained in influence after his death. By 1904 we know that Vlaminck was taking an interest in primitive art, and Vlaminck infected Derain with his enthusiasm, and Derain infected Matisse. Both Matisse and Derain began to collect Negro sculpture before 1907. Then came *Les demoiselles d'Avignon* and a series of paintings, by Picasso, Braque, Derain and others, which grew increasingly geometrical in style, and finally developed into cubism: cubism analytical and synthetic, and then abstract and uncontaminated by any representational element.

Meanwhile another development was taking place which was to have its repercussions on modern art. About the same time that Gauguin was discovering primitive art, Freud was discovering the unconscious. I have no documentary evidence of the first contact between art and psychoanalysis, but I suspect that it took place in Munich between 1908 and 1910. There is some research to be done on this question, but I think it would establish that both Kandinsky and Klee had some knowledge of psychoanalysis before 1910, and certainly the group of artists who assembled in Zürich on the outbreak of war in 1914 and established the Dada group were familiar with some of Freud's ideas. This group was presently reinforced by a trained psychiatrist, André Breton, and from the interpenetration of primitive art, psychoanalysis, the poetry of

Rimbaud and Lautréamont, post-Hegelian philosophy and I know not what else, the movement known as Surrealism was born.

The surrealists from the beginning took a serious and indeed a scientific interest in all forms of primitive art, and in Paris at any rate there was a close understanding between the surrealist artists, the psychoanalysts, and the anthropologists. The general effect of this was to reveal a common basis, in the unconscious, for those irrational forms of art in which the contemporary, no less than the primitive man, felt impelled to express himself.

These historical considerations are perhaps unduly pedantic, but the dimensions of the relations between modern art and primitive art are not fully appreciated. I hope I have shown that it has not been a superficial flirtation; that on the contrary there has grown up, over a period of sixty years, an intimate connection which, on the one hand, has led to a revaluation of ethnological material, a great portion of which has now been rescued from the scientific lumber-room and elevated to a worthy place among the creative achievements of mankind; and on the other hand has given to the modern artist a new mode of expression which he finds in accordance with his emotional or spiritual needs. And that brings me to my last point.

I have been criticized for using the word *Angst* [anguish or dread] in this context, and for suggesting that the similarities which exist between certain types of primitive art and certain types of modern art are due to a common psychological condition. Perhaps I did not make my meaning clear, but it seems to me beyond doubt that the trend of modern art away from representational realism and towards some degree of abstraction or symbolism is but a reflection of those philosophical and religious trends which, themselves no doubt determined or at any rate intimately related to economic trends, have led mankind into a state of religious unbelief, of psychological imbalance, and social unrest. If there is one word which succinctly defines the universal condition of mankind today, it is the word *insecurity*—mental insecurity, social insecurity, metaphysical insecurity.

I am not going to suggest that the same or a similar word can be used to characterize primitive man. This term is far too inclusive for our purposes, and we need some classification of primitive races before we can venture to generalize about their metaphysical characteristics. But there is the general division which I have already referred to—that between tribes whose art is naturalistic, and tribes whose art is geometrical or symbolic. It is roughly, as I have said, the distinction between paleolithic art and neolithic art, between what is usually called bushman art and what is usually called Negro art. At this point I would quite sincerely ask for the anthropologist's guidance, because it does seem to me that we lack any thorough correlation of types of religion and types of art. I am assuming, however, that such a correlation would reveal a parallel between religions of fear, terror, propitiation and retribution to which would correspond arts of symbolic or geometric tendency; and between religions of ritual and sympathetic magic based on a belief in the beneficence of nature and of the gods to which would correspond a naturalistic or representational art.

If such a correspondence does in fact show itself throughout the history of mankind, then it is very easy to explain the return of the modern artist to forms of art similar to those we call "primitive". The reason lies in mankind's return to a "primitive" state of mind. To call the state of mind of a contemporary existentialist "primitive" is perhaps paradoxical; but when the existentialist (and we must remember that he represents the up-to-date Christian theologist as well as the up-to-date atheist philosopher)—when the existentialist begins to talk about the anguish or uneasiness which overcomes him when he faces up to the problem of man's cosmic predicament, he is merely using elaborate linguistic signs to describe the same feelings which overcome primitive men, but which they can only express in emotive symbols. Well, the modern artist, not being an adept in philosophical verbalization, is reduced to expressing himself in concrete symbols—that is to say, in works of art that are the objective correlate of his inner emotional tensions. That is the central fact to be grasped in this debate—I mean the fact that modern man, and the modern artist in particular, is no mere eclectic monkey, trying to imitate for his occasional amusement the artifacts of primitive races; on the contrary, he is, spiritually speaking, in a tough spot himself, and the more honest he is with himself, the more resolutely he rejects the traditional shams and worn counters of expression, and the more nearly, and the more unconsciously, he finds himself expressing himself in a manner which bears a real and no longer superficial resemblance to so-called "primitive" art.

37

Graham Sutherland

HENRI MICHAUX remarks, in his book of travels, that the Chinese consider "*la racine comme plus 'nature' que le tronc . . . Tout ce qui est tortueux dans la nature lui est une douce caresse*". This is not an oriental eccentricity; it is typical of an aesthetic that finds more power and significance in the generation of life than it its florescence. There is vitality in both root and branch, but the element that searches the earth, extending its form in opposition to hard particles of rock, by that very struggle seems to win a superior grace. By contrast, how banal seem to be those regular or symmetrical forms that have matured in the unresistent air.

This image comes to mind when we contemplate the paintings of Graham Sutherland. Not that he is an orientalist, either in style or philosophy; but his work shows the same desire to reveal the directions taken by hidden germinal forces, to record the unexpected shapes assumed by life in its blind proliferation. The painter's eye is a revealing, not merely a recording organ. But the revelation is also a transformation, for the artist is not a mere discoverer (that would be to confuse his job with the scientist's), but an interpreter. His forms are aesthetic, which means that he uses the power he takes from living things to give vitality to the creatures of his imagination.

Such abstract formulas of criticism are invented only when the artist has finished his work of creation. He himself is guided by instinct. His eye, searching the solid darkness where life germinates, is suddenly aware of phosphorescent shapes, dim analogues of roots, of larvae, of knots, joints, scarred bark, succulent fibres; of leaves, too, and branching twigs; of thorns and flowers. Rarely of men or animals, for they do not have the rooting, tentative quality of vegetation. An artist like Sutherland is not, is *essentially* not, a humanist. (His portraits assimilate the human being to thorny, spicular forms of life, as though a first frosted sheath of crystallization had already glazed the skin.) Sutherland is a landscapist, like so many of his English predecessors. This English obsession, which began more than two hundred years ago as a simple topographical interest, scientific in its motivation, became under the influence of the Romantic poets, a transcendental philosophy of nature. Landscape-painting, with Turner, is already a symbolic representation of cosmic reality—of the Spirit of Nature. But such a romantic revelation is always coloured by the mood of the revealer. Turner was the least philosophical of men, but he had a naïvely direct mystical vision which belongs to the same *Weltanschauung* as Words-worth's and Coleridge's, which it is not merely fanciful to associate with Schelling or Novalis. Sutherland, a hundred years later, has entered another philosophical climate, and though his relations to a Heidegger or a Sartre may be as remote as Turner's was to Schelling or Novalis, the growing fearsomeness of the symbols reflects the now prevailing cosmic anxiety. These colours, to a philosophical temperament, may be a shade too acid; these lines and forms too hesitant or too agitated; but a painter whose sensibility is acutely aware of the metaphysical mood of the age no less than of the occular vision of the scene, must transform the fragments of his per-ception into a coherent language of the spirit. To do less is to be false to the destiny of the artist, which is always to rend the veil of Maya, reckless of what the action may reveal.

Sutherland's naturism is opposed to the humanism of Moore, but these two examples of contemporary philoso-phical art are properly regarded as complementary; together they represent England's distinctive contribution to the art of the twentieth century. The position they occupy is not exclu-sive, even of other artists in England. If we assume that these two figures have a representative function at the present moment, we are at the same time conscious that they stand, not only for a general spirit of the age, but also for many other artists who speak the same language, with accents that may be different but not necessarily less significant. The range and consistency of Sutherland's work gives it a more than regional significance. Indeed, Sutherland is possibly the first English painter since Turner who has been bold enough to take up an independent position as an artist, and to maintain it with conviction in the presence of his European contemporaries.

38

Kokoschka

THOUGH HE is undoubtedly one of the major artists of our time, the work of Oskar Kokoschka is not so well known in the United Kingdom and America as it should be. It is true that the Museum of Modern Art in New York has two superb paintings in its permanent collection, and most of the important art galleries in the United States possess one or more examples of his work. In England, the Tate Gallery has a portrait and a landscape, and there is a single example of his work in the National Gallery of Scotland. But in all these places considerably more space is given to artists of considerably less stature.

To explain this neglect might lead us into social undergrowths which cannot be explored in a short and would-be gracious tribute. In a world of competing interests, of conflicting nationalisms, of the increasing commercialization of art, the fame of any one particular artist is a counter, thrown into the game of wits. A poet is good if he sings the praises of the dominant party leader; a painter is good if he depicts the inevitable progress of the working classes or flatters the vanity of the rich; and poet and painter sink or swim with the political fortunes of the country where they happen to be domiciled. If the country is a stable one, it may still be a question of the relative value of its exchange rate: for art is an export of potential value. The dealer plays a part, the press plays a part. What seldom gets a chance, in this sordid trafficking, is the unprejudiced sensibility of the people—of those people who can respond to the appeal of a work of art without the stimulus of fashion or fortune.

But even supposing we were back in a state of such inno-cency, and art was to be enjoyed for itself alone, it is idle to pretend that the work of Kokoschka would everywhere have an immediate appeal for the unsophisticated. That work does undoubtedly meet with uninstigated resistance in some quarters, and particularly in England. We feel abashed by such relentless realism. Even if we are not sentimentalists, we shrink from the exposure of nerves—our own nerves no less than the twitching nerves of the painter's victim. It is for this reason that a critic so typically English as Roger Fry could not wholly accept Rembrandt—or Picasso. It is a Quakerish restraint in us. But then, we are not consistent. We accept El Greco, in spite of the quivering limbs, the distorted features, the fingers pointed with agony. We accept El Greco partly because we have been told to accept him by impressive critics, partly because his mysticism and masochism are expressed in Christian symbols. But there is no artist of the present time so near to El Greco as Kokoschka. I am not saying that the styles are related—stylistic comparisons are not part of my present purpose. It is the ideals that are related. Once we have discounted the symbols, which are useful conventions to which an artist may be driven by the circumstances of his time—then it is the essential humanism of the two artists that brings them together: they are both artists of love, of suffering, and of redemption.

Love is, of course, a soiled word. In Kokoschka it is instinctive identity; identity with the colour of the flower, the iridescences of fish scales and shells, the fluctuation of light over hills, or its splendour as it strikes the massed roofs of some city. It is the plastic artist's peculiar power of translating his sensations into living forms, and that power is effective in the degree that the love of the objects which arouse the sensations is pure and intense. There is no pride in such love, no judgment. The flayed carcass belongs to the same order of existence as the flower. But beyond love is suffering, and it is that perception which makes Kokoschka an exceptional artist in our age. His portraits reveal the mute suffering of the individual, of the person crucified on the codes of false social values. A few larger symbolic paintings resort to symbolism, not Greco's symbolism, but rather Goya's, to depict the suffering of oppressed peoples, the tortures of war.

And then beyond is the note of redemption. In this case it is not the divine redemption of the Christian religion, but a human redemption which Kokoschka takes over from his master and countryman, Comenius—redemption by education, by creative activity, by art. This theme is not, of course, explicit in Kokoschka's paintings. But it is the practical aspect of his humanism. It is implied in the love of man and in the belief that man can participate, through art, through creative activity, in the world of objective beauty—can become a part of that universal harmony which the great artist sees so clearly revealed in the world of objective fact.

39

The Problem of the Zeitgeist[1]

IN ANY AGE there exists a confusion of values, due to temporary conditions of an economic or social character, psychic disturbances which interfere with the clear perception of what is enduring in human creation. That is to say, a given age always looks at its contemporary art with contemporary prejudices. When, in the course of time, these prejudices disappear, the art of that given age is revalued and again with contemporary prejudices—the prejudices of a new age. We need not deny that certain values persist through all ages; but we must recognize that it is always difficult at any historical moment to distinguish them clearly.

What we have to recognize is the existence, in every age, of a state of intellectual consciousness which is in fact an illusion. For reasons which so far remain obscure certain works of art are elevated temporarily to the highest rank of esteem or popularity, and even the best minds of a period are deceived by them. The duration of the fame of such works varies, but it rarely seems to exceed fifty years, and may be much less.

All the arts exhibit such phenomena, but they can be observed with most clarity in literature (books have a better chance of material survival—it is very difficult to trace the works of a once famous painter, such as Benjamin Robert Haydon). A typical example of a temporarily inflated genius is James Macpherson, whose Ossianic poems aroused worldwide enthusiasm between 1760 and 1800. Homer and Milton were evoked for comparison, and the best minds of the time

[1] Originally given as an introduction to a discussion at the IVth International Congress of Art Critics, Dublin, July 20–26, 1953.

316

(Goethe's, for example) were deceived. The popularity of Ossian was associated with a general movement—a newly discovered and widely diffused interest in the culture of primitive peoples, to which we owe literary monuments of permanent value such as Percy's *Reliques*. That movement may be regarded as the expression of an atavism which was a natural reaction to the prevailing rationalism of the eighteenth century—the Zeitgeist had provoked a revolt in the collective unconscious. But what provokes the Zeitgeist, that particular combination of curiosity and excitement which leads to a blind and unbalanced judgment of certain contemporary artists?

It is a very complex problem, and it is doubtful if it can be solved without recourse to some form of group analysis which would lay bare the workings of unconscious collective motives.[1] It is not my intention to provide any such general hypothesis—indeed, I merely wish to *pose* the problem, with particular reference to contemporary art and literature.

We might say that in any age there are certain conventions (accepted canons of art) and certain prejudices (ethical or religious) which constitute the taste of that age. We know that in the middle of the eighteenth century, for example, the prevailing taste was "classical", and according to that taste certain poets and painters were esteemed above all others. But this does not explain the anomalies *within* that situation. Exact statistics are always lacking, but we know, for example, that a poet like Abraham Cowley had a reputation out of all proportion to the merit of his equally classical contemporaries. In his own day he was probably esteemed more than his contemporary Milton, and certainly more than another contemporary, Andrew Marvell, whom we now find much more genuinely poetic than Cowley. Cowley was an infant prodigy,

---

[1] A first attempt from a psychological point of view has been made by Dr. Erich Neumann. Cf. "Kunst und Zeit", in *Eranos-Jahrbuch*, 1951, pp. 11-56, Zürich, 1952.

and early had a great reputation for his cleverness. Indeed, it seems very difficult for an age to distinguish between cleverness and genius among its contemporaries: the works of genius are probably at first more strange and obscure, and cleverness is always immediately dazzling.

I have just said that we nowadays find Marvell "more genuinely poetic" than Cowley. Sir Herbert Grierson's opinion, that apart from Milton Marvell "is the most interesting personality beween Donne and Dryden, and at his best a finer poet than either", expressed in 1921, would have been inconceivable in 1721 or 1821 (though by the latter date he had been "discovered" by Hazlitt and Lamb). The vagaries of taste in respect of Donne, and even Shakespeare, are well known, and may be due to a multiplicity of factors. But we must ignore this secondary, historical process, to concentrate on the problem of the Zeitgeist, which is always of its time, and immediate.

That it is not merely a question of the prevailing level of taste (in other words, of the Zeitgeist being selective and arbitrary) may be observed by contrasting the fate of two writers who aroused the same universal enthusiasm *at the same time*—Macpherson already mentioned, and Laurence Sterne. Macpherson's name is not remembered by the general public, but Sterne has stood the test of time: he has never gone out of fashion, and has even been a fruitful influence in our own day (on Joyce, for example). Obviously Sterne did not survive because he gave conscious expression to some eternal values which were distinct from the fashionable values represented by Macpherson. He, too, was a creature of his time, but he has survived because he gave expression to a new development of consciousness (made his readers aware of hitherto unexpressed nuances of sensibility), and invented a technique appropriate for the purpose.

Ossian and Sterne may be compared with painters like Bouguerau and Cézanne, but there is this difference: Sterne was immediately recognized, but Cézanne was not adequately recognized until after his death. This may be explained as a difference in the speed of diffusion in the respective arts of painting and writing.

The case of Sterne leads me to suggest as a tentative hypothesis that the "eternal" works of art—those exempt from the mortality of taste and fashion—are those which are based on individual sensibility, to the exclusion of all conceptual or "ideological" motives. But this still leaves the individual at the mercy of those unconscious forces which we call taste or fashion, unless genius is precisely the capacity to evade those forces, to be "*detache de son époque*", as Lionello Venturi has suggested.

Whether "eternal values" exist or not, in the aesthetic realm or the ethical realm, is a philosophical question which I will not discuss now. But in the realm of aesthetic values we know that each age has its own definition of beauty; and if the aesthetic value of "beauty" is denied, then we are ready with a substitute value which we may call "vitality" or "realism". In my own opinion there are a limited number of such values, some of which are essential to the survival of a work of art.

We have admitted that the values of art are subject to variations in esteem, and what is for the moment fashionable may seem eternal. There are no values in art that have not, at one time or another, been challenged. But this general condition or relativity should not blind us to the fact that the world keeps returning to certain specific values. These values may be few, but they seem to be fundamental. I would mention as examples the geometrical proportions which are common to forms of organic life as well as to the forms of art—the so-called Divine Proportion, etc.—and those invariable qualities of harmony and serenity to which mankind returns after every period of storm and stress. If these values are regarded as eternal, then the variations may be ascribed to certain distortions of a temporary nature.

The origin of such distortions must no doubt be sought in the economic sphere, which is the most unstable element in human society. The cultural values of a dominant class do not always correspond to its social status. In any period of revolutionary upheaval, a hiatus will exist for at least a generation between society and culture. A rising *élite* in the economic sense brings with it a low level of taste—perhaps has no taste at all. It is not at ease in manners, speech, clothes, or any form of expressive possession. Hence for a time this new social class, its own taste uncertain or unformed, will attempt to "buy culture". The middleman intervenes. He exploits a favourable situation. Dealers have their "hunches" or intuitions; fashions are more or less deliberately created to feed a new market. In such a situation the Zeitgeist is born—a spirit, an illusion, an *ignis fatuus*.

It follows that the Zeitgeist is not a phenomenon susceptible of rational explanation. At a certain moment there exists a favourable conjunction of events—of wants, desires, objects to satisfy these wants and desires, middlemen to act as catalysts in this portentous situation. The collective unconscious is in need of certain *stimuli*, of certain releases of tension. A significant pattern exists in the social psyche—a synchronicity of otherwise discrete phenomena. The Zeitgeist finds expression in certain expressive forms, in works of art that are suddenly fashionable, and that no power of reason or good taste can prevent from becoming fashionable. The likelihood is that even we, men of good taste that we are, will be deceived.

What is the moral of all this—what lesson of humility should we learn from a sober realization of the facts of cultural history? Two, I think:

First, that the fashionable is always suspect—the fame of the greater part of the most fashionable artists of any period does not survive that period.

Second, which is the contrary proposition, that the greater part of the best artists of any period have a posthumous fame out of all proportion to their contemporary fame.

Finally, in view of these general considerations, can we venture to characterize the features of our own Zeitgeist? It is a hazardous proceeding, but I will suggest four of them:

1. *Egoism*—the prevailing subjectivism of all forms of art: the general Zeitgeist of Romanticism, now two hundred years old.
2. *Erethism*—by which I mean excessive excitation of the sensibility, the absence of serenity.
3. *Eclecticism*—the tendency to make, both of poetry and painting, a mythological salad, I might instance, without any critical intention, poems like "The Waste Land", paintings like "Guernica", the theatre of Giraudoux and Cocteau.
4. *Escapism*—the tendency to evade the human dilemma; denial of the tragic sense of life.

But it is easier to describe the general characteristics of our Zeitgeist than to decide which particular artists best represent it. In any case, I do not propose to undertake such an invidious task. Of these four features of contemporary art, I would say that it is unlikely that we can now escape from subjectivism without some great change in human consciousness, such as occurred at the beginning of the Romantic Movement—and it would have to be an *extension* of human consciousness, such as the Romantic Movement was, and not a mere return to a narrower outlook. Secondly, we must remember that vitality is essential to any enduring art—it is the excess of excitement we must guard against, not its presence.

It is the third and fourth characteristics of our culture which should give us most concern. Though there is a traditional element in all civilized art, and though Shakespeare and Milton are "eclectic" in no small measure, nevertheless there is a directness and originality about all "eternal" works of art: the myth is used as a paradigm or as an archetype, not as an exotic mine to be exploited. As for escapism, there is no compromise possible on this issue: to escape from life is to escape from art.

40

The Faith of a Critic

AT THE BASIS is *pathos*. Sympathy and empathy—feeling *with* and feeling *into*: these are the essential psycho-physical processes without which all criticism is null and dull.

It follows from this that there are no immutable canons of criticism, no perfect critics. Criticism is good and sane when there is a meeting of intention and appreciation. There is then an act of *recognition*, and any worthwhile criticism begins with that reaction.

Recognition is inhibited by constitutional limitations in the critic. These may be defects of sensibility (e.g., insensibility to the sensuous quality of words) or imperfect sympathy due to pathological inhibitions. Contrast the critical reactions of two such eminent critics as John Ruskin and Lord Acton to the same author—George Eliot.

Ruskin on *The Mill on the Floss*: "There is not a single person in the book of the smallest importance to anybody in the world but themselves, or whose qualities deserved so much as a line of printer's type in their description . . . the rest of the characters are simply the sweepings out of a Pentonville bus."

Acton: "No writer has ever lived who had anything like her power of manifold, but disinterested and impartially observant sympathy. If Sophocles or Cervantes had lived in the light of our culture, if Dante had prospered like Manzoni, George Eliot might have had a rival."

The sources of such a disagreement must be sought in the psychology of the critic. In this case there would be a general agreement that Acton was right, Ruskin wrong. If we seek for an explanation of Ruskin's blind spot, it would not be difficult to find. It is part of the same complex that wrecked his marriage. His reaction to Byron, on the other hand, is, unexpectedly, passionately favourable; and has its basis in an identification of himself with Byron. "With this steadiness of bitter melancholy, there is joined a sense of material beauty . . . which in the iridescence, colour-depth, and morbid (I use the word deliberately) mystery and softness of it—with other qualities indescribable by any single words, and only to be analysed by extreme care—is found, to the full, only in five men that I know of in modern times: namely, Rousseau, Shelley, Byron, Turner, and myself . . ."

All critics do not so confidently expose their sympathies, or their antipathies, but nevertheless they always exist, and they are inevitable. We should not confuse criticism with the expression of imperfect sympathies, however much this is disguised in pseudo-scientific jargon. It may be retorted that the same mistake must not be made about the expression of perfect sympathies, but this is not the case. Perfect sympathy may lead to exaggerated partiality (Swinburne's for Victor Hugo, for example); and love may make us blind to many faults in the beloved. But then the performance is no longer critical.

I have said that sympathy is the basis of criticism; the structure above ground-level is intellectual. Sympathetic criticism is not necessarily favourable criticism. We can sympathize with the intention and at the same time reject the execution of it, or object to certain details in this execution. Coleridge on Wordsworth is the best illustration of this truth: the perfect sympathy is not in doubt, but the critic can admit that the object of his sympathy may on occasion be *out of his element*—"like the swan, that, having amused himself, for a while, with crushing the weeds on the river's bank, soon returns to his own majestic movements on its reflecting and sustaining surface". "Though," says Coleridge, here defining the critical principle, "though, to appreciate the defects of a great mind *it is necessary to understand previously its characteristic excellencies*, yet I have already expressed myself with sufficient fulness, to preclude most of the ill effects that might arise from my pursuing a contrary arrangement. I will therefore commence with what I deem the prominent *defects* of his poems hitherto published."[1]

The word *empathy*, indispensable to modern criticism, needs some explanation. It is no longer necessary to give it formal definition—it has entered into our critical vocabulary. But it should be used in *literary* criticism with caution. The process, as the psychologists from Lipps to Koffka have recognized, is so sensational that strictly speaking it only takes place in the plastic arts. We feel ourselves occupying with our senses the

[1] *Biog. Lit.*, ch. xxii.

Gestalt of the rising column or the spatial design of a picture. There may be a true empathetic relationship to the sound and shape of a poem—our response to metre, for example. But in general our use of the word in literary criticism can only be analogical—as when Acton says: "George Eliot seemed to me capable not only of reading the diverse hearts of men, but of *creeping into their skin, watching the world through their eyes,* feeling their latent background of conviction, discerning theory and habit, influences of thought and knowledge, of life and of descent, and having obtained *this experience,* recovering her independence, *stripping off the borrowed shell,* and exposing scientifically and indifferently the soul of a Vestal, a Crusader, an Anabaptist, an Inquisitor, a Dervish, a Nihilist, or a Cavalier without attraction, preference, or caricature."[1] The phrases I have italicized undoubtedly describe the empathic process in images that avoid the use of critical jargon.

Scientific method in criticism, in my creed, is only admissible as a secondary activity. The critic with a head but without a heart, armed with instruments of precision but without love, is the monster who killed Keats. He has had a numerous progeny, and I fancy that the species has found a particularly congenial habitat in American universities (but we have enough to spare for export in England). In so far as he confines himself to textual criticism, he can perform a very useful service. Analysis of Hopkins's metre, exegesis of Eliot's mythology—these are types of necessary activities that one must not for a moment despise. But they should not be confused with criticism proper, which is a philosophical activity, concerned, in Acton's words, with the "latent background of conviction, discerning theory and habit, influences of thought, and knowledge, of life and descent".

For the same reason criticism proper must be dissociated

[1] *Letters to Mary Gladstone,* pp. 60-1.

from sociological criticism of the Marxist type. Again, one cannot object to such criticism as a secondary activity; to demonstrate, for example, "Balzac's profound comprehension of the contradictorily progressive character of capitalist development" may be of great importance to the sociologist; and if a great artist like Tolstoy "creates immortal masterpieces on the basis of an entirely false philosophy", the Marxist may legitimately deplore the fact, but the literary critic may ignore the fact (if it is a fact).[1]

Finally, and most important, the true critic will not indulge in moral judgments. With Bradley he will distinguish between moral judgment and moral perception. Moral perception is a mode of sympathy: we have to participate in the moral dilemmas presented by the poet, and we may justly criticize the way in which they are presented. "When we are immersed in a tragedy," wrote Bradley in his *Shakespearean Tragedy*, "we feel towards dispositions, actions, and persons such emotions as attraction and repulsion, pity, wonder, fear, horror, perhaps hatred; but we do not *judge*." How difficult it is for a critic, committed to some code of ethics or politics, to observe that prime precept of criticism! How many of the pundits of literature, from Dr. Johnson to Irving Babbitt, have failed for precisely that reason! How often we, who claim to be sympathetic critics, have been false to our imaginative experience!

A creed does not admit of qualifications, and I have none to make. It is difficult, however, to convey the meaning of imaginative experience to those who have no such experience; and to claim such experience for oneself savours of vanity. It is a question of organic sensibility. It would be rash to assume that this is a common possession, even in critics. I know from my own attitude to music, an art for which I have

[1]Both examples from George Lukács: *Studies in European Realism*.

no organic sensibility, how easy it would be to formulate a
critical system without imaginative experience. I could begin
from my experience of other arts, and argue (for example)
that since Stendhal whom I admire as a writer of brilliant
critical intelligence expressed a passionate love for the music
of Mozart and Cimarosa, that therefore that kind of music is
likely to be the right kind of music. I have been tempted to
extol the music of Cimarosa simply because there is an impressive amount of evidence to show that in his time he was
greatly admired by people of sensibility and intelligence; and
because I have never found anyone today who could explain
the disappearance of Cimarosa from our opera houses and
concert halls. That greatest of modern musicologists, Sir
Donald Tovey, had no explanation to offer when I once
questioned him on the subject. I am not making out a case
for Cimarosa because I have neither the necessary knowledge
of his music, nor the sensitive equipment to acquire such
knowledge. But I have been temped, without these necessary
tools, to indulge in critical fantasies about Cimarosa; and I
am sure that in literature, where exposure of such an organic
defect is much more difficult, at least half the criticism in
existence is a hollow structure of this kind. The cadences of
poetry are just as sensational as the tones of music. Many
people will readily admit to being tone-deaf in music. I have
met very few people who will admit to being tone-deaf in
poetry.

There remain those overriding considerations which Arnold,
rendering Aristotle's meaning, called higher truth and higher
seriousness. Goethe, a little more concretely, spoke of clarity
and serenity. I do not think the critic can do much more than
announce the presence of such qualities in a work of art. It is
doubtful if the qualities that give Homer, Dante and Shakespeare their supremacy can be reproduced by lesser minds.

The *accent* of high seriousness, said Arnold (and he was wise to call it an accent) comes from absolute sincerity. That is true, but how do we define sincerity? We should not make the attempt. We recognize, we *feel*, such a quality, and if such an action seems like an abdication of the critical intelligence, I can only suggest that there are in the House of Art certain tabernacles which the critic should enter with lowered eyelids, so dazzling is their glory.

NOTES

I HAVE endeavoured to trace the original appearance of the essays and articles reprinted in this volume, but in two or three cases my memory is at fault. To the editors of these forgotten periodicals I tender my apologies; and to those listed below my thanks for giving first hospitality to my opinions.

2. Broadcast, Third Programme, B.B.C., April, 1952. The passage from Fromentin (pp. 23–4) is from *The Masters of Past Time* translated by Andrew Boyle (London, J. M. Dent & Sons, Ltd., 1913). The passage from Wölfflin's *Principles of Art History* (pp. 26–7) was translated by M. D. Hottinger (London, G. Bell & Sons, 1932). The passage from André Malraux, *The Psychology of Art* (pp. 28–9) was translated by Stuart Gilbert (New York, Bollingen Series and London, A. Zwemmer, 1949).

3. *Art News Annual* (New York), 1955.

4. Broadcast, Third Programme, B.B.C., February, 1951.

5. Broadcast, Third Programme, B.B.C., November, 1949. Translations from *Goethe: Wisdom and Experience*, selected by Ludwig Curtins and translated by Hermann J. Weigand (New York and London, 1949).

6. Introduction to *Naum Gabo* (London, Lund, Humphries & Co., 1957).

7. *World Review.*

8. Broadcast, Northern Region, B.B.C.

10. *Architectural Review; New Republic,* November, 1953.

11. Broadcast, European Service, B.B.C., November, 1948.

12. Broadcast, Third Programme, B.B.C., November, 1955.

13. *London Magazine,* March, 1957.

14. *The Listener.*

15. Francis Bergen Memorial Lecture, Yale University, February 19, 1954; printed in *Encounter*.
16. *The Adelphi*, 1946. I have used the Henry Reeve text edited by Phillips Bradley and published by Alfred A. Knopf, New York, 2 vols., 1945.
17. *B.B.C. Quarterly*.
18. *New Statesman & Nation*, February 2, 1957; with additional paragraphs from a review.
19. Presented by the Columbia Broadcasting System in honour of the Bicentennial of Columbia University, 1754–1954. Printed in *The London Magazine*.
21. Broadcast, Thrd Programme, B.B.C., February, 1947. Translations from *The Complete Works of Friedrich Nietzsche*, ed. Oscar Levy, Edinburgh, 1916.
22. *The Complete Plays of Henry James*, edited by Leon Edel, were published in Philadelphia by the J. B. Lippincott Company, and in London by Rupert Hart-Davis (1949).
23. Introductions to reprints of *The Wings of the Dove* (London, Eyre & Spottiswoode, 1948) and *The Golden Bowl*.
24. *The Hudson Review* (in part). Translations by R. F. C. Hull from *The Collected Works of C. G. Jung* (New York and London, several volumes of various dates); or from *Psychological Reflections*, an anthology from the writings of C. G. Jung, selected and edited by Jolande Jacobi, Bollingen Series, New York and Routledge & Kegan Paul, London, 1953.
25. Broadcast, Third Programme, B.B.C., April, 1950.
26. Introduction to *Barbara Hepworth: Sculpture and Drawings*. (London, Lund Humphries & Co., 1952.)
27. Broadcast, Third Programme, B.B.C., 1951, with additional material from a review in *The New Republic*
29. Congress of the International Association of Art Critics, Amsterdam, 1951.
30. From an address to the English Society, Durham University.
31. *The Architect's Yearbook*, 1956, and *Casabella* (Milan). Statements by Mies van der Rohe from a volume edited by Philip G.

Johnson and published by the Museum of Modern Art, New York, 1947.

32. *The Listener.*

34. *The Listener.* A new edition of *On Growth and Form* was published by the Cambridge University Press in 1942.

35. *Encounter.*

36. *The New Republic,* September, 1953.

37. Introduction to a British Council catalogue.

38. Introduction to *Oscar Kokoschka* by Edith Hoffmann (London, Faber & Faber, 1947).

39. *Encounter.*

40. *The Kenyon Review.*